A PRACTICAL GUIDE

Managing Switched *Local Area* Networks

A PRACTICAL GUIDE

Managing Switched *Local Area* Networks

Darryl P. Black

ADDISON-WESLEY
An Imprint of Addison Wesley Longman, Inc.

Reading, Massachusetts • Harlow, England • Menlo Park, California
Berkeley, California • Don Mills, Ontario • Sydney
Bonn • Amsterdam • Tokyo • Mexico City

The publisher offers discounts on this book when ordered in quantity for special sales. For more information, please contact:

Corporate & Professional Publishing Group
Addison Wesley Longman, Inc.
One Jacob Way
Reading, Massachusetts 01867

Library of Congress Cataloging-in-Publication Data

Black, Darryl.
    Managing switched local area networks : a practical guide / Darryl Black.
        p.   cm.
    Includes bibliographical references and index.
    ISBN 0-201-18554-7
    1. Local area networks (Computer networks)—Management.
    2. Telecommunication—Switching systems.   I. Title.
    TK 5105.7.B57   1998
    004.6'8—dc21   97-36656
                                                                              CIP

ISBN 0-201-18554-7

1 2 3 4 5 6 7 8 9—MA—0100999897

First printing, November 1997

To my dear wife, Betsy,

and my

book-loving children, Spencer and Olivia

Contents

PART TWO Components of a Switched LAN

Preface

Introduction

I suppose it all started at the age of seven when I took apart my mother's vacuum cleaner to see how it worked. One thing led to another, and for the last several years, understanding how networks work, how they're managed, and how useful tools are built has satisifed my aroused curiosity.

This book is about taking control of your switched Local Area Network (LAN). It provides a guide to understanding the key management aspects of switched LANs and specific strategies, techniques, and tips for successful LAN management of them. The book includes many lists of common networking problems and possible solutions. It goes through the classic problems encountered with a LAN and provides a step-by-step approach to isolating and solving these problems. It presents a complete, albeit strategically concise, presentation of network management for your switched LAN including the following:

- key background knowledge you must know
- problems you will encounter
- solutions and network policy which you will want to consider

This book gives you the blueprints necessary to build a switched LAN and to manage it like a networking system—a well-tuned, well-maintained networking machine.

The style of this book is most likely quite different from what you may be used to. It is not a textbook because textbooks tend to be dry and boring; it is not a book for so-called "dummies" since those books often lack "meat." Rather, it follows an informal style, designed both to hold your interest and simultaneously to cover a lot of information. Significant information is condensed and tailored for the busy professional, student, or individual who is looking for a focused, pragmatic approach to understanding switched LAN management.

The book follows a "cookbook" style. The "ingredients" of switched management are first presented by surveying significant ground, that is a concise introduction to network management—the standards, networking technologies, switching, routing, switching futures, and connection to the WAN. The book then presents the "directions" for management. It includes problems associated with switched LAN management and provides problem scenarios and step-by-step lists and tables on troubleshooting. The book concludes with the complete "picture" of your finished product—guidance on developing a custom network management system for your own LAN.

Another factor that makes this book unique is that it stays vendor neutral. Networks are typically made up of components from different vendors, using the tools of many vendors to manage these networks. In addition, LANs are customized based on corporate policies and organizational needs. For example, rather than telling you precisely what you need to buy, this book provides you with the background, in concise, bulleted lists, that you need in order to make your own decisions, and, where appropriate, gives World Wide Web (WWW) pointers to vendor-specific information. This makes for a more useful, up-to-date book and provides you with what you need to make switched LAN purchasing decisions (and where you should apply pressure to your vendors for management needs) rather than giving you a prewritten "shopping list."

And so you ask, At what level is the text written? Easy? Difficult? The text varies and is tuned to "what you need to know to manage a switched LAN." Wherever possible the book attempts to simplify the information; but to be perfectly honest, some network management and networking concepts are easy to understand, whereas some are difficult. This book attempts to smooth out the ride and keep the road straight without meandering onto every back road of network trivia. The text tries to keep things interesting by being informal in style and introducing some real-world comparisons along the way.

Prerequisites? Although I try to fill in the salient points of TCP/IP with respect to network management, a basic understanding of TCP/IP will be very helpful to you. TCP/IP is a rich and popular protocol suite about which many fine books have been written. Please consult the bibliography for my favorites.

Network management is evolving with the rapid advances in networking technology. New advances result in new management problems to solve. It wasn't all that long ago that "switching" within the LAN was introduced, placing new requirements on management. Current movements to supporting multimedia and exponentially increasing traffic levels are placing new challenges on management. The goal of this book is to get you up to speed quickly on network management and to extend this base to managing switched LANs.

Be prepared to get refueled within the next few years, though, as technology advances quickly. Network management is an exciting and challenging discipline that continues to grow in terms of need, complexity, and scope.

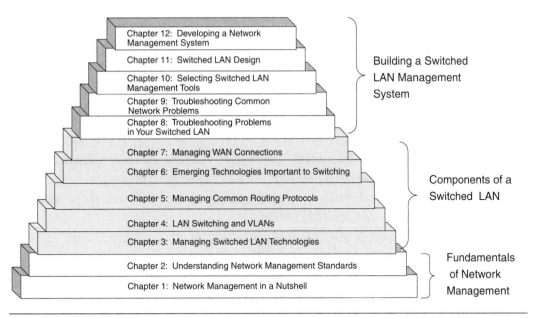

Figure I.1 Building-block approach to this book

Organization of the Book

The book consists of twelve chapters organized into three parts, as shown in Figure I.1:

- Fundamentals of Network Management
- Components of a Switched LAN
- Building a Switched LAN Management System

Although each chapter and part can stand alone (with only occasional referencing), the book uses a building-block approach. You will receive the greatest benefit by reading the book all the way through in the order in which it was written. Of course, if you are very knowledgeable about the material in a particular chapter or part, you may decide to skip over those pages.

The first two chapters cover Part One, Fundamentals of Network Management.

- Chapter 1 provides a quick, yet pretty complete tour of network management.
- Chapter 2 presents the standards of network management, the basics about reading a Management Information Base (MIB), and the fundamentals of how network management applications communicate with your network devices.

The next five chapters comprise Part Two, Components of a Switched LAN:

- Chapter 3 is quite long and is an important chapter in the book. It goes through MAC layer protocols like Ethernet, Fast Ethernet, FDDI, Token Ring, and ATM LANE (LAN Emulation).
- Chapter 4 discusses switching and routing and gets into specific details about switching.
- Chapter 5 describes the management of common routing protocols: IP, IPX, and AppleTalk. Routing is a fundamental component of switched LANs and therefore requires a fair amount of coverage.
- Chapter 6 looks at emerging technologies that will shape switched LANs over the next few years.
- Chapter 7 presents the fundamentals of connecting to the WAN, a necessary part of most LANs.

The last five chapters apply the knowledge learned in the previous parts of the book providing a solid base for Part Three, Building a Switched LAN Management System:

- Chapter 8 presents the techniques for solving problems and an inventory of common problems in the switched LAN.
- Chapter 9 walks through solving the classic and all-too-common problems experienced in the LAN in a step-by-step way.
- Chapter 10 makes you a smart tool shopper by providing you with the motivation for needing tools and showing you what to look for when shopping for tools.
- Chapter 11 focuses on building your switched LAN and creating a manageable switched LAN design.
- Chapter 12 concludes this book by discussing how to build a comprehensive, well-tuned network management system.

Audience

It is pretty evident that LANs are moving toward switching technologies in a big way. The sale of switches, number of switch vendors, and trade journal coverage have grown substantially over the past few years in an effort to support the popularity of switching within the LAN. Switched LANs offer the necessary infrastructure for today's LAN needs as well as a rich base for tomorrow's. This book provides you with the background for understanding this new wave of LANs and sets you up for understanding how to manage and grow a networking system.

Although the focus of this book is on managing switched LANs, it has general applicability for many. Since the foundation of switched LAN management is traditional network management, you will find this book useful, even if your network isn't completely switched; it may help you to *switch* over. In addition, anyone who really wants a short book about how LANs work and what problems are associated with LANs will find this book appealing. And last, the student or the inquisitive soul who once took apart a vacuum cleaner or any other complex device should enjoy this text.

Acknowledgments

The richness of a book is greatly influenced by the people who surround the author. Over the years as an engineer I have been fortunate to have linked up with some of the greats. In my previous jobs there were Luther Barber who taught me how to build professional software; Elizabeth Ricci with whom I share software patents; Jim Perry, my best friend and colleague (a true, network management diehard); and Dan Carr, an organizational genius—someone who can get any effort off the ground. In my current job are my previous manager, Nelson Ronkin, who supported and encouraged this effort; Ko Baryiames and Jing Xiang, two outstanding engineers who technically prereviewed most of the text prior to sending it to my publisher, and Andrew Ward, an outstanding sage who does network management for a living. I'd also like to thank all of the fine technical reviewers provided under the direction of Addison Wesley Longman: Chuck Black, Jeff Burgan, Jeffrey D. Case of SNMP Research, Inc., J. Alan Gatlin of Livingston Enterprises, Bob Natale, Radia Perlman, Ravi Prakash, Linda Richman, and Peter Stutz. This team helped me make the text as technically accurate as possible with correct focus and flow. And last but clearly not least, I would like to thank Karen Gettman, Mary Harrington, Melissa Lima, and the entire Addison Wesley Longman team. This team helped greatly in the process of writing this book.

PART ONE

Fundamentals of Network Management

CHAPTER 1

Network Management in a Nutshell

1.1 Introduction

This chapter captures the essence of network management of a LAN. The emphasis is on presenting a quick, focused, yet thorough tour of traditional network management that serves as the foundation for the management of switched LANs. At the end of this chapter you should have a good understanding of what traditional network management is and how switched LAN management builds off and extends it.

1.2 A "Simple" Network

Currently the communications industry is experiencing explosive growth. Having your business "networked" is no longer an option; it is a requirement. Advances in technology have made building a "simple" network much easier than it was in the past.

PCs now come with integrated Network Interface Cards (NICs) ready to be plugged into a network. Setting up a network is no longer a daunting task; three PCs with integrated NICs, three lengths of Unshielded Twisted Pair (UTP) wire, and a small workgroup hub or switch constitute a simple LAN.[1] Figure 1.1 illustrates a simple network.

The network is extended by adding additional users, electronic mail, a shared printer, or a database server. Internet access to the World Wide Web (WWW) is provided by adding a modem (or on a larger scale by adding a

---

1. This completes a "simple" LAN from a hardware perspective. However, to make the LAN operational from a software point of view, you need a Network Operating System (NOS). PCs today are pre-installed with NOSs (Windows 95, Windows/NT) as Operating Systems (O/Ss) have evolved to subsume this task. In Chapter 5 we will talk more about some of the software aspects of making the "simple" network work from a software perspective.

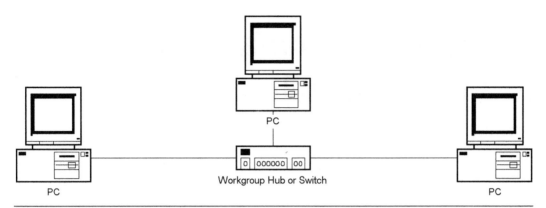

Figure 1.1 Simple network

router with a firewall) and subscribing to an Internet Service Provider (ISP). An Intranet may be formed connecting many sites via leased lines using network routers. Soon the simple network of three PCs becomes several PCs, workstations, and file and print servers. To satisfy the need for more networking horsepower, the workgroup hub is replaced by a switch. This significantly improves the overall network bandwidth for devices on the network. The network continues to grow with the organization. Soon the small business becomes a business built around the network. Keeping the network up, well-tuned, and capable of supporting more and more users becomes a job— simply stated, the network must be managed.

Network management must support diverse networks with varied network devices, have an intuitive user interface, place low overhead on the network, and be resilient to network breakage. Clearly a tool that uses 30 percent of all available bandwidth to manage only a single device is of limited use. Likewise a Graphical User Interface (GUI) that could easily double as an adventure game may be entertaining but not terribly useful. Last, a tool that fails to work when a network device "times out" is of questionable value.

Networks based on switching technology present new challenges to network management. Each switched interface may be a separate LAN or may be directly connected to an end station providing a "private LAN." One can no longer get the entire pulse of the network by monitoring any link in the network. In addition to understanding the fundamentals of traditional network management, the manager of the switched LAN must understand switching and the many technologies that comprise a switched LAN environment.

1.3 The Model

Network management is built largely upon three models:

- **International Organization for Standardization (ISO) 7498-4 Standard** has become the industry standard for dividing network management into functional areas.

- **Open Systems Interconnection (OSI) Reference Model** serves as the foundation for dividing the functions of a network into layers. The fields of both networking and network management revolve around this standard.

- **Management station/agent model** provides network device control and monitoring. The management station serves as the controlling point (network view) to various network device agents. In turn these network device agents provide the interfaces to the network devices that comprise your network.

Once you understand these three models, you are well on your way to understanding network management.

1.3.1 ISO Functional Areas of Management

The International Organization for Standardization (ISO) has partitioned network management into five functional areas. Figure 1.2 presents a quick checklist on how you may assess the overall health of your network based on these five areas:

- Configuration management
- Fault management
- Performance management
- Security management
- Accounting management

These are the areas of management that you need to focus on in order to manage any network successfully. You can emphasize various levels of management of each of these areas. I have organized them in order of most to least importance based on the requests I have received for functional features over the past years.

- **Configuration management** is the process of initially setting up your network, baselining this configuration (taking a snapshot of the configuration so that you have a record of each network device's customization), and responding to network changes (for example, new

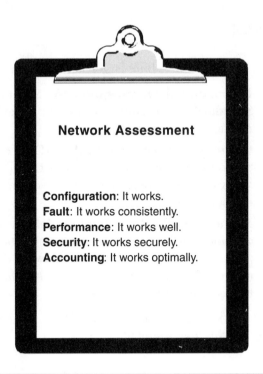

Figure 1.2 Network management checklist

users, network expansion, new network services), which requires subsequent network setup or modifications. Configuration management is by far the most important aspect of network management because, if your network is not properly configured, it may not work at all, may fail unexpectedly, or may not be giving you optimal network performance.

An example of configuration management is updating the embedded software of a switch or many switches within your LAN. Another example is setting up the name of the system contact (the person responsible for the network device) on one or more switches in your network.

- **Fault management** refers to the discovery, isolation, and resolution of network problems. This is the second most important area of management because faults can cause portions of your network to malfunction, to work only intermittently, or to fail completely in the future. By properly managing faults, you can often resolve user problems (like loss of network connectivity) and prevent future problems from occurring.

An example of fault management is responding when a network device reboots. The response may be sending urgent mail or automatically interfacing with the network manager's beeper. If a core network device persistently reboots, network "brownout" may be imminent. Another example may be a fault in a port's transmitter, resulting in high error rates. In this case the error rate can cause cascaded failures by causing a protocol like spanning tree to constantly reconfigure itself.

- **Performance management** ties with security management as third in importance. How you perceive the network to perform is often the most critical metric for an organization. Performance is managed by measuring the network utilization and end-to-end response time at various points in your network. Network utilization is the fraction of a network component used for transmitting data at any given moment. End-to-end response time is the amount of time it takes for data to go from one point in your network to another. The TCP/IP Packet Internet Groper ("ping") tool is commonly used to approximate end-to-end response time.

  An example of performance management is tracking Ethernet utilization on all switched interfaces and determining the top "N" most active interfaces and the top "N" most underutilized interfaces (where N is often 10). This data can help you tune your network.

- **Security management** refers to keeping the data in your network in the correct hands or out of the wrong hands. Naturally if you have a WWW site or provide remote access for your users, you need to ensure via a firewall (a data access barrier) or proper passwording that unknown users do not have access to your corporate network. Likewise in certain organizations, certain data are restricted, and you must ensure that the proper level of encrypting and passwording is used for these data.

  An example of security management is adding and maintaining password protection to certain database servers that store sensitive data. Another example of security is installing a firewall between your LAN and the Internet.

- **Accounting management** refers to tracking usage of your network resources. A common example of accounting management is password administration. Sometimes accounting software is used to track network usage so that you may potentially reconfigure "power" users with higher bandwidth or restrict use of WAN connections as dictated by your organization's networking policy. By tracking network usage on an individual basis, you can often tune your network to perform better.

Another example of accounting management is recording traffic levels for individual ports or recording traffic composition (the number of IPX packets, IP packets, or AppleTalk packets) going across a given network link and then modifying your configuration to result in better performance. You may also wish to record only average aggregate bandwidth and charge network users based on network usage. Last, tracking software licenses across your network is a final example of an accounting management function that will become more and more important as networks grow.

A S I D E . . .

With the advent of the WWW, expect an increased emphasis on security! Your organization's security policy will vary depending on your organizational needs and requirements.

1.3.2 The OSI (Open Systems Interconnection) Seven Layer Reference Model

Divide-and-conquer is a widely deployed technique used in the development and debugging of software. The OSI Reference Model, which includes seven communication layers (a standard defined and approved by ISO), is an attempt to divide and conquer the complexities of communication into manageable units. Although at times the seven-layer split may seem nebulous, the field of networking constantly references these layers. Subsequently, understanding the subdivision and the general motivation for these layers is fundamental to understanding the task of managing a network. My advice: Memorize this chart. Then, when the next person says it's a layer 2 problem, you will know precisely what the person is talking about.

Coupled with the OSI Reference Model seven layers (see Table 1.1), you will see every communication stack "retrofitted" (they never fit exactly) to depict the functional parallelisms. One stack, the TCP/UDP over IP communication stack, is a popular and widely deployed stack used in LANs. Simple Network Management Protocol (SNMP), the main vehicle for managing network devices, typically runs using IP (or IPX) over UDP. SNMP is discussed in detail in the next chapter.

Layers 1, 2, and 3 deserve extra attention as these layers are where most network management takes place today.

Table 1.1 OSI Reference Model

Layer Number	OSI 7 Layers	TCP/IP Layers	Responsibility
7	**Application**		Provides access to network services. (Applications like Telnet, FTP, and e-mail span layers 5–7.)
6	**Presentation**	There is no clear distinction between these layers in TCP/IP.	Provides workstation-based interpretation of display formatting according to application requirements.
5	**Session**		Coordinates communication connections between applications across the network.
4	**Transport**	**TCP, UDP**	Provides end-to-end management. For example, TCP provides flow control, acknowledgment, sequencing, checksumming, and error correction; TCP also provides connection-oriented, "reliable" communication. UDP provides connectless-communication (datagram) service, a very thin layer on top of IP. UDP also provides "unreliable" communication—the data may get to its destination, or it may not.
3	**Network**	**IP, ICMP, ARP** (address resolution protocol), **RARP** (reverse ARP)	Is responsible for routing of packets (which encapsulate frames) across the network.
2	**Data Link**	**Data link** (Ethernet, ATM adaptation, FDDI, Fast Ethernet, Token Ring, and Gigabit Ethernet *span both the **data** link and **physical layers**.*)	Regulates access to the network. Provides point-to-point frame formation and management for various protocols. All frames contain source and destination addresses.
1	**Physical**	**physical**	Controls physical attachment including wiring and signaling.

Layer 1 is responsible for delivering data across a network link; think of it as providing a "stream of bits" across a wire. Layer 1 must regulate signaling and ensure that the signal stays strong. *Repeaters* and *concentrators* are network devices that operate at layer 1. Repeaters are used between two lengths of wire to regenerate a signal, and concentrators (a special type of repeater) are used to share a single signal among many stations. It is important to follow the rules associated with the maximum span of wire and wire type associated LAN technologies like Ethernet, Token Ring, and FDDI. We talk about cable management in Chapter 8.

Layer 2 is responsible for transmitting frames of data across a layer-1 physical connection. Data frames are checked for errors and contain source and destination addresses. Two distinct layer 2 segments may be linked together with a bridge that operates at the layer-2 level. Switches, sometimes referred to as *multiport bridges*, operate at layer 2. We discuss layer 2 protocols in Chapter 3 and switching in Chapter 4.

Layer 3 is responsible for routing packets (comprised of one or more individual frames) across one or more links, enabling stations to communicate across the network. Primarily this layer must determine the appropriate route between stations. This layer is also responsible for fragmentation and reassembly of data and network congestion. *Network routers* operate at the layer-3 level. We discuss layer 3 in Chapter 5.

A S I D E . . .

Most routers today also do packet filtering (filtering out certain packets based on information in the packet header like source or destination address) that is technically part of layer 4.

It is important to note that the OSI seven layers exist on each side of network communication. Each layer "talks" with its counterpart, ignoring the "communication" of adjacent layers. The following diagram (Figure 1.3) depicts this communication, combined with the common network devices that facilitate connectivity. These devices are the fundamental core of a LAN.

Another ASIDE . . .

The division of layers also facilitates interoperability. For example, different physical implementations allow both FDDI (fiber) and CDDI (copper) to exist within a LAN.

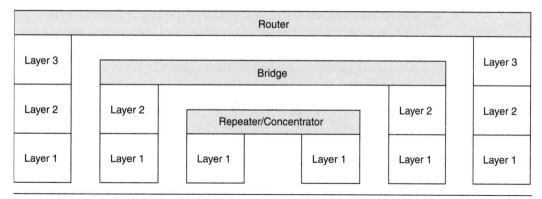

Figure 1.3 Relationship between network devices and OSI Reference Model

1.3.3 TCP/IP Layers

TCP/IP combines the efforts of layers 3 (network layer) and 4 (transport layer). TCP/IP serves as the backbone to the Internet (and subsequently the WWW), is widely used in LANs, and is the foundation for SNMP. There is *a lot* to TCP/IP. The following definitions provide you with the terms defined in the OSI/TCP/IP layer chart shown previously. These definitions give you a minimal working set of TCP/IP knowledge—throughout the book we will build on this simple base.[2]

- **Transmission Control Protocol (TCP)** provides reliable, end-to-end connections and is responsible for error control and recovery. TCP is designated as a reliable connection-oriented service. Telnet, File Transfer Protocol (FTP) and remote log in (rlogin) run on top of TCP, ensuring a reliable terminal emulation session or file transfer session.

- **User Datagram Protocol (UDP)** provides a simple connectionless service. This service does not establish a connection with its counterpart prior to communicating and supports only limited optional error checking. UDP is often designated as an unreliable connectionless service. SNMP runs on top of UDP.

- **Internet Protocol (IP)** provides a connectionless routing service. It is responsible for packet fragmentation and reassembly, routing, and data encapsulation.

---

2. This book does not, however, provide comprehensive TCP/IP coverage. There are many fine books that do. Please consult the bibliography for selected books.

■ **Address Resolution Protocol (ARP)** operates at layer 2. It provides a mechanism to find a Media Access Control (MAC) address (address of the format xx-xx-xx-xx-xx-xx—for example, 00-20-AF-12-34-56) given an IP address (address of the format xxx.xxx.xxx.xxx—for example, 192.168.1.43). The ARP command on your PC or Unix workstation can be used to list the association between MAC and IP addresses.

■ **Reverse Address Resolution Protocol (RARP)** provides a mechanism to find an IP address given a known network address (MAC).

A S I D E . . .

A MAC address is a unique address across your network, typically burned into the network interface card (NIC) on your computer. The IP address is an assigned address that enables a network to be segmented based on traffic flow and other network management policy. Chapter 5 will discuss TCP/IP addressing.

■ **Internet Control Message Protocol (ICMP)** provides communication of control data (information and error recovery data) between IP nodes in the network. Ping, a simple TCP/IP tool used to determine connectivity, is built on top of ICMP.

1.3.4 Management Stations and Agents

Network Management involves *management stations* and network device *agents*. A management station provides a text or graphical view into the network, based on information retrieved or sent from one or more device agents. Agents provide information about a network device and an interface into the device for configuration changes. Some network devices have multiple agents running inside and enable you to proxy (gain access) to a specific agent using the same network address by a different password (or community string in SNMP lingo). You may have several management stations operating concurrently providing different views (or the same view in multiple geographically distributed locations) of your network. Figure 1.4 illustrates a management station running a management application that is "talking" to the agent of a network device.

Through a management station you can

■ change the configuration of your network,

■ react to network faults,

■ observe your network's performance,

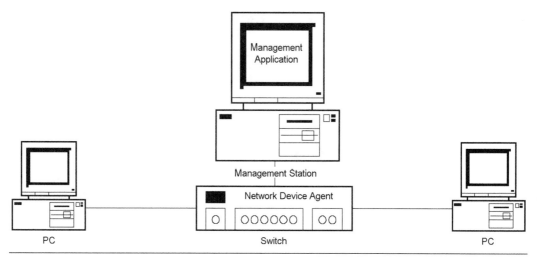

Figure 1.4 Management components

- monitor your network's security, and
- track your network usage.

The management station provides you a window into the network where you monitor and control your network.

Agents provide access to network devices—a "view" into the internals of a device and a way to modify the way a device works. An agent provides an interface to track certain key counters (such as those necessary to calculate utilization), to tweak parameters (allowing you to customize a device to work with your network), or to forward events (traps) when faults occur.

Agents are typically specific to a network device. Generally speaking, each network device in your network has its own interface and its own set of manageable attributes (there are exceptions—especially with stackable network devices). Manageable attributes are known as objects in network management and are defined in Management Information Bases (MIBs); MIBs are discussed in the next chapter. Note that there are many objects that are *common* to all network devices and are defined in standard MIBs. Common objects make it possible to compare the characteristics of several distinct network devices across your network.

This combination of management stations and agents makes it possible for you to take control of your network.

1.4 Traditional Management Techniques, Strategies, and Tools

This section discusses traditional LANs. It is useful to understand the components of traditional LANs since switched LANs build off many of the same fundamental underpinnings.

1.4.1 Traditional LANs

Most traditional LANs use shared media technology. Using shared media, all nodes are physically or logically connected on a few shared media segments. The major disadvantage of shared media is scaling; as the number of users increases, so does the contention (with Ethernet) for network access. Having only a few segments does, however, simplify network management. This is because *all* network traffic can be monitored by probing only a few points, enabling you to easily get the "pulse" of your network. Figure 1.5 provides an example of a traditional LAN.

Traditional LANs are constructed mainly using three network devices: repeaters, bridges, and routers. These devices form a hierarchy as shown in Figure 1.6.

As mentioned previously, *routers* are devices that operate at layer 3 of the network which have many networking capabilities. Routers provide a mechanism to:

- segment your network based on policy and traffic flows (in TCP this is called subneting; see Chapter 5 for details).
- connect to the WAN.
- add a firewall to stop certain traffic from flowing.
- connect one or more dissimilar LANs.

In Figure 1.5 we have shared devices on a separate LAN. Routers contain broadcast traffic (traffic destined for all network devices on the LAN) within each LAN they connect.

Bridges connect two segments. Local traffic on each side of the bridge stays local; traffic destined for the other side is forwarded. Bridges restrict traffic to a given segment and enable you to grow a network by adding more segments. Bridges also enable you to connect two dissimilar LANs, such as Ethernet and Token Ring.

Repeaters are used to extend an Ethernet segment simply by amplifying and regenerating the physical signal. Repeaters enable the physical length of the shared media to be extended.

Network Interface Cards (*NICs*) provide the interface to the network for

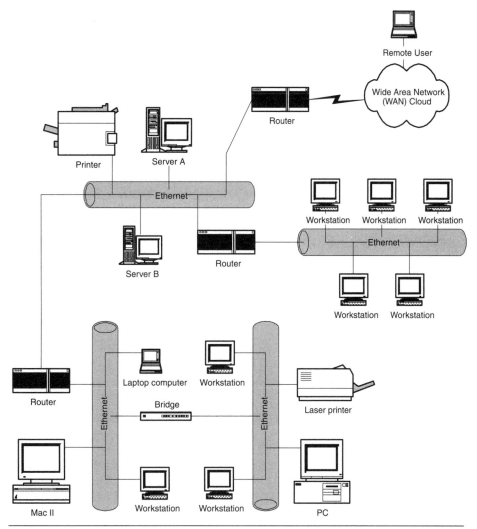

Figure 1.5 Example of traditional LAN. Notice shared Ethernet segments.

your workstations, PCs, and MACs. *Cables* and *cable connectors* connect all your network devices together. Popular cabling options are Unshielded Twisted Pair (UTP), fiber, and coaxial cable. Certain higher speed technologies require better cable, for example, Fast Ethernet requires CAT 5 UTP or 4 pairs of CAT 3 UTP. Cabling distance is also important due to signal attenuation.

1.4.2 Traps, Sets, and Polling

Bridges and routers within a traditional LAN are managed with three primary mechanisms: traps, sets, and polling. Figure 1.7 shows our simple network with

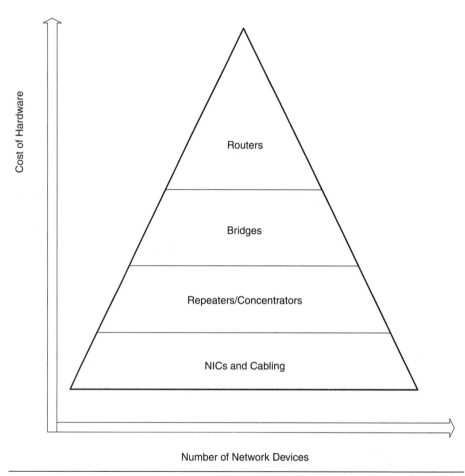

Figure 1.6 Traditional network hierarchy of devices

the data flow of these three mechanisms. These mechanisms are facilitated through Simple Network Management Protocol (SNMP), discussed in the next chapter.

Traps are equivalent to events. An event is a condition that is reported to one or more network management stations that are "listening" for the event. Events happen at nonregular intervals; they are often used to report "something-has-gone-wrong—direct-your-attention-here" type of messages. For example, an agent sends a trap when its device reboots; some agents emit a trap when a certain utilization threshold has been exceeded. In many cases it may be desirable to start a polling operation based on the receipt of a certain trap—this is often called *trap-based* polling.

Sets are used to modify or initially establish configuration information. For example, when you set up a device you typically will want to define which management stations will receive traps when the network device is experiencing

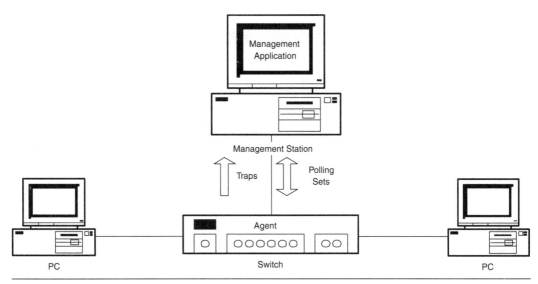

Figure 1.7 Simple network with management data flow

problems. Or perhaps you set up the designated system administrator for each device; you may also need to set up routing parameters that typically need to be synchronized across your network.

Polling is used to monitor your network. You can monitor your network's configuration (for example, take a snapshot of the current configuration and compare it against an established baseline), or you can monitor your network performance (for example, retrieve the necessary attributes on a network interface to calculate network utilization).

You can also monitor network usage for security and accounting purposes. Remember that polling takes network bandwidth and that management requests take CPU cycles to process by the network device you are monitoring. Consequently, you need to poll for information judiciously.

1.4.3 Network Device Management

Network device management refers to management of a single device within your LAN. A device has a physical representation to it; in a switched LAN a device refers to any member of the device hierarchy—repeater, stackable hub, chassis hub, bridge, router, or backbone switch.

Device management may involve all areas of network management and is typically facilitated with a graphic "mimic" of the device showing operation state and providing access to key statistics such as interface utilization. See Figure 1.8.

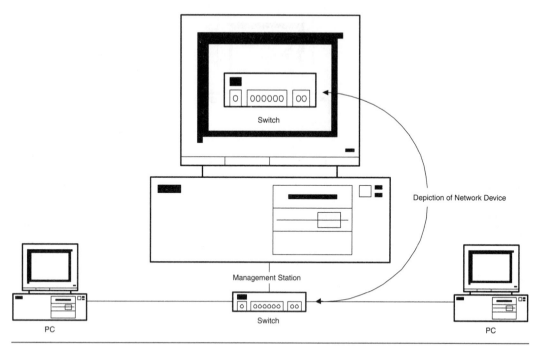

Figure 1.8 Simple network with device management of single switch in network

1.4.4. Enterprise Management

Enterprise management refers to providing a network-wide management view that may optionally be divided into one or more network domains in order to segment management responsibilities cleanly. Segmentation is especially useful in large, distributed organizations because it provides a way to manage independently the details of a domain locally and to limit the amount of data that is rolled up (often over a WAN connection) to the enterprise view.

Selected events and polled data are rolled up to the enterprise. Much of the data stays within its local domain. Data sharing and appropriate data rollup are important aspects of enterprise management. Regardless of the size of the network or number of domains, enterprise management looks at the network as a single entity, as a system made up of network devices that together provide network connectivity for many users and applications within the organization.

1.4.5 Browsers, Platforms, and Vendor Solutions

Common network management platforms are Hewlett-Packard's OpenView, IBM's NetView for AIX, Sun Microsystems' SunNetManager, and Cabletron's

Spectrum. Platforms are aimed at providing a single management view of your entire network enterprise. This view is typically a graphical map that is first discovered via the platform and then later refined by you to depict the physical outlay of your network. See Figure 1.9 for an example of a map.

Typically the network includes the network backbone (or the core of the network), WAN access points, edge routers, and end nodes. Color is used to denote device state—green may indicate okay, yellow may be used for warning, red is often used for critical errors, and blue may be used when the device is unreachable. From this graphical map you can make device queries, launch vendor-specific network management (for example a front-panel view of a device), and customize how the manager should handle key device events.

All platforms have an event log for traps that are sent to the management station. Platforms typically collect raw attributes (or objects) on periodic sampling intervals, optionally evaluate custom algebraic expressions, and alert you via color coding or event logging of conditions. You can completely customize this collection. An example of an expression may be to collect a number of cyclic redundancy check (CRC) errors on an Ethernet segment. When a segment exceeds a certain value, turn the network device red.

All platforms have device "browsers" that enable you to look at generalized network device objects (or objects specific to a network device) by walking down the browser tree and making a query. One problem with platforms is that they are general purpose; they do not provide comprehensive coverage of all the objects in each network device that you need to monitor in order to manage your network. Vendor-specific solutions attempt to fill this void. See Figure 1.9.

Vendor-specific solutions are network management applications that are tailored for a device or family of network devices. 3Com's Transcend Enterprise Manager, Cisco's CiscoWorks, and Bay Network's Optivity are examples of vendor-specific solutions. These solutions often loosely integrate with the common network management platforms; that is, you can launch the application with map context and provide comprehensive management for a vendor's device. If you purchase equipment from many different vendors, you will need to become familiar with many different applications to manage your network.

1.5 Switched LAN Management

Although switched LAN management builds on the foundations of traditional network management, there are many differences worth noting. This section first defines what a switch is and then discusses the components of both switched and traditional LANs with a focus on switched LANs.

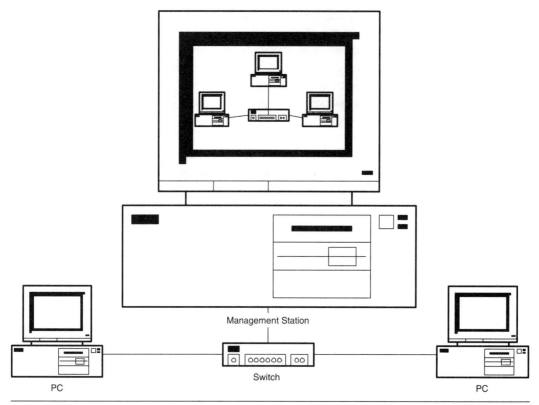

Figure 1.9 Simple network with platform map-based management of itself

1.5.1 What is a Switch?

A switch is a network device designed to greatly reduce network congestion and network contention (Ethernet) commonly found within traditional shared LANs; switches often result in a significant performance improvement within your LAN. Switches work by providing a *central integration point* (the switch) for many *separate LANs* (ports/interfaces on the switch). Each port is a separate LAN with its own dedicated pipe into the LAN; LANs are interconnected by "switching" across a high-speed backplane (typically many gigabits). For example, an Ethernet switch may have several Ethernet ports (each providing a 10 Mbps-dedicated bandwidth) that are switched across a 3-gigabyte (3000 Mbps) switch backplane. Switches often "switch" together many technologies including Ethernet, Fast Ethernet, FDDI, and Token Ring, making it relatively simple to use a variety of technologies in a LAN. Figure 1.10 shows how a traditional LAN segment may be converted to a switched LAN, each PC having its own segment.

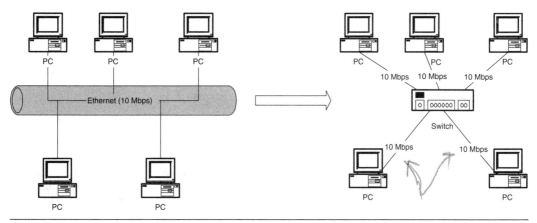

Figure 1.10 Traditional LAN segment (left) transitioned to a switched LAN (right)

*where each device is
on a seperate segment*

1.5.2 Switched LANs

Switched LANs use switching technology to facilitate increased bandwidth at the desktop and backbone necessary for network-hungry applications. Switched LANs build off the same technologies used in traditional LANs: repeating, bridging, and routing; switching itself is based on bridging technology. Switching does not require wholesale network replacement—many of the advantages of switching can be realized by replacing routers, local bridges, and hubs with switches using existing wiring within traditional networks, transparent to the user at the desktop. Switching often can be used to complement an existing network infrastructure. Figure 1.11 illustrates a switched LAN.

Switching enables easy traffic segmentation by providing discrete LAN interfaces that are interconnected to form a bigger LAN. For example, an Ethernet port to which you connect as few as one user essentially results in a dedicated 10 Mbps pipe for that user—free of frame collisions of others. Interconnection occurs through an intelligent switching fabric (massively parallel interconnection devices) that directs traffic to its destination (another part on the switch), greatly reducing the contention characteristic of traditional Ethernet LANs. By use of optimized buffering schemes, switching fabric often switches frames at line speed—this, coupled with the reduced contention found within shared media, greatly reduces network bottlenecks. Switched LANs can easily be extended by adding more interfaces. See Figure 1.12.

Switches *switch* all the current and imminently emerging technologies: Ethernet, Fast Ethernet, FDDI, Token Ring, ATM, and Gigabit Ethernet. As technology advances, central switch upgrades can be done to increase performance, again largely transparent to the user. If the user has a 10/100 Mbps NIC and Category 5 wiring, a central change from a 10 Mbps port to a 100 Mbps

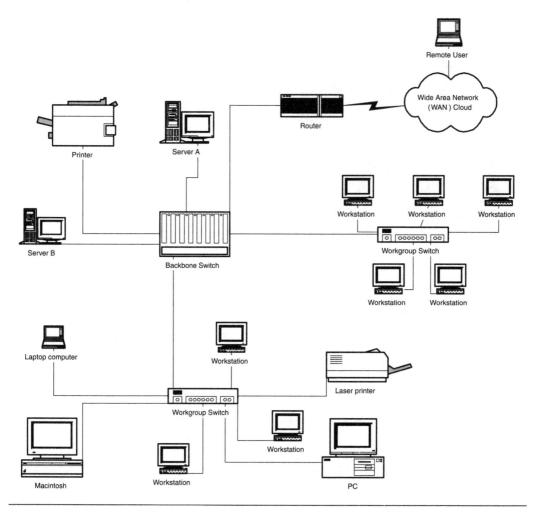

Figure 1.11 Example of switched LAN

port will increase the user's bandwidth by a factor of 10 without even going to the user's office. Figure 1.12 shows a switch connected directly to a few PCs.

Switch LANs are made up of the following hierarchy of components (or-dered by power and price, highest to lowest), as shown in Figure 1.13.

- **Routers:** (Same function as in a traditional LAN.) Often routing tech-nology is integrated into backbone or workgroup switches, providing "a network in a box" with complimentary switching and routing.

- **Backbone Switches:** High-end switches that are deployed at the core of a network and use switching technology. These switches aggre-gate data from hubs and workgroup switches providing interconnec-

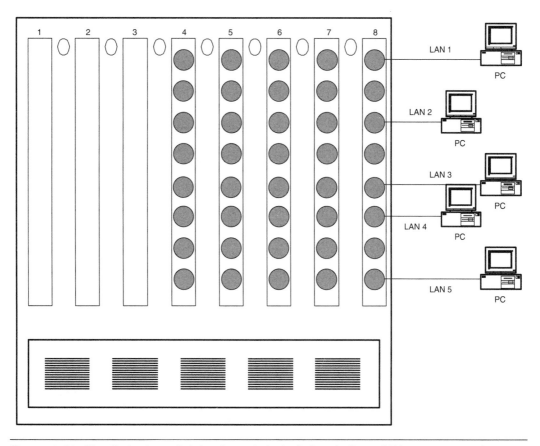

Figure 1.12 Simplistic view of eight-slot switch depicting dedicated Ethernet connections to five PCs in slot 8

tion among these devices. Backbone switches typically accept various cards that contain various network options; FDDI, Ethernet, Fast Ethernet, Token Ring, and ATM are usually supported by card options. These switches typically have one or more high-speed interconnections such as FDDI, Fast Ethernet, or ATM. Gigabit Ethernet will be initially deployed at the backbone.

■ **Workgroup Switches:** Lower-end network devices that aggregate multiple shared segments by using switching technology. Workgroup switches are typically deployed at the desktop level. An example of a common switch is a 12-port Ethernet switch that provides 1.2 GB aggregate bandwidth and can be thought of as 12 discrete Ethernet LANs. Often a workgroup switch switches onto a high-speed backbone connection such as FDDI or Fast Ethernet.

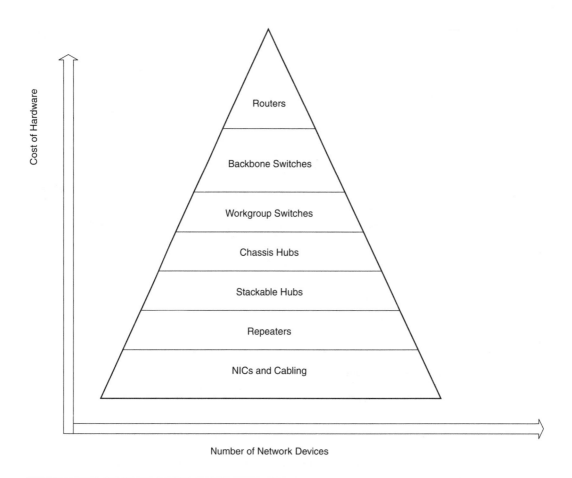

Figure 1.13 Switched network hierarchy of devices

- **Chassis Hubs:** "Big iron" boxes that can contain a variety of network modules. A chassis hub is a box with a power supply and high-speed backplane capable of housing repeaters, bridges, switches, or concentrators. The high-speed backplane is used to store data between plug-in modules. Often a network module will be sold either as a "plug in" to a chassis hub or as a standalone in a box with power supply.

- **Stackable Hubs:** Devices that provide shared media access by logically extending the *backplane*. (The backplane is a shared bus across the stackable units over which data can be transmitted.) Stackables share aggregate bandwidth among many ports, performing the same function as a repeater to many ports at once. Unlike a repeater, stackable hubs may be stacked to add more ports to the same aggregate bandwidth. A 16-port Ethernet hub is commonly stackable. Often stackables can be managed as one logical entity even though there may be several physically separate devices stacked.

- **Repeaters:** (Same function as in a traditional LAN.)
- **NICs and Cabling:** (Same function as in a traditional LAN.)

1.5.3 Differences from Traditional Network Management

The main difference between managing a switched LAN and a traditional LAN is the level of granularity at which you must manage. Platforms tend to manage at the device level rather than at the interface level—managing at the interface level is a requirement of switched LAN management.

In a traditional network consisting of repeaters, bridges, routers, and end nodes, you can adequately represent the network's state in a platform map. A traditional repeater restores the network signal enabling the network to span greater distances. If the repeater is manageable (and not all repeaters are) and a failure occurs, network connectivity between nodes connected by the repeater will be severed. A traditional bridge connects two local area networks. If the bridge fails, the two local area networks will lose connectivity between them. A traditional router provides interconnection between LAN subnets and/or the WAN. If the router that provides the default route off a subnet fails, nodes on that subnet will not be able to connect to systems beyond the subnet. All of these states and conditions can be depicted with the granularity of a platform's network map. Figure 1.14 shows a management station running a network map application of our simple network.

In a traditional network one can also monitor performance and security, as well as do accounting by monitoring the network at only a small number of points—the points at which traffic flows. The data highway of a traditional LAN typically has a few points of intersection (the more routers, obviously, the more points of intersection) at which you need to focus your network monitoring.

In a switched LAN, each switched device by itself contains several LANs. A switch is a bridge that has several interfaces (FDDI, 10 Mbps Ethernet, 100 Mbps Ethernet, ATM). Each interface is a separate manageable entity, a separate "LAN." Many LAN switches switch traffic between each of these interfaces at line speed and contain local traffic (traffic between interfaces on the same switch) within the switch. Managing switched devices with a platform often breaks down, since, even though overall switched device status is important, you really need to know the status of each interface (or part) on the switched devices (or ports) to determine the overall health of your network.

Bandwidth management, improved network security, fault recovery, simultaneous configuration across many ports, and simplication of user moves,

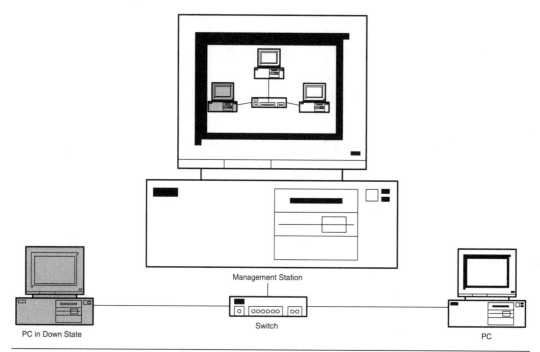

Figure 1.14 Simple network with a self-depicting map showing a PC in down state

adds, and changes are key to switched LAN management. Network modeling (that is, being able to predict the impact on network growth and change) is expected to grow in importance as networking continues to explode. Subsequent sections in this book will go into detail on these subjects.

1.5.4 Scaling

Switched LAN management tools must scale. It is typical for a single network device (for example, a backbone switch) to contain over 100 interfaces that need to be managed. If you have a large network with several hundred network devices, you may have in excess of 10,000 interfaces to manage. So ask yourself: What are the characteristics of tools that scale?

Tools that scale offer both decentralized polling and leverage trap-based polling and minimize the frequency of polling as much as possible:

- *Decentralized polling* is another name for distributed management. Rather than poll raw network information from one point in your network and incur the large hit of traffic to one location, distributed pollers locally collect raw network data (like counters and states) and roll up information to the central site. This technique minimizes the amount of raw data that goes across the network (network management traffic is localized), gives some fault tolerance by having multiple data collectors (if one poller goes down, collection does not stop for the entire network), and enables the network manager to control more readily the polling frequency across devices (poll the backbone more frequently). Decentralized polling is necessary in LANs in large corporations.

- *Trap-based polling* relates to polling on demand rather than on timed intervals. This type of polling is largely dependent on the richness of traps supported by the network device. Also, since traps do not guarantee delivery, there is some risk of not collecting data when they are needed. Often a combination of less frequently scheduled polling with trap-based polling works well.

- *Minimized polling* is possible by placing more intelligence in the device. Rather than collecting raw data, you collect information. Device support of Remote Network Monitor (RMON) and Remote Network Monitor Version 2 (RMON2) at the interface level has recently become very popular because of this switched network management requirement.

1.5.5 Enterprise, Device, and Interface Granularity

Switched LAN management must present a network health picture of the network at various levels. Is my entire network performing well? Does Building X supported by Switch A have adequate bandwidth? Is the LAN defined by Switch A, Slot B, Port C experiencing high utilization?

By adequately monitoring all interfaces on your switched LAN and rolling up data appropriately, you can answer all of these questions with confidence. Strong switched LAN management tools provide you the granularity to view and manage your network from multiple vantage points, giving you a health statement at any time. Strong tools also record data so that you can historically track trends, proactively manage growth, and prevent future breakdowns.

1.5.6 Logical versus Physical

The physical layout of your network does not necessarily reflect the logical way your network is used or should be managed. One of the criticisms of moving to a switched LAN infrastructure is that, when you flatten your network essentially to a bridged network, you open up the broadcast domain to a much larger area—this can dramatically increase the amount of broadcast traffic each NIC must sort through and intensifies the problem of broadcast storms. Virtual LANs (VLANS), as discussed in Chapter 4, are a solution to create logical groupings of interfaces across the network. In the same way that interfaces can be grouped in a VLAN, they can be managed as a logical group, spanning many devices. VLANs contain broadcast traffic and provide a way to secure network access. This is much different from conventional network management, which manages the network as a single collection of devices.

1.5.7. Switched Performance Management

Switched performance management involves the same utilization metrics as conventional LANs; there are just a lot more places of measurement. It is important for the network manager to monitor all interfaces that represent LANs at some level of a management scheme; for example, backbone interfaces should be monitored more frequently. By observing utilization of an extended period, you can denote network bottlenecks, trends of network usage, and places where interfaces may be underutilized. This information can be used to tune your network and to determine future network requirements.

1.5.8 Switched Configuration Management

Switched configuration management involves the management of many interfaces, across many devices. This calls out for *bulk* network management— management of many interfaces at once. For example, you may want to change the community strings (read or write network device passwords) on weekly intervals for security management. Doing this by telneting into 100+ devices and traversing several different menu structures gets old very fast and is prone to error. Tools that allow you to apply a network management task across many devices and record the results simultaneously are important for configuration management of switched LANs. In addition, having tools that enable you to take a snapshot of a device's configuration (complete with the configuration of all of its interfaces) that can be later used as a template for a new network device is a useful feature for network management.

1.5.9 Troubleshooting a Switched LAN

Since a switched LAN is really a collection of many interfaces or LANs, it is important that each of these interfaces is monitored for areas that indicate current problems and areas that indicate a likely source of future problems. For Ethernet, it is important to monitor the number of collisions and the number of frame check sequence (FCS) errors. For FDDI, it is important to monitor the link error rates; high-link error rates may be indicative of a bad connector.

By monitoring interfaces and logging traps, a network manager can identify problem areas before a pending network crisis. In addition, periodic reports can be instrumental in quickly identifying and resolving problems in times of network crises.

1.6 Summary

With the advent of switched LANs, the requirements of network management increase significantly. It is still important to manage the five key functional areas as identified by ISO. It is also important to focus on your network using the OSI Reference Model, since the bottom three layers (physical, data link, network) are how all switched LANs are constructed and the OSI Reference Model layers provide the common nomenclature used to talk about networking and network management.

All network management applications should have an intuitive interface, place a low overhead on the network, and work (at least to some degree) when the network is in trouble.

The platforms, browsers, and device mimics serve as a useful base to network management of all networks. With switched LANs, however, they lack the granularity needed to get an accurate view of the network and to manage the network adequately.

Switched LAN management involves management at a much finer granularity. Since each interface within a device may represent a LAN in itself, each interface must be independently managed. The management of individual interfaces, then, should be intelligently rolled up to present a view of the device and further focused to a view of the network. Tools that manage at the interface level and allow bulk and template operations will help you manage your network. Switched LAN management is new and evolving, and although it builds off the old, it opens the door to the new.

CHAPTER 2

Understanding Network Management Standards

2.1 Introduction

This chapter provides a concise summary of fundamental network management standards. The discussion focuses on practical management application, not on comprehensive coverage. For example, the fine details of data encoding and decoding are intentionally omitted; in addition, an in-depth discussion of every specification key word and esoteric Simple Network Management Protocol (SNMP or SNMPv1), tidbit is not presented. You could easily write a book on the material highlighted in this chapter (many have)—here we attempt to focus on the "must know" for understanding network management.

We start off by discussing Internet standards and dive right into how to read a Management Information Base (MIB). (MIBs are virtual databases of information used to define the functional and operational aspects of network devices.) We then discuss SNMP and its role in facilitating communication between the management station and network devices. A brief discussion on the emerging SNMPv2 standard follows, concentrating on the features that improve upon the original. We then discuss some standard MIBs, particularly focusing attention around MIB-2 and RMON, the classics for network management. We conclude with a discussion of RMON2, which provides network management up to the application layer.

This chapter presents the core SNMP infrastructure upon which network management is constructed. At the end of this chapter you should have a good idea about what the important network management standards are, how SNMP works conceptually, what RMON and RMON2 are all about, and where to find more detailed information about any specific standard. The chapter will leave you with the information necessary to understand what standard data exist for managing a network via SNMP.

2.2 Internet Standards

All Internet Standards are written in the form of Request For Comments (RFCs). RFCs are documents used by the Internet community initially to draft and then later (optionally) to ratify a standard; they are publicly available to anyone. A master index for all RFCs is in a file called `rfc-index.txt` that can be found on the node `ds.internic.net` under the RFC directory. This master location of RFCs is replicated across many sites throughout the world. Using anonymous **ftp** (log in as user anonymous using a password of your e-mail address), you can retrieve the index and any standard that you are interested in. Or, if you do not have ftp access but do have WWW access, you can get the RFCs at `http://ds2.internic.net/rfc/`.

RFCs go through several states before becoming a standard. RFCs start off as a preliminary draft upon which anyone can comment; they then go on to a proposed standard state, followed by a draft standard, and finally become a full standard. An RFC can stop anywhere along the way, because composing an RFC's draft in no way guarantees that the draft will become a standard. Likewise, a given RFC can literally take years to become a standard. The length of time it takes depends largely on how widespread the standard is expected to become. It is perfectly normal for an RFC to take a year to become a standard—this gives lots of time for refinement along the way.

The rigorous, arduous process of turning a draft into a standard is controlled by the Internet Engineering Task Force (IETF). The world's leading networking experts—mostly engineers from various network vendors—comprise this task force. Commenting on a draft is open to anyone. If you contribute valuable, unique comments on a draft, you are likely to be recruited to serve on the task force formed to ratify the RFC as a standard.

There are thousands of RFCs and new ones emerge weekly; reading new RFCs is a good way to stay abreast of what's new in networking and in the field of network management.

2.3 Network Management Standards

SNMP Version 1 is a widely accepted and deployed standard for managing network devices. The SNMP standard is described in the following four important RFCs:

- RFC 1155
- RFC 1212
- RFC 1157
- RFC 1213

Network management revolves around the concept of a MIB. Very simply stated, a MIB is a structured database of information that is physically located on a network device. Access to the information is provided by Simple Network Management Protocol (SNMP). MIB-2 is a common database of information that many network devices support. We now go through the standards that provide the *structure* (SMI), the *access* (SNMP), and a *set of common data* (MIB-2) used to manage your network.

2.3.1 The Structure of Management Information Standard

RFC 1155 defines the Structure of Management Information (SMI). SMI presents a global tree structure for management information and the original conventions, syntax, and rules for building MIBs.

RFC 1212 is logically grouped with RFC 1155 as it builds upon RFC 1155 by providing a more concise description of the SMI data representation mechanism. RFC 1212 further restricts the possible data constructs in order to keep management simple.

MIBs are concisely defined databases of information that characterize the functional and operational aspects of a network device. MIBs contain objects for each functional aspect of a network device that needs to be managed. This information provides the common "view" and structure of management capabilities shared between the management station and the network device's agent. Figure 2.1 shows an agent and management application "synchronized" by the MIB.

There are many MIBs in existence; some MIBs are vendor-specific and others are common. Common MIBs (for example, MIB-2, RMON, and RMON2) are very important in network management; they provide objects that are supported across many diverse devices, giving the network manager a consistent mechanism to manage a network device regardless of its vendor.

All MIB objects have a unique *object identifier* (OID). This object identifier is composed of a series of dot-separated positive integers (0...255) that define the object position within a global management tree. You need to know the OID for the object in order to access a MIB object from a network device. The global MIB tree is completely extensible to new MIBs as there are an infinite number of branches that can be added below designated branches (`private` and `experimental`) by the IETF. This structure results in objects with codes that are universally unique. Figure 2.2 illustates the global management tree.

The top of the SMI tree (`iso` (1), `org` (3), `dod` (6), `internet` (1), `mgmt` (2) or `1.3.6.1.2`) is used repeatedly in OIDs. This is often designated to be the global root prefix of every MIB object (see Table 2.1).

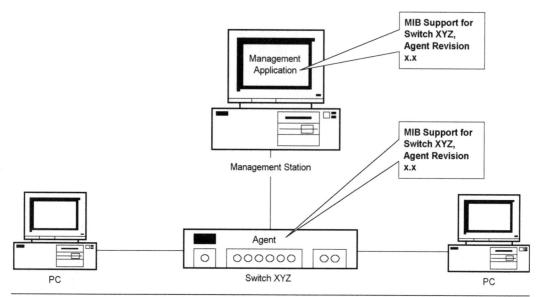

Figure 2.1 MIB shared between management application and agent

> ### A S I D E . . .
>
> One way to help you gain an understanding of the structure of MIBs is to use a MIB browser to "walk" various MIBs. MIB browsers are generally packaged with network management platforms. See Chapter 10 for more information on network management platforms.

2.3.2 The SNMP Standard

RFC 1157 defines the SNMP used between management stations and agents (or a probe, as we will see when we discuss RMON). SNMP provides network access to all MIB objects supported by a network device. This protocol facilitates polling the device in order to check for key device states, set operational characteristics of a device, and receive event notification for important device state changes that may require management attention. SNMP was defined to be a simple protocol in order to gain widespread acceptance, and it has. We will talk more about SNMP in the next section.

All SNMP-based management data are encoded and interpreted based on MIBs defined using the SMI (RFC 1155 and RFC 1212). The actual data going across the wire are encoded in a subset of Abstract Syntax Notation One

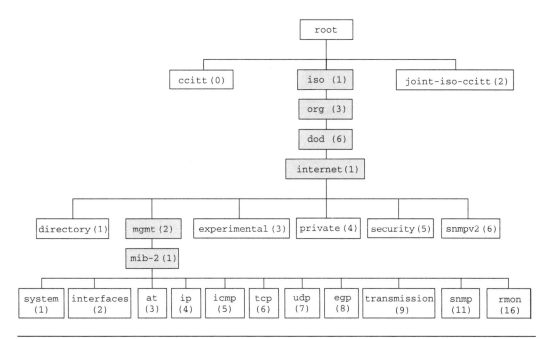

Figure 2.2 Object identifier global tree (shaded boxes indicate global root prefix down to MIB-2)

Table 2.1 Global root prefix

```
iso = 1
   org = 3
       dod = 6
             internet = 1
                  mgmt = 2
```

(ASN.1), but here we will not get into the details of the encoding. Figure 2.3 illustrates the relationship between SNMP, the management station, and the network device's agent.

2.3.3 The MIB-2 Standard

RFC 1213 defines MIB-2. MIB-2 is *the MIB* (all other MIBs are technically MIB extensions) for SNMP. MIB-2 replaces an early standard, MIB-1, and provides a core set of managed objects used to manage devices.

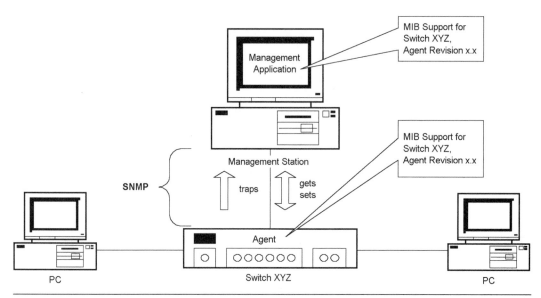

Figure 2.3 MIB shared with SNMP data flow

MIB-2 is widespread within the Internet. Nearly every device in a network supports MIB-2, so it can be thought of as a common denominator for most network devices. This is important because MIB-2 provides a core set of standard management capabilities across many diverse network devices. Figure 2.4 shows a single management application providing management across many network devices based on a common MIB.

2.4 Reading a MIB

The SMI provides the basic rules and conventions used to define a MIB and the tree-identifier structure of manageable objects. Manageable device attributes are represented as unique objects. Each object includes the following:

- name (using the SMI-defined object naming conventions)
- datatype (whether the object is represented as an integer, text string, or other form)
- description (a human-readable description of the object)
- object access (whether this is a readable and/or writable object)
- object identifier (a way to identify an object uniquely within the MIB tree)

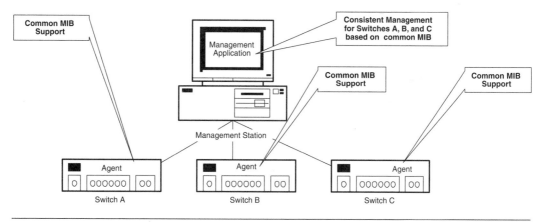

Figure 2.4 MIB shared between management application and many agents

Objects are bundled together in a MIB. An example of a MIB object is system description (`sysDescr`), found within MIB-2.

2.4.1 Determining the Object Identifier

One of the keys to reading and understanding a MIB is grasping where the objects fit within the global MIB tree. This object identifier is necessary to access and change (if the object is writable) the value of any object. The following code snippet from MIB-2 (Table 2.2) shows the SMI-based syntax used to represent `sysDescr` and the position of `sysDescr` within the global MIB tree.

The unique object identifier for sysDescr is `1.3.6.1.2.1.1.1`. Let's see how we get this object identifier from the MIB.

First notice the `IMPORTS` section of the MIB. This section includes references to other MIBs that provide definitions external to this file. These external definitions are necessary to complete other definitions without duplicating them in this file. Calling up `IMPORTS` is a way to create a daisy chain of files necessary to complete definitions. It has the advantage of allowing many different files to be constructed independently yet ensures certain data are not replicated across files. This is especially important to ensure that the global tree remains intact as it eliminates mistakes made by including the same *nearly* redundant data in many files. Since all MIBs reference back to the root SMI MIB for the first few integers of their object identifiers, we easily retain the global root. The mgmt object identifier is defined in `RFC1155-SMI` as

```
internet OBJECT IDENTIFIER ::= {iso org(3) dod(6) 1}
mgmt     OBJECT IDENTIFIER ::= {internet 2}
```

Table 2.2 MIB-2 Snippet

```
RFC 1213=MIB DEFINITIONS ::=BEGIN
IMPORTS
     mgmt, NetworkAddress, IpAddress, Counter, Gauge,
     TimeTicks
          FROM RFC1155-SMI
          OBJECT-TYPE
          FROM RFC-1212;

— This MIB module uses the extended OBJECT-TYPE macro as
— defined in [14];

— MIB-II (same prefix as MIB-I)

mib-2 OBJECT IDENTIFIER ::= { mgmt 1 }

...

system OBJECT IDENTIFIER ::= { mib-2 1 }

              sysDescr OBJECT-TYPE
              SYNTAX DisplayString (SIZE (0..255))
              ACCESS read-only
              STATUS mandatory
              DESCRIPTION
                 "A textual description of the entity. This
                 value should include the full name and
                 version identification of the system's
                 hardware type, software operating-system,
                 and networking software. It is mandatory
                 that this only contain printable ASCII
                 characters."
              ::= { system 1 }
```

If you reference the global tree, as shown in Figure 2.2, you will see that the internet subtree of object identifiers starts with the prefix 1.3.6.1. Since mgmt begins with the internet subtree and extends it with a 2, the mgmt subtree starts with the prefix 1.3.6.1.2. MIB-2 (mib-2) builds off mgmt; the mib-2 subtree is 1.3.6.1.2.1; mib-2 contains a system group that builds on mib-2 by adding a 1 to the tree (1.3.6.1.2.1.1). Finally the sysDescr object is added to form the globally unique ID 1.3.6.1.2.1.1.1. Table 2.3 shows an example of the way all object identifiers are constructed.

Table 2.3 sysDescr

```
iso = 1
    org = 3
        dod = 6
            internet = 1
                mgmt = 2
                    mib-2 = 1
                        system = 1
                            sysDescr = 1
```

2.4.2 Other Object Attributes

Let's go back to the syntax shown in the previous section and explain the rest of the sysDescr definition.

SYNTAX indicates the datatype of the object. In this case, the sysDescr object is a DisplayString, defined in the SMI as a text string from 0 to 255 characters. There are many other data types defined in a subsequent section.

ACCESS for sysDescr is read-only. This means that the object can only be read, not written, by the management station from the network device's agent. ACCESS may be read-only, read-write, write-only (for objects like passwords), or not-accessible for objects that exist within the agent but are not externally accessible.

STATUS describes the state of the object. A mandatory status indicates that a device claiming support of this MIB group must support this object. A status may be optional, obsolete (phased out), or deprecated (being phased out). Support of the sysDescr object is mandatory if a device supports the MIB-2 System group.

DESCRIPTION provides a textual "human-readable, albeit not necessarily understandable" description of the object. In the case of sysDescr, the description tells you that this object provides a textual description of the network device.

2.4.3 Scalar and Tables

SysDescr is an example of a scalar object. There is only one instance of a given scalar object within any network device. Thus there is only one SysDescr within a network device.

A S I D E . . .

When retrieving a scalar object using SNMP, you must append a "0" to the end of
the object identifier. This indicates that the object is the zeroth instance of the object, i.e., the only instance. Do not append a "0" to the end of the object identifier
when you retrieve tables. You use the object identifier as is.

Many network devices have several instances of the same object, represented in the form of tables. Tables have one or more indexes used to make
each row unique. A good example of a table is the interfaces table found within
MIB-2, which has an instance for each interface in the box.

The key words INDEX and SEQUENCE are used when specifying tables.
An index makes each instance unique—simple tables have one index; more
complicated tables have multiple indexes. Sequence specifies an ordered
group of objects associated with each instance, or row, of the table. For example, the ifTable within MIB-2 is found with the interfaces group (the
root identifier for interfaces is 1.3.6.1.2.1.2.2). See Table 2.4.

The ifTable contains ifNumber of interfaces; each entry in the table,
called a row, is indexed by ifIndex. IfIndex is an integer from 1 to ifNumber.
A row contains all the objects defined by the IfEntry object. A table uses the
ASN.1 SEQUENCE encoding for each row in the table (see Table 2.5).

The following Object IDs uniquely identify all the interface types of all
the interfaces in a network device, as shown in Table 2.6 and 2.7.

A n o t h e r   A S I D E . . .

Scalars are typically retrieved with an SNMP GET PDU, whereas tables typically are
traversed with an SNMP GET NEXT PDU. The section on SNMP talks about the
GET and GET NEXT PDUs.

Table 2.4 IfTable

```
iso = 1
   org = 3
      dod = 6
         internet = 1
            mgmt = 2
               mib-2 = 1
                  interfaces = 2
                     ifTable = 2
```

Table 2.5 Interface Table Objects

Interface Table Objects	Object ID
ifTable	1.3.6.1.2.1.2.2
ifEntry	1.3.6.1.2.1.2.2.1
ifIndex	1.3.6.1.2.1.2.2.1.1
ifDescr	1.3.6.1.2.1.2.2.1.2
ifType	1.3.6.1.2.1.2.2.1.3
ifMtu	1.3.6.1.2.1.2.2.1.4
... (rest of table entries)	1.3.6.1.2.1.2.2.1.x
ifSpecific	1.3.6.1.2.1.2.2.1.22

Table 2.6 Object IDs

Interface	Object ID for ifType, interface x
1	1.3.6.1.2.1.2.2.1.3.1
2	1.3.6.1.2.1.2.2.1.3.2
3	1.3.6.1.2.1.2.2.1.3.3
...	1.3.6.1.2.1.2.2.1.3.x
ifNumber	1.3.6.1.2.1.2.2.1.3.ifNumber

2.4.4. Common Datatypes

The SMI provides many object datatypes, the most common of which are the following:

- Integer: a positive or negative whole number, limited to 32-bit precision.
- Octet String: an ordered sequence of 0 or more octets.

Table 2.7 Object Type

```
ifTable OBJECT-TYPE
    SYNTAX SEQUENCE OF ifEntry
    ACCESS not accessible
    STATUS mandatory
    DESCRIPTION
        "A list of interface entries. The number of
        entries is given by the value of ifNumber."
    ::= { interfaces 2 }

ifEntry OBJECT-TYPE
    SYNTAX IfEntry
    ACCESS not accessible
    STATUS mandatory
    DESCRIPTION
        "An interface entry containing objects at the subnetwork
        layer and below for a particular interface."
    INDEX { ifIndex }
    ::= { ifTable 1 }

IfEntry ::=
    SEQUENCE {
        ifIndex
            INTEGER,
        ifDescr
            DisplayString,
        ifType
            INTEGER,
        ifMtu
            INTEGER,
...

        ifSpecific
            OBJECT IDENTIFIER
}

ifIndex OBJECT-TYPE
    SYNTAX INTEGER
    ACCESS read-only
    STATUS mandatory
    DESCRIPTION
        "A unique value for each interface. Its value ranges between
        1 and the value of ifNumber. The value for each interface must
        remain constant at least from one re-initialization of the
        entity's network management system to the next reinitialization."
    ::= {ifEntry 1 }
ifDescr OBJECT-TYPE
    SYNTAX DisplayString (SIZE (0..255))
    ACCESS read-only
    STATUS mandatory
    DESCRIPTION
        "A textual string containing information about the interface.
        This string should include the name of the manufacturer, the
        product name and the version of the hardware interface."
    ::= { ifEntry 2 }
```

- `Display String`: a octet string containing all printable ASCII characters.

- `Object Identifier`: a unique identifier in the MIB tree, for example, the `sysDescr` object identifier of is `1.3.6.1.2.1.1.1`.

- `Object Descriptor`: textual printable form of an object identifier. Whereas an object identifier is an array of integers, the object descriptor is a printable string of the array of integers separated by decimal points (.).

- `Sequence`: a group of one or more ordered objects, referred to as a row in a table.

- `Ipaddress`: a 32-bit IP address represented as a 4-byte octet string.

- `Counter`: a nonnegative integer that increases until it reaches its maximum value, 2^{32-1} or 4,294,967,295. When this occurs, it wraps back to 0.

- `Gauge`: a nonnegative integer that may increase or decrease. When the maximum value (2^{32-1}) is reached, it *latches*. Latching implies that it does not wrap back to zero; it stays firmly on the maximum value, or it goes back down.

- `TimeTicks`: a nonnegative integer that counts the time in hundredths of a second from a specified starting point.

2.5 MIB-2

When a network device supports MIB-2, you have access to a collection of common, useful management data. When you have many discrete, diverse network devices that support MIB-2, you have access to the same collection of common, useful management data across many network devices. This is important as it gives you many counters and other data that can be formulated into statistics to be interpreted identically across many different network devices.

For example, MIB-2 provides the counters necessary to calculate Ethernet or Token Ring utilization. Utilization provides a measurement of the percentage of time a resource is used over a given time interval. A network manager (or more likely a management application) can retrieve the counters for an interface on network device X and calculate utilization. It can then retrieve the counters for an interface on network device Y and calculate utilization. The same formula can be used to calculate the statistics. Assuming the same time interval and interface types (such as Ethernet) are used, the network manager can compare the results fairly. The results can be compared and even plotted on the same graph, even though the devices may have been built by two different vendors. Since networks are typically constructed of devices from many vendors, this capability is invaluable. Support of such standards is often a "buy/no buy" decision because of management requirements.

2.5.1 MIB-2 Functional Areas

RFC 1213 has arranged manageable objects into the following groups. With each group there is an object prefix and an indication as to whether implementation of the group is mandatory. For example, all objects within the system's group have the prefix "sys." Implementation of the system's group (if MIB-2 support is claimed) is required.

System (object prefix sys, mandatory) contains general information about a network device. Many of the objects are settable by the network manager. The group is small enough yet important enough to list each of the objects it contains.

- sysDescr defines a textual string for the network device.
- sysObjectID indicates a vendor-specific identification of the network device, (often including hardware type and agent-software revision.
- sysUpTime is the time in hundredths of a second from the time the network device was booted.
- sysContact is a field that can be used to define a textual string containing the name of the person responsible for the network device.
- sysName defines a textual string that represents a name for the network device.
- sysLocation defines a textual string that represents where the network device is located.
- sysServices defines an integer that tells which layers the network device supports. RFC 1213 defines the formula as $2^{(L-1)}$ where the L may be the following:
  - 1 physical (for example, repeaters)
  - 2 datalink/subnetwork (for example, bridges, switches)
  - 3 internet (for example, routers)
  - 4 end-to-end (for example, IP hosts)
  - 7 applications (for example, mail relays)

Since a network device may support more that one layer, a summation is used.

For example, Table 2.8 shows a network device that supports bridging and routing.

Table 2.8 `sysServices` Value

$$2^{(2-1)} + 2^{(3-1)} = 2 + 4 = 6$$

`Interfaces` (object prefix "`if`," mandatory) contains both a row of information for each of a network device's interfaces and a count of these rows (`ifNumber`). Some of the important objects within each row are the speed of an interface (`ifSpeed`) (for example, "ethernet-csmacd"—10 Mbps Ethernet—or `FDDI`), the type of interface (`ifType`), the operational status of the interface (`ifOperStatus`), and frame and error counters. This group is critical when you manage a switched network device that typically has many interfaces.

`Address Translation` is deprecated and therefore should no longer be used.

`IP` (object prefix "`ip`," mandatory) contains information useful to manage a network device at layer 3. The `ipRouteTable` contains information for determining how to route packets—for example, routing destination, various routing metrics (cost of route), and the routing protocol (`ipRouteProtocol`) whether it is `rip`, `icmp`, `ospf` (open shortest path first), or some other protocol. The `IP table` also contains the `ipNetToMediaNetAddress` that is useful for mapping layer-2 physical addresses to layer-3 network addresses. For example, MAC address 00-20-AF-12-34-56 maps to IP address 192.168.1.43.

`ICMP` (object prefix "`icmp`," mandatory) contains information useful for monitoring the ICMP protocol; packet counts and error rates are included. The popular "ping" executable used to determine reachability runs on top of ICMP, so all ICMP statistics include ping processing.

`TCP` (object prefix "`tcp`," mandatory, if device implements the TCP protocol) contains information useful for managing TCP. One important table continued within the TCP group is the connection table (`tcpConnTable`). This table contains local to remote address mappings and port mappings and the connection state (`tcpConnState`)—for example, closed or established.

`UDP` (object prefix "`udp`," mandatory, if device implements the UDP protocol) contains information useful for managing the UDP protocol such as data and error counts.

`EGP` (object prefix "`egp`," mandatory, if device implements EGP) contains information useful for managing the Exterior Gateway Protocol (EGP), a protocol used to exchange routing information among routers in a network. This group contains various neighboring router state and address information.

A S I D E . . .

EGP is used to exchange routing information across network domains—logically contained, network bubbles that often span across the WAN to connect multiple-site LANs. Internal Gateway Protocols (IGPs) are used to exchange information within a domain. Routing Information Protocol (RIP) and ARP are examples of IGPs.

Transmission (object prefix "transmission," mandatory entry for each transmission media supported by network device) is not really a group; it is more correctly a node position in the MIB-2 tree. For every new transmission standard there is a subtree management MIB. For example, there are subtrees for FDDI, Token Ring, (802.5, represented as dot5), and Ethernet (802.3, represented as dot3).

SNMP (object prefix "snmp," mandatory, if SNMP is supported) contains useful information for SNMP accounting such as number of SNMP packets—snmpInPkts (inbound); snmpOutPkts (outbound); and a number of SNMP errors, gets, and sets.

2.5.2 Using MIB-2 in a Switched Environment

As stated in the previous chapter, the main difference between traditional shared-media LANs and primarily switched LAN environments is that, instead of a managing a few interfaces, you have many interfaces to manage. For example, for one large backbone device that has several hundred Ethernet ports, you need to calculate the utilization for all of these ports—indexing each port by its interface (if) number. MIB-2 still applies; you just have many more interfaces to manage.

MIB-2 breaks down a little when network devices have more than one SNMP agent. This is not at all uncommon; the motivation is to subdivide a network device with a single power supply and backplane into multiple logical devices. Since MIB-2's "if" table provides only one-dimensional indexing (indexes are global across the box), a multiagent implementation typically needs to provide a way to map an "if" index into a subdevice/index. For example, a box with many separate switches (multiport bridges) in it may have a bridge index associated with each bridge. Vendors have come up with proprietary solutions to accommodate their multiagent network devices. Since there is not a standard solution, you must learn each vendor's own solution.

A S I D E . . .

There is currently work, called "AgentX," going on within the IETF. It addresses the problem of a single network device having more than one agent.

2.6 What is SNMP?

SNMP is the management protocol that facilitates communication between the management station and the agent of a network device. SNMP runs over the UDP/IP (or IPX) communication stack. Over UDP, SNMP uses well-known port numbers 161 and 162. Port number 161 is used for normal SNMP messages; port number 162 is used for trap messages. Over IPX, 36879 and 36880 are used for SNMP messages and trap messages respectively. On UNIX these port numbers are defined in "/etc/services."

A S I D E . . .

TCP/IP provides the concept of well-known ports. Essentially, well-known ports are a set of numbers ranging from 1 to 1023 managed by the Internet Assigned Numbers Authority (IANA), see RFC 1700. Well-know ports are designated as being UDP or TCP well-known ports. These ports provide access to standard services like SNMP (UDP port 161), SNMP traps (UDP port 162), or Telnet (TCP port 23).

SNMP works by sending packets, including an SNMP header (for authentication), with ASN.1-encoded Protocol Data Units (PDUs). Request and response packets go in both directions, from the management station to the agent and from the agent to the management station, respectively. There are five operations for SNMP version 1 (SNMPv1), each with its own PDU: SET, to set a device attribute; GET, to retrieve a device attribute; GETNEXT, to get a sequential row (or table) of device attributes; SET or GET RESPONSE, to answer a SET, GET, or GETNEXT request; and TRAP to send asynchronously (by the agent) state change information (exceeded threshold, system reboot, and so on) about the network device. PDUs contain Variable Binding Lists (VBLs), structures used to package a bunch of objects into one request.

There are currently two versions of SNMP: SNMPv1 and SNMPv2. SNMPv1 is widely deployed, whereas SNMPv2 is an emerging standard.

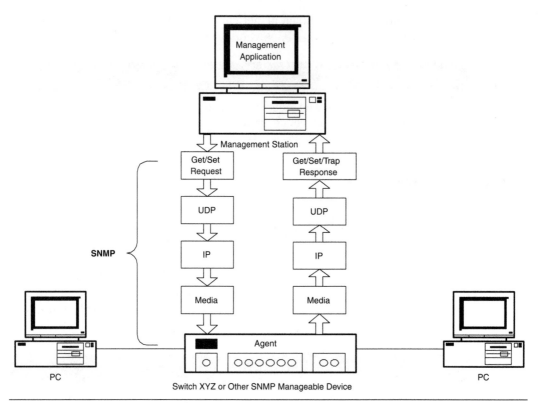

Figure 2.5 SNMP data flow

SNMPv2 extends SNMPv1. For clarity I will use SNMPv1 for information specific to v1 throughout the remainder of this section. Figure 2.5 shows the layer by layer flow of SNMP requests and responses.

2.6.1 **SNMP Data Interpretation**

So, you might ask, how does the management station stay in sync with the agent? How does the management station know how to interpret the data returned by the agent?

The first thing to note is that all data sent to and returned from the agent are in the form of a PDU. Each PDU comes with a VBL, which can be thought of as an array of "N" data items (where "N" is some number of data items that fits within a single SNMP packet) that are returned based on a request (GET) of "N" data items. (In the case of a set, if the set is successful, "N" data items are returned with the values set to the values you gave.)

The datatypes and associated coded values for manageable objects are stored in MIBs that provide a common repository describing device attributes.

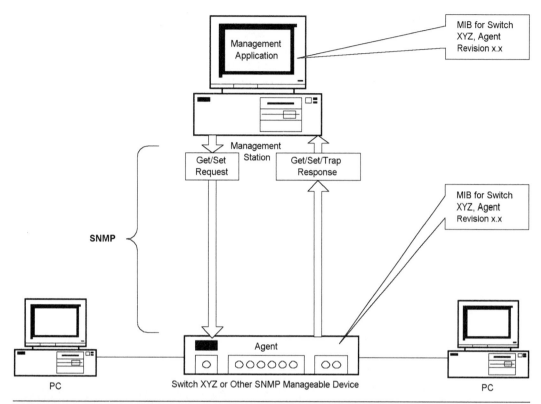

Figure 2.6 SNMP data flow

MIBs are used by both the agent and the management station, keeping the network device and the agent in sync. Note that as the device is augmented and the MIB is changed, the version of the agent is incremented. It is therefore important that the management station match its MIB version to the particular agent revision with which it is communicating. Since the MIB provides the structure of the agent's information, the MIB revisions must be carefully synchronized between the agent and the management station. See Figure 2.6.

2.6.2 SNMPv1 Community Strings

SNMPv1 has weak authentication. It relies on community strings (represented as a fully readable text string) contained within the packet header. There is a read community string and a write community string. The read community string enables read access to a network device's objects while the write community string enables both read and write access to a network device's objects. These community strings pass through the network without any encryption; then provide only weak authentication.

2.6.3 SNMPv1 Traps

Traps are unsolicited events that are generated and dispatched via SNMP to all management stations registered to receive the trap. Typically a management station registers to receive certain traps by performing a series of set requests to the device.

There are six "generic" trap types and one more for enterprise-specific traps. They are as follows:

- coldStart: The network device is rebooting; configuration may be reset.

- warmStart: The network device is reinitializing; configuration will not be reset.

- linkDown: One of the agent's links has experienced a failure.

- linkUp: An agent link has come up.

- authenticationFailure: An improperly authenticated message has been received.

- egpNeighborLoss: An Exterior Gateway Protocol neighbor is down.

- enterpriseSpecific: This trap is specific to a certain vendor's device.

A S I D E . . .

A common problem when running multiple management applications on the *same* management station is trap sharing. Since only one application can open port 162 at any one time, an application that opens this port for exclusive use will lock out and prevent all other applications from receiving traps. WINSNMP (a standard SNMP interface used by many vendors' network management applications) provides a solution for this problem by acting as a trap broker for all applications using WINSNMP.

Another A S I D E . . .

Devices with a rich set of enterpriseSpecific traps are good for trap-directed polling. Trap-directed polling is a technique used to minimize the amount of device polling by polling only when a certain event or trap occurs. With trap-based polling you only "drill down" into the device when a trap that is indicative of a potential problem comes in. One caveat with traps, however, is that they are over UDP and do not require acknowledgment; that is, traps may not make it to your management station or go into the bit bucket if you are not listening. Both of these factors make traps unreliable!

2.6.4 SNMPv1 Errors

When a request returns, there will be either `NoError` (code 0) or any one of five errors that follow:

- `tooBig` (code 1): The response to a `GET`/`GETNEXT` is larger than the agent can handle. Typically this code results when a UDP packet size is exceeded.

- `noSuchName` (code 2): One of the requested variables does not exist; an index of the offending variable within the VBL is returned.

- `badValue` (code 3): A set request is made to set an object to an inappropriate value; an index of the offending variable within the VBL is returned.

- `readOnly`: A set request is made to an object that doesn't permit write access; an index of the offending variable within the VBL is returned.

- `genErr`: A variable cannot be retrieved for some general reason other than the errors mentioned above; an index of the offending variable with the VBL is returned.

2.6.5 SNMP Requests

All SNMP requests contain an SNMP header that contains a version ID, authentication information, and the type of request. Requests are directed at the IP (or IPX) address of the network device's agent. Some network devices have multiple agents and hence multiple IP addresses. Typically a device with multiple agents has a main agent that can proxy to all other agents. There are three SNMP requests (and corresponding PDU types): `GET`, `GETNEXT` and `SET`.

The `GET` PDU is used to retrieve one or more objects from a network device. For example, to retrieve all the MIB-2 objects in the system group, you would first build a VBL with object identifiers (with ".0" appended since the objects in this example are all scalar) and appropriate datatypes for `sysDescr`, `sysUpTime`, `sysContact`, `sysName`, `sysLocation`, and `sysServices`. You would then create a `GET` PDU and put your VBL into the PDU. Finally, you would send out the `GET` packet providing the IP address of the agent with the appropriate read community string. Asynchronously, a return "request response" would come back. Alternatively if the device is unreachable or the wrong community string is given, the request will be timed-out (a request is timed-out by the management station if it takes too long to return). Assuming the request response returns and is error-free, you would unpack the PDU and retrieve from the VBL the values for the requested variables.

The `SET` PDU is used to change the value of one or more objects for a network device. For example, to set the sysContact, sysName, and sysLocation within the MIB-2 system group, you would build a VBL with the object identifiers (with ".0" appended since the objects are all scalar), datatypes, and new values for each of the three variables. You would create a SET PDU and put your VBL into the PDU. Finally, you would send out a packet providing the IP address of the agent with the appropriate write community string. Asynchronously, a return SET RESPONSE would come back, or if the device was unreachable, the request would be timed-out. Assuming the SET RESPONSE returns and is error free, you would unpack the PDU and validate that values that you set are returned correctly—after setting objects, the agent reads the values and stuffs the read values into the VBL for validation by the setter.

The GETNEXT PDU is used to retrieve a table of information about one or more objects within a network device. For example, to retrieve the ifIndex, ifType, ifSpeed, and ifOperStatus for many interfaces within the MIB-2 Interfaces group, you would build a VBL with the object identifiers and datatypes (with no ".0" appended since the objects are not scalar). You would then create a GETNEXT PDU and put your VBL into the PDU. Finally, you would send out the GETNEXT packet providing the IP address of the agent with the appropriate read community string. Asynchronously a return GETNEXT response would come back, or if the device was unreachable, the request would be timed-out. Assuming the GETNEXT response returns and is error free, you would unpack the PDU and use the object identifiers returned to retrieve the next instance within the table (if you are not at the end of the table). When the end of the table is reached, either you will get a noSuchName error, or the object identifiers will go to the next object within the MIB.

A S I D E . . .

Should you need to get down to the programming level, we recommend WINSNMP. WINSNMP is a standard Windows DLL that provides a nice Application Programming Interface (API) that hides all the encoding and decoding. Although WINSNMP is a Windows standard with both 16- and 32-bit stacks, there are efforts in place now to port this stack to Unix platforms. At the time of this writing, ports to UNIX exist for AIX (IBM) and Solaris (ACE*Comm).

2.7 What is SNMPv2?

SNMPv2 is an attempt to address the deficiencies of SNMPv1. Some of these deficiencies address tradeoffs made to keep SNMPv1 simple; others address the growing complexities of networks and the need for a more sophisticated network management protocol.

SNMPv2 dates back to 1992. It became an RFC draft a year later, but, due to an inordinate level of complexity imposed by security features, it didn't fly. I remember attending a seminar with Jeff Case, one of the founders of SNMPv1 and an active but very dissatisfied contributor to SNMPv2. He demonstrated that the imposed security levels made it impossible even to manage a network device. In short, the original version of SNMPv2 was a fiasco.

In 1996 a new SNMPv2 became an RFC—this time without security. Vendors lobbied for an SNMPv2 with "usable" security, not total elimination. At the time of this writing, the standard is being reactivated. It is hoped that this round of the RFC is successful, because SNMPv2 offers a lot of features that greatly improve upon the original SNMPv1 standard. We should know the results within a year or so. The next section provides the highlights worth tracking.

A S I D E . . .

As a result of SNMPv2 disagreements, *technically* two SNMPv2 standards emerged: SNMPv2u and SNMPv2*. At the time of this writing, work on SNMPv3 has commenced. The SNMPv3 workgroup will work on the next generation of SNMP with a goal to converge on a single approach. It is hoped that SNMPv3 will come up with an agreed-upon solution for security!

2.7.1 SNMPv2 New Features

SNMPv2 is intended to build off the foundation of SNMPv1. Some of the new features are

- **Security:** SNMPv1 is not secure, especially since community name strings are in the message header as plain text; any packet analyzer can easily view them. Having an unsecure protocol in use for managing the devices that keep your network operational is problematic. Anyone with access to your network can easily make configuration modifications that might cause total network failure.

- **Bulk operations:** SNMPv2 adds a `GetBulkRequest` PDU. This PDU gives network management applications the ability to retrieve lots of data at once. This is especially important when retrieving large tables, which, with SNMPv1's `GETNEXT`, are retrieved one table entry at a time. The `GetBulkRequest` PDU will fill the response buffer up to the maximum message size. This means that there is less traffic on the network for management and fewer requests required by the management application—making the management application more responsive. This is critical in switched-LAN management since there is potentially one or more instances of data to collect for each interface in a network device.

- **New Trap Format:** In SNMPv1 the format of a trap PDU is unique. An SNMPv2 trap simplifies trap processing by using the same exact format for the PDU as used by a GET or SET.

- **Manager-to-Manager Communication:** By adding a new Inform-Request PDU (a trap that must be acknowledged), SNMPv2 is able to facilitate communication using SNMPv2 between management stations. This allows for a hierarchical style of management often needed in large organizations to localize network traffic and roll up only certain critical information to the parent manager. This management style reduces overall management traffic and the amount of information that must be digested at the parent manager.

- **New 64-bit Datatype:** To facilitate faster networks with counters that would wrap, or start over due to lack of datatype significance (like old car odometers when they reached 100,000 miles), a 64-bit counter has been added. This datatype should be used for counters that would wrap in an hour as a 32-bit representation.

- **Improved Gets:** Instead of one invalid GET causing an entire packet of GETs to fail, "good" variables are processed, and "exceptions" are indicated in the VBL returned in the GET RESPONSE PDU.

2.8 What is RMON?

Remote Network Monitoring (RMON) (RFC 1757) defined by Steve Waldbusser of Carnegie Mellon University became a standard in February 1995. RMON is viewed as a major extension to MIB-2, and it greatly improves the level of network management possible within a network.

RMON's improvements are largely due to the functional level of information that it makes available. In MIB-2, the information that can be retrieved is rather "raw." That is to say, in order to provide the information to monitor the device, it is necessary first to retrieve several counters and crank them through a formula. If you wish to see the information change over time, you need to poll the data continuously and store it in a database for comparisons. Even if you rely on trap-based polling, there is significant polling overhead involved when the traps come into the management station.

What's so bad about this? For one thing, you can create a significant strain on your network by flooding your available bandwidth with periodic polling for management data necessary to facilitate historical analysis. You not only need to poll for lots of counters, but you need to poll very frequently—as frequently as every minute of every day. You need to run the counter samples through the formulas; you then need to save the information in perhaps a database (which may be remote in order to be centrally accessible—more network activity). This can also strain the management application because it can take a significant number of CPU cycles to process the data. So what happens when you have in excess of 100 interfaces per device—like in switched LANs? This illustrates the multiplier effect; switched LANs greatly exacerbate the problem of lots of polling.

In a switched LAN, where you need to poll many unique interfaces for each network device, you can quickly see how much management traffic will result. This flooding is further intensified in environments with multiple distributed management stations (not at all uncommon), polling for the same data. In short, polling frequently for lots of data on lots of interfaces does not scale well.

RMON addresses the problem of simultaneously servicing many network devices with the same data by a technique called remote management. With traditional SNMP-based polling, if you lose connectivity to your device, you are no longer polling your device, and hence you are no longer managing your device. With RMON you *remotely* manage network devices.

RMON divides data collection into two parts. The data are collected by the RMON agent (usually a probe) that may be on a segment near the device or embedded within the network device. One or more management stations talk to the RMON agent (using SNMP), rather than talking directly to the network device. This design facilitates data sharing among multiple-management stations. Even if a management station loses connection to the probe (or even periodically connects), collection would still proceed as long as the probe is connected to the network it is monitoring.

Having the probe be discrete from the management station offers the flexibility of "attaching" a management station to a probe from anywhere in the network. This allows many different management stations to view the RMON data collected, perhaps collected many hours before. This is great in the event of network failure when you may not be running your management station or if your management station became detached.

RMON provides a higher level of standardization—standardization of information. In the same way that MIB-2 provides standardization of many raw counters, RMON provides standardization of many historical statistics. If you are relying heavily on many different vendors to provide you with "information" (that is, the applications to turn "raw" data into useful management data), you may need to run several slightly different applications to collect the data you need. If you rely on RMON, you get standard "roll up"—you have fewer applications to run, and you are comparing similar items.

RMON provides statistical and diagnostic "information"—intelligence in (or close to) the network device—near to the source of the "raw" counters. This minimizes network data traffic, reduces the impact of losing connectivity, services many management stations simultaneously, and provides a standard set of metrics that can be used across many devices supporting RMON.

2.8.1 Functional Areas

RMON is under MIB-2 in the global OID tree, as shown in Figure 2.7.

RMON supports monitoring of layers 1 and 2 of the OSI stack. This enables RMON to provide traffic statistics at the MAC level of Ethernet and Token Ring networks where bridging (or switching) happens.

RMON is functionally divided into nine groups. A tenth group was later added for Token Ring support. The following is a concise summary of the groups:

1. `Statistics`: provides key statistics for specific media types.
2. `History`: provides control for periodic statistical sampling.
3. `Alarm`: provides event generation when periodic statistical samplings exceed defined thresholds.
4. `Host`: provides statistics about source and destination MAC addresses seen in the network.
5. `HostTopN`: provides a list of rate-based statistics pertaining to a group of hosts. The list is ordered by some parameter and typically contains only a top number of hosts, usually ten. It utilizes the `Host group`.
6. `Matrix`: provides statistics about conversations between any two MAC addresses.
7. `Filter`: provides the ability to filter out packets that satisfy a given filter equation.
8. `Packet Capture`: enables the capture of packets based on a given filter equation.
9. `Event`: provides the ability to generate and log events.
10. `Token Ring`: provides four additional parameters for Token Ring networks: Ring Station, Ring Station Order, Ring Station Configuration, and Source Routing Statistics.

2.8.2 RMON Design

The RMON MIB is designed for use in conjunction with a RMON probe. A RMON probe is a dedicated network-management device. Its purpose is to

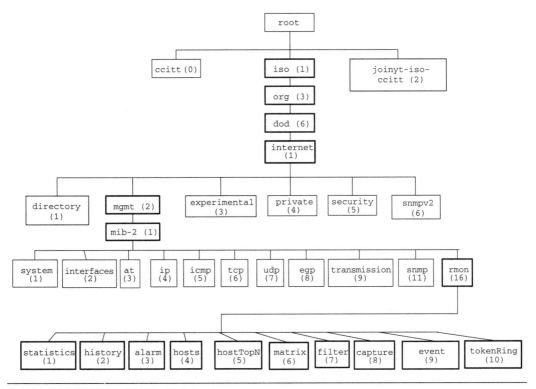

Figure 2.7 RMON within the global tree

configure the collection of RMON statistics, which can be quite complicated, and to provide access to the summary data to one or more (usually remote) management stations. Recent trends in switching have embedded RMON setup and collection directly into the network device.

RFC 1757 offers the following design goals:

- **Offline Operation**: allows the collection configuration to perform diagnostics without constant communication with a management station. This provides flexibility in LAN environments in the event of network failure.

- **Proactive Monitoring**: enables continuous monitoring of network faults indicative of pending network failure. This facilitates proactive management. In addition RMON provides the ability to save historical data that can later be analyzed.

- **Problem Detection and Reporting**: provides the capability to detect and log error conditions based on the interpretation of "raw" data.

- **Value Added Data**: provides data that are not just a bunch of raw counters to be interpreted and correlated with the rest of the network. By correlating data, a RMON probe has the opportunity to provide data that take into account the relationship of more than one network device.
- **Multiple Managers**: facilitates access of RMON data by multiple managers simultaneously and provides a locking protocol for configuring the collection by one manager at any given time.

2.8.3 Using RMON in a Switched Environment

RMON was originally written for a shared media environment, a traditional LAN. RMON sees only traffic on the LAN segment to which it is attached; in the case of a switch, this is often a single port. Since a switched device usually has several ports and RMON probes aren't cheap, attaching a probe to every port becomes prohibitively expensive. Two solutions have emerged for managing switched interfaces with RMON—having the roving RMON capability (focused RMON collection on any designated port) within a switch or having RMON support embedded in the switch.

With a roving RMON, the probe can attach to a port, do some sampling, and then automatically rove (or are manually moved) to the next port. The advantage with this capability is that you get support for all nine groups—+1 if Token Ring (TR)—and there is no impact on the performance of the switch. The disadvantages are that you give up a port and your statistics are based on sampling, not on dedicated monitoring. See Figure 2.8 for an illustration.

Embedding RMON at each port is another popular solution. Embedded RMON has the advantage that you can manage each switched port. Typically, only the first four or five groups (for example, `statistics`, `alarms`, `hosts`, `host TopN`, and `history`) are provided because the calculations are processor-intensive and therefore can be a drain on the switch that is simultaneously attempting to move data at line speed. Another issue is the limited amount of historical data that can be stored based on available memory.

Nonetheless, RMON has a bright future in the switched arena. RMON provides so much useful information to manage your network proactively without the drain of collecting much raw data across your network. Over the next few years we will see more management intelligence embedded into the device, eliminating network management failure that is often associated with a failed network. Work has already begun on defining switch-based RMON (SMON). SMON is discussed later in this chapter.

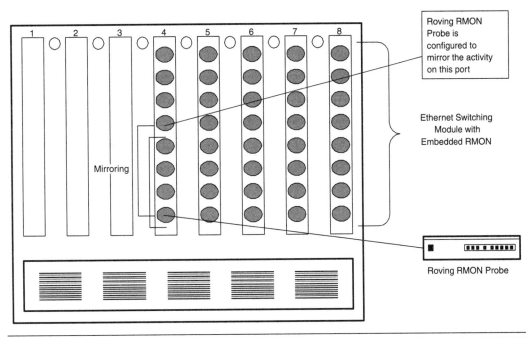

Figure 2.8 Eight-slot switch depicting roving RMON probe and module with embedded RMON

A S I D E . . .

One alternative for attaching a standalone probe to an Ethernet switch port on a network device without roving capabilities is to use an intermediate hub or multi-port repeater temporarily. If the port is already fanned out to a hub, plug the probe in directly to a spare port.

2.9 What is RMON2?

RMON2 is a 1994 draft standard that extends RMON by providing management at layer 3 and above, whereas the original RMON standard was limited to layer 2 data. In particular, RMON2 enables monitoring of network layer traffic (for example, IP, ARP, IPX, or AppleTalk) and application-level traffic (for example, notes, e-mail, or WWW access).

RMON2 enables a network manager to determine the mix of traffic on a network, making it possible to do some reconfiguration based on traffic patterns. If, for example, there is a lot of database traffic for a particular application going through several hops, it may make sense to relocate the database closer to the application users. Likewise if you add a few new applications and suddenly the network is slow, you can often identify which application is the culprit. RMON2 enables you to see your network traffic and to tune your network based on traffic patterns.

Since RMON2 works across layer 3 and above, you can monitor through routers and, most important, your WAN connections. These connections tend to be expensive resources that you want to be sure are optimally utilized. You may want to make special provisions for file transfer requests (using FTP) during the day, permitting other access across the WAN to be more responsive (FTP of large files tends to consume lots of bandwidth by transmitting many packets of the maximum size). You also can monitor your WWW traffic with RMON2 and determine how much nonbusiness-related traffic you have and to what Web servers your traffic is destined. Or you can use RMON2 to do application-level accounting on a per-user basis.

The RMON2 draft extends RMON with the following ten new groups:

1. **Protocol directory**: provides a list of protocols that the probe can support.

2. **Protocol distribution**: provides a breakdown of octets and packets for each of the protocols detected.

3. **Address mapping**: provides inventory of MAC to network address bindings inventory.

4. **Network layer host**: counts traffic in both directions for each network address discovered by the probe.

5. **Network layer matrix**: counts traffic sent between pairs of network addresses.

6. **Application layer host**: counts traffic in both directions by protocol between pairs of network addresses.

7. **Application layer matrix**: counts traffic by protocol sent between pairs of network addresses.

8. **User history**: uses alarm and history group mechanisms to provide user-specific history collection.

9. **Probe configuration**: provides standard mechanism to configure the various operating parameters of a probe.

10. **RMON conformance**: describes the requirements for conforming with the RMON2 MIB.

These groups are the basic units of conformance. As in RMON, if a group is implemented, all objects in that group must be implemented. See Figure 2.9.

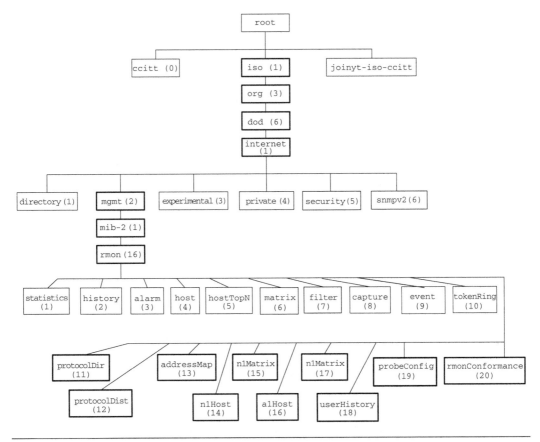

Figure 2.9 RMON2 extensions within the global tree

2.10 Other Standard MIBs

There are literally hundreds of MIBs in existence. Use the WWW URL to get MIBs (defined in the first part of this chapter) and to get the up-to-date MIB index (`rfc-index.txt`). The following are a few MIBs that are widely used in conjunction with managing switches:

- **RIP Version 2 (RFC 1389)**: is a MIB providing management of Routing Information Protocol (RIP), a widely used routing protocol. Provides access to interface configuration table and RIP statistics.
- **Ethernet MIB (RFC 1398)**: provides management of Ethernet-like objects. Provides statistics group and collision statistics group.

- **Bridge MIB (RFC 1493)**: is a MIB used to manage 802.1d bridges. Provides control of Spanning Tree Protocol (STP) and forwarding table management.

- **FDDI-SMT73 MIB (RFC 1512)**: is a MIB used to manage FDDI. Provides access to port, path, MAC, and station management (SMT) objects associated with the FDDI protocol.

- **Repeater MIB (RFC 1516)**: provides management of repeater devices. Includes port table and port statistics.

- **Source Routing Bridge MIB (RFC 1525)**: is a MIB used to manage 802.1d Source Routing Bridging. Provides access to port, root port, source routed ports, and Spanning Tree Protocol (STP) objects associated with Source Routing Bridging.

- **UPS Management MIB (RFC 1628)**: is a MIB providing management of Uninterrupted Power Supplies (UPS).

- **ATM Management MIB (RFC 1695)**: is a MIB providing ATM interface management. Provides configuration and traffic management.

- **AppleTalk MIB II (RFC 1742)**: is a MIB providing management of AppleTalk routing protocol. Includes management of the Zone Information Protocol (ZIP) Router Group.

- **Token Ring MIB (RFC 1231)**: provides management of Token Ring interfaces.

- **Open Shortest Path First (OSPF, RFC 1850)**: is a MIB used to manage increasingly popular routing protocol. Provides access to address/host tables, routing metrics, and routing interfaces.

2.10.1 Emerging Standards

There are several active IETF Working Groups developing new standards important to managing switched LANs. The following are worth mentioning:

- The Switch-Based Monitoring (SMON) MIB Working Group focuses on evolving RMON for switching. A "testPoint" concept is being introduced to help reconcile inconsistencies between switch architectures that make switch management difficult to standardize. This concept introduces a table that indicates various test points where a box can be monitored. These points may be ports, backplanes, aggregation of ports, aggregation of backplanes, or other box-specific locations that should be monitored. The "testPoints" are described by OIDs.

- The Physical Topology (PTOPO) Working Group attempts to standardize a set of managed objects around physical topology information.

Providing an up-to-date map of a network is one of the fundamental requirements of network management. As networks become more dynamic and switching increases in popularity, this becomes increasingly difficult because the information currently available in bridging tables and router caches is insufficient to provide the required level of granularity necessary to generate a decent map. The PTOPO team is working on defining a common MIB that provides a local view of topology from each network device's vantage point. By taking the data from multiple vantage points, an approximate physical topology can be made.

- The Interfaces MIB Working Group is considering adding an `ifCounterDisconTime` (a `sysUptime`) per interface. This would provide useful granularity (currently the entire device must rely on `sysUpTime`) for managing each interface in a switched LAN device.

- A Distributed Management Working Group is working on a distributed management framework, script MIB, and a threshold monitoring MIB. These efforts follow on the popularity of RMON's distributed concept and the requirement for standardized threshold monitoring. Getting more proactive management closer to the device is a major theme of this workgroup.

- The IETF charter for the Entity MIB (RFC 2037) Working Group defines its goals as standardizing a set of managed objects for representing logical and physical entities with relationships between them. This facilitates management of a network device (physical entity) that contains more than one instance of a single MIB (each instance represented as a logical entity within the device).

- The AgentX MIB, as mentioned previously, is designed to facilitate SNMP Agent extensibility. The IETF charter for the AgentX Working Group has a mandatory goal to develop a standard protocol for SNMP agent extensibility. There are two optional goals for the group: to develop a MIB to standardize management of the extensible agent environments and to produce an API that facilitates the development of AgentX subagents. An AgentX implementation consists of a "master-agent" that represents a single interface to external SNMP developed "sub-agents" that are, in turn, highly focused on their specific managed element (for example, NIC, storage devices, printers, application, and so on), and are not required to handle SNMP directly.

2.11 Summary

MIBs define the functional and operational aspects of network devices and provide the common information store necessary to keep management applications and device agents synchronized. SNMP is the communication vehicle, allowing network management applications to get and set the operational characteristics of a network device. Traps provide asynchronous notification of events that may require management station attention. SNMPv2 is an emerging standard designed to overcome the shortcomings of SNMPv1 with new features.

MIB-2 is the mother of all MIBs. MIB-2 provides a set of managed objects useful for managing TCP/IP-based Internets. Since objects can be viewed as "standard" across many devices, MIB-2 enables a management application to compare similar items across many different networking devices.

RMON and RMON2 provide a significant amount of valuable data for the network manager, not just "raw" counters. RMON and RMON2 are complementary technologies—RMON2 extends the capabilities of RMON. Both standards facilitate remote management by providing historical statistical collection and event generation to one or more than one management stations independent of the significant traffic poll-based statistics can generate.

With RMON you can monitor error rates, packet-size distributions, unauthorized users, and conversations between devices. RMON provides many important management capabilities for layer 2. With RMON2 you can monitor congestion, non-routed requests, packet distribution, many topN statistics, and traffic across routers. RMON2 provides layer 3 and above management, enabling you to determine the end-to-end destination and the source of packets. RMON2 helps you to fine-tune your network by repositioning servers and users to reduce traffic bottlenecks and to increase network response time.

PART TWO

Components of a Switched LAN

CHAPTER 3

Managing Switched LAN Technologies

3.1 Introduction

One interesting thing about switches is that they bring so many technologies together. This amalgamating provides a lot of flexibility when you design and grow your network; it also provides protection of investment as you can integrate and build upon established LANs within your organization and extend your existing switched LAN without wholesale replacement.

The big management challenge that comes with this flexibility is the requirement to know the essence of so many technologies. You cannot manage something you do not understand, and therefore you need a working knowledge of many technologies in order to manage your switched LAN effectively.

This chapter provides a whirlwind survey of each of today's popular layer-2 technologies with a focus and twist on "What do I need to know to manage this technology effectively?" Be warned: *This chapter covers a lot of ground and condenses a significant amount of material into diagrams and tables.* When you make it through this chapter, however, you should have a pretty good idea of what each technology is, how it basically works in a LAN, what the key terminology is, and what the fundamentals of management are. Note that there are many fine books written on each of the technologies that you may consult for more comprehensive coverage (see the bibliography at the end of the book).

Note, too, that ATM is covered only in a limited, very focused LAN sense. This technology is very rich, and I bet I've seen 25 different books written on it. After surveying ATM, I decided to include it here but to limit discussion to what currently is most widely deployed.

Finally, although I do present some of the actual MIB objects that are useful to manage your network, I do not expect that you will be looking at or changing many of these objects with a MIB browser. Rather, I want to give you a "taste" of what management objects are available and a sample of what's possible and fundamental for switched LAN management. This gives you a "leg up" on what to expect in the form of tools that incorporate some of these objects from your switch-device vendor(s). There is no substitute for reading MIBs; time spent with the MIBs will help you understand other possibilities. My advice: Read or browse the MIBs, and keep your switch-vendor honest.

3.2 Switching Happens at Layer 2

For the most part, the technologies discussed in this chapter cover layers 1 and 2 of the OSI model. All of the technologies have their own way of defining and further dividing each of the layers. Although this information is interesting, these divisions are not paramount to understanding management, and therefore they will not be discussed in detail. Note that we revisit cabling in Chapter 8 when we discuss switched LAN troubleshooting.

It is important to know that Ethernet,[1] Token Ring, and Fiber Distributed Data Interface (FDDI)—all use the same 802 IEEE specified Logical Link Control (LLC) layer at the top of their stacks. This makes it relatively easily to "switch" frames among the technologies. This LLC layer provides a common interface across the technologies and is used to multiplex and demultiplex frames received from any of the three protocols. The MAC layer provides an access point to the medium and how the medium is shared. Because the LLC layer serves as a common integration point, these technologies can be used together; in fact, this is precisely where switching comes in. As mentioned previously, switching (or multiport bridging) happens at layer 2.

All the technologies divide the physical layer into a media-dependent layer and media-independent layer. This makes it easy to support multiple media without changing the interface. Table 3.1 outlines these technologies related to the OSI Reference Model.

There are several other technology distinctions worth noting. These include the following:

- Both FDDI and Token Ring have built-in network management which FDDI calls Station Management (SMT) and Token Ring calls Network Management (NMT). SMT provides management of the MAC and Physical layers of FDDI; NMT provides management from the LLC, MAC, and Physical layers of Token Ring.

- ATM is a connection-oriented protocol; the other technologies are connectionless. ATM sets up a pipe prior to communicating while the other technologies just fire frames that may or may not arrive at their destination (higher-layer technologies take care of this problem).

---

1. This is true for 802.3 SNAP, 802.3, 802.2 but *not* for Ethernet II frame formats.

Table 3.1 OSI Reference Model Technologies

OSI	Ethernet	FDDI	Token Ring	ATM
Layer 2	LLC	LLC	LLC	Adaptation
Data Link	MAC	MAC	MAC	Layer (AAL)
Layer 1 Physical	Physical	Physical	Physical	Physical

- In order for ATM to work with Ethernet and Token Ring, LAN emulation was defined. LAN emulation (LANE) provides the same MAC-level interface used by Ethernet and Token Ring, making it possible for these shared-media technologies to run over ATM transparently. Translational bridging is used to support FDDI and Fast Ethernet which interfaces with slightly different 802 standards, namely 802.1g and 802.10 respectively.

3.3 Switching Different Technologies

With the advent of switching, there is significant flexibility within the LAN. Switching enables you to incorporate many technologies into your network by transparently bridging traffic from technology to technology. Switching from Ethernet to an FDDI backbone has become very popular over the past few years; currently switching from Ethernet to Fast Ethernet or ATM is gaining popularity. Switching clearly makes it possible to leverage and customize your LAN based on traffic flows and management requirements.

Generally you position higher-speed technologies at the backbone of your network and lower-speed technologies at the edges—this is no different than having four- or six-lane highways to connect major cities and secondary roads to get you to your home. FDDI, ATM, Fast Ethernet, and the emerging standard, Gigabit Ethernet, are well positioned for the backbone, whereas Ethernet and Token Ring are commonly used to fan out to the desktop. Figure 3.1 shows a network design that incorporates all the technologies. Note that it is clearly not necessary (especially for manageability reasons) to use all the technologies; there are many installations built just with Ethernet. When determining how to lay out a network, you should consider cost of ownership (including understanding and managing the technology), traffic flows, and future requirements. Chapter 11 discusses switched LAN design considerations.

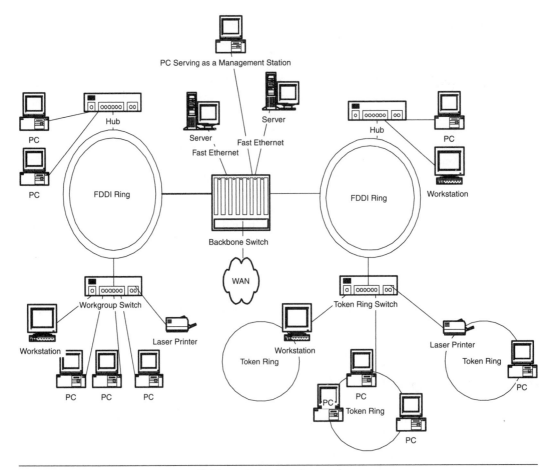

Figure 3.1 LAN using many available switched technologies

3.4 Some Background Information

There are many abbreviations used within the industry to describe networking technologies. Although this practice isn't unique to networking, this chapter certainly is filled with new acronyms and abbreviations. The advantage of learning a subset of abbreviations is that you will know a good deal about the technology just by learning the acronyms. If you understand the *termi*nology, you understand the *tech*nology.

For convenience there is a general acronym table at the end of the book. In addition, this chapter includes acronym tables specific to each technology we discuss.

3.4.1 Bit Ordering and Addressing

Whenever you put a network analyzer on your network, you need to be aware of bit ordering and address formats. Within Ethernet, FDDI, and Token Ring frames, there are source and destination addresses. These addresses, called Media Access Control (MAC) addresses, are normally 48 bits (6 bytes)[2] in length and are commonly represented in hexadecimal strings separated by dashes (-) or colons (:). FDDI and Token Ring use Most Significant Bit (MSB) order, represented lexically by colons. Ethernet use Least Significant Bit (LSB) order, represented lexically by dashes. MSB is also referred to as "Big Endian," and LSB, also called the canonical form of an address, is referred to as "Little Endian." Table 3.2 summarizes MSB and LSB MAC layer address structuring.

It is useful to note that, normally speaking, the first three bytes[3] of the six-byte source and destination MAC addresses are Organization Unique Identifiers (OUIs) of the many different manufacturers of networking equipment. This can help you determine what type of device produced a network frame when troubleshooting a network problem. For example, all MAC addresses with the 00-20-AF prefix or 02-60-8C are 3Com devices, all addresses with 00-00-0C are Cisco devices, and so on. With company acquisitions and volumes of network devices produced, many vendors have several MAC address prefixes.

The prefixes shown in LSB format in Table 3.3 are taken from *The*

Table 3.2 MAC Address Stucturing

FDDI or Token Ring	MSB	Big Endian	Noncanonical	xx:xx:xx:xx:xx:xx where xx represents a single-byte hexadecimal value, such as AB or 15.
Ethernet	LSB	Little Endian	Canonical	xx-xx-xx-xx-xx-xx where xx represents a single-byte hexadecimal value, such as AB or 15.

2. Two-byte addressing is also used (though no longer common) in FDDI, Token Ring, and Ethernet.

3. In some cases the first three bytes are not representative of the equipment manufacturer. Rather these prefixes are used *locally* to indicate such things as multicast addressing. With six-byte addressing, if the first bit is turned on, it implies that the address is a group address—this is used to multicast (send a frame to many addresses at once). The second bit also has special significance; if it is 1, it implies that the address is local; if it is 0, it implies that the address is global (for example, the address burned into the NIC by your NIC manufacturer). Note that 16-bit addresses do not have the global/local bit, but they do have the group address/nongroup address bit.

Table 3.3 MAC Address Prefixes for Different Manufacturers

Global Prefix	Manufacturer	Global Prefix	Manufacturer
00-00-0C	Cisco	00-00-A7	Network Comput Dev.
00-00-0E	Fujitsu Limited	00-00-A9	Network Systems
00-00-0F	NeXT	00-00-AA	Xerox
00-00-10	Sytek	00-00-B0	RAD Network Devices
00-00-15	Datapoint Co.	00-00-B3	CLIMLinc
00-00-1B	Novell	00-00-B5	Datability
00-00-1D	Cabletron	00-00-B7	Dove
00-00-20	Data Industrier AB	00-00-BB	TRI Data
00-00-22	Visual Technology	00-00-BC	Allen-Bradley
00-00-2A	TRW	00-00-C0	Western Digital/SMC
00-00-32	GPT Limited (GEC)	00-00-C5	Farallon
00-00-44	Castelle	00-00-C6	HP I.N.O./Eon Systems
00-00-46	ISC-Bunker Ramo	00-00-C8	Altos
00-00-4F	Logicraft	00-00-C9	Emulex
00-00-5A	S & Koch	00-00-D7	Dartmouth College
00-00-5D	RCE	00-00-D8	Novell (~1987)
00-00-5E	US DoD (IANA)	00-00-DB	British Telecom
00-00-62	Honeywell	00-00-DD	Gould
00-00-65	Network General	00-00-DE	Unigraph
00-00-69	Concord Communications	00-00-E2	Acer Counterpoint
00-00-6B	MIPS	00-00-E5	Sigmex

Continued

Table 3.3 MAC Address Prefixes for Different Manufacturers (*Continued*)

Global Prefix	Manufacturer	Global Prefix	Manufacturer
00-00-6E	Artisoft	00-00-E8	Accton Technology Corp.
00-00-6F	Madge	00-00-EF	Atlantec
00-00-77	Interphase	00-00-F0	Samsung
00-00-7A	Ardent	00-00-F3	Gandalf Data Limited
00-00-7B	Research Machines	00-00-F4	Allied Telesis Inc.
00-00-80	Dataco	00-00-FD	High Level Hardware
00-00-81	Synoptics	00-01-02	BBN
00-00-84	ADI System Inc.	00-01-63	National Datacom Corp.
00-00-86	Megahertz Co.	00-01-68	Wandel & Goltermann
00-00-89	Cayman Syst Gatorbox	00-17-00	Kabel
00-00-93	Proteon	00-20-AF	3Com
00-00-94	Asante	00-40-0D	LANNET
00-00-95	Sony/Tektronix	00-40-C8	Milan Technology Corp.
00-00-98	CrossComm	00-60-8C	3Com
00-00-9F	Ameristar Technology	00-80-0F	Standard Microsyst Corp.
00-00-A0	Sanyo Electronics	00-80-10	Commodore
00-00-A2	Wellfleet	00-80-19	Data Comm Co.
00-00-A3	Network Application Technology	00-80-1B	Kodiak Technology
00-00-A4	Acorn	00-80-21	Newbridge Networks Corp.
00-00-A5	Compatible Systems Corporation	00-80-29	Microdyne Corporation

Continued

Table 3.3 MAC Address Prefixes for Different Manufacturers (*Continued*)

Global Prefix	Manufacturer	Global Prefix	Manufacturer
00-00-A6	Network General	00-80-2B	IMAC
00-80-2D	Xylogics	08-00-20	Sun
00-80-2E	Plexcom Inc.	08-00-22	NBI
00-80-34	SMT-Goupil	08-00-23	Matsushita Denso
00-80-51	ADC Fibermux	08-00-25	Control Data Corp.
00-80-5C	Agilis	08-00-26	Norsk Data
00-80-64	Wyse Tech/Link Tech	08-00-27	PCS Computer Systems
00-80-7C	FiberCom	08-00-28	Texas Instruments
00-80-87	Okidata	08-00-2B	Digital Equipment
00-80-8C	Frontier Software Devel.	08-00-2E	Metaphor
00-80-A1	Microtest	08-00-2F	Prime
00-80-B2	Network Equipment Technology	08-00-36	Intergraph
00-80-C2	IEEE 802.1	08-00-37	Fujitsu-Xerox
00-80-C7	Xircom	08-00-38	Bull
00-80-C8	D-Link/Solectek	08-00-39	Spider Systems
00-80-D3	Shiva Corporation	08-00-3E	Motorola
00-80-D8	Network Peripherals	08-00-41	Digital Com. Associates
00-AA-00	Intel	08-00-44	DAVID Systems Inc.
00-DD-00	Ungermann-Bass	08-00-45	Xylogics
00-DD-01	Ungermann Bass	08-00-46	Sony
02-04-06	BBN	08-00-47	Sequent

Continued

Table 3.3 MAC Address Prefixes for Different Manufacturers (*Continued*)

Global Prefix	Manufacturer	Global Prefix	Manufacturer
02-07-01	Interlan/Micom	08-00-49	Univation
02-60-86	Satelcom Megapac	08-00-4C	Encore
02-60-8C	3Com	08-00-4E	Isolan/BICC
02-CF-1F	CMC	08-00-51	Experdata
08-00-01	Computer Vision	08-00-56	Stanford University
08-00-02	Bridge Inc. (3Com)	08-00-58	DECsystem-20
08-00-03	Advanced Comput Com	08-00-5A	IBM
08-00-05	Symbolics	00-00-60	Industrial Networking
08-00-07	Apple	08-00-67	Comdesign
08-00-08	BBN	08-00-68	Ridge/Bull Univation
08-00-09	Hewlett-Packard	08-00-69	Silicon Graphics
08-00-0A	Nestar Systems	08-00-6A	AT&T
08-00-0B	Unisys	08-00-6E	Excelan
08-00-0D	ICL	08-00-70	Mitsubishi
08-00-0E	NCR	08-00-74	Casio
08-00-11	Tektronix	08-00-75	Dansk Data Elektronik
08-00-14	Excelan	08-00-7C	Vitalink
08-00-17	NSC	08-00-80	XIOS
08-00-1A	Data General	08-00-81	Crosfield Electronics
08-00-1B	Data General	08-00-83	Seiko Denshi
08-00-1E	Apollo	08-00-86	Imagen/QMS

Continued

Table 3.3 MAC Address Prefixes for Different Manufacturers (*Continued*)

Global Prefix	Manufacturer	Global Prefix	Manufacturer
08-00-1F	Sharp	08-00-87	Xyplex
08-00-89	Kinetics	48-44-53	HDS
08-00-8B	Pyramid	80-00-10	AT&T
08-00-8D	XyVision	80-AD-00	CNET Technology Inc.
08-00-8E	Tandem	AA-00-00	DEC obsolete
08-00-90	Retix	AA-01-01	DEC obsolete
40-52-43	American Research Corp	AA-00-02	DEC obsolete
44-46-49	DFI	AA-00-03	DEC Global physical
AA-00-04	DECnet Local logical	———	———

Table 3.4 MAC Address Prefixes for Multicast (Group Destination) Traffic

Local Prefix	Meaning	Local Prefix	Meaning
01-00-5E	Multicast Internet	09-00-56	Stanford V Kernel
01-80-C2	Spanning Tree	09-00-77	Retix Spanning Tree
09-00-02	Vitalink	09-00-7C	Vitalink
09-00-09	HP Probe	0D-1E-15	Hewlett Packard
09-00-1E	Apollo Domain	AB-00-0X	DECnet Multicast
09-00-2B	DEC	CF-00-00	Ethernet Test Loopback
09-00-4E	Novell IPX	———	———

Evolving Ethernet by Alexis Ferrero (p. 108). They represent a partial list; see the WWW at URL: `ftp://ftp.ieee.org/info/stds/ouilist.txt` and RFC 1340 for online prefixes.

The prefixes shown in Table 3.4 are also taken from *The Evolving Ethernet* (p. 110). They represent a partial list of registered prefixes used by multicast (group) traffic.

3.5 Ethernet

Table 3.5 summarizes the key characteristics of Ethernet. Note that there are many other Ethernet standards over different media, using different connectors. The following are the most popular.

Ethernet is the oldest and most widely deployed LAN technology. It's popular because it's simple and efficient. A major criticism is that it is nondeterministic; you cannot guarantee bandwidth to a user of a shared Ethernet segment.

The advent of switching has done much to ameliorate the nondeterministic nature of Ethernet. Within a switched environment you can assign dedicated ports to each user. Each user has his or her own Ethernet segment; there will be no collisions with other users on that segment. This greatly improves the responsiveness of the network.

From the original Ethernet standard (IEEE 802.3), dating back to the 70s, a slightly different standard evolved—the DIX (Digital, Intel, Xerox)

Table 3.5 Ethernet Characteristics

Ethernet Technology	10BASE-T	10BASEF/FOIL
Standard	802.3i	802.3j
Important MIB(s)	Ethernet MIB, MIB-2, RMON	(same)
Speed	10 Mbps	10 Mbps
Medium	2-pair Category 3 Twisted Pair	2 strands multi/single mode fiber
Segment Length	100 m (12 stations per segment)	2000 m
Frame Size	64 to 1518 8-bit bytes	64 to 1518 8-bit bytes
Physical Topology	Star	Star

Ethernet standard. The principal difference between the two standards is the third field in the frame. DIX Ethernet treats the field as a type field, whereas 802.3 Ethernet treats the field as a length field. Today 99 percent of all NIC vendors conform to DIX Ethernet.

Over the years there have been several 802.3 standards to accommodate new media and speeds; each standard is differentiated by appending a lower-case letter to 802.3. For example, the popular 10BASE-T standard is 802.3i.

3.5.1 Physical Topology

Standard Ethernet provides 10 Mbps aggregate bandwidth, shared among all users on a common communication channel. In traditional LANs this communication channel is called a *bus* (see Figure 3.1). A bus is a segment of cable of a limited length to which many devices connect along the way. In a switched environment the physical topology used is a star configuration, but it may be a star of trees if multiple devices are attached to the same Ethernet port using a repeater. A *star technology* (used in switched LANs) refers to a configuration in which all devices connect back to a common connection point using a separate length of cable. The 10BASE-T Ethernet standard restricts segment length to 100 m. Greater distances can be achieved by going to fiber; the 10BASEF/FOIL standard extends segment length to 2000 m.

Ethernet switching supports dedicated end node connections, fanning out a port to many by introducing a hub (that is, a repeater) or backbone port to port connections. When a port is fanned out to a hub to many ports, the Ethernet bandwidth is shared, and the collision domain is presented by the number of active users at any one time attached to the hub. When a switched port is dedicated to a workstation, the user's collision domain is limited to the single workstation. Naturally dedicated is better and more expensive than shared. In a switched LAN, one common parameter used to decide upon a network configuration is cost per port. For obvious reasons backbone connections should be dedicated.

Regardless of whether the connections are shared or dedicated, the connections are said to form a star at the switch or repeater. All connections go back to a central point (hub or repeater) rather than daisy chain (like Christmas-tree lights) off a shared bus. See Figure 3.2 for an example of an Ethernet LAN installation.

One nice additional feature to Ethernet found in many switched connections is full-duplex Ethernet. Full-duplex Ethernet provides 20 Mbps aggregate bandwidth—10 Mbps in each direction. Full-duplex is available only in point-to-point links using fiber or some twisted pair media since each 10 Mbps channel is supported using a separate wire. *Simplex* (half-duplex) is the term used to define bandwidth shared between both directions.

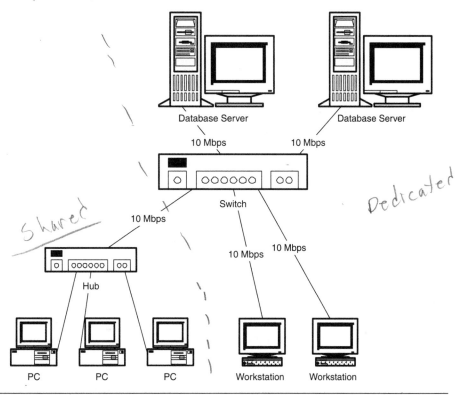

Figure 3.2 Simple network showing three PCs sharing 10 Mbps Ethernet hub; workstations and servers with dedicated 10 Mbps each

3.5.2 Operation

Ethernet relies on Carrier Sense Multiple Access with Collision Detection (CSMA/CD) to arbitrate bandwidth. CSMA/CD is analogous to the protocol used in a meeting with several people. If a person wishes to talk (we'll assume that this is a well-behaved meeting in which only one person talks at a time) and no one else is talking, he or she begins to talk. As long as the person has something to say, he or she is given the floor or the medium to communicate. If two people begin to talk at the same time (a collision), one stops and the other continues. All the people in the meeting share a common communication channel; access to this channel is gained by simple arbitration. As the number of people in the meeting increases, so does the number of communication collisions. Ethernet works largely in the same way. When two users sharing the same segment attempt to "talk" simultaneously, a collision is detected and both of them "back off." Each user waits a random period of time and then retransmits. Segments with more users have more collisions.

3.5.3 Fast Ethernet

Fast Ethernet is essentially the same as Ethernet, but ten times faster. Fast Ethernet achieves this speed by increasing the clock speed and using a different encoding scheme—both of which require a better grade of wire than standard Ethernet. Two pairs of (category 5) or four pairs of (category 3/4/5) wire are required. As an alternative, you still can use multimode fiber, which is less expensive than single-mode fiber, for 2000 m of distance or use single-mode fiber for the long haul (10 km).

Fast Ethernet also provides full-duplex communication. Full-duplex Fast Ethernet provides 200 Mbps aggregate bandwidth—100 Mbps in each direction. Like Ethernet, full-duplex Fast Ethernet is available only in point-to-point links using fiber or twisted pair media since each 100 Mbps channel is supported using a separate wire.

Fast Ethernet is relatively new; the 802.3u standard came out in 1995. Because it employs the same technology as Ethernet, it can be managed in the same way as Ethernet, taking into account the line speed for performance calculations like utilization.

One elegant feature of Fast Ethernet is *autonegotiation*. Autonegotiation is a scheme that facilitates automatic adaptation to the highest possible communication speed found at both ends of the cable. This enables you (assuming you originally installed data grade, category 5 UTP) to use a 10/100 Mbps Ethernet NIC within your networked database server and later to upgrade the server connection to 100 Mbps within the wiring closet by simply moving the wire from a 10-Mbps port to a 100-Mbps Fast Ethernet port. Since 10/100 NICs are becoming less and less expensive, current trends are moving Fast Ethernet to the desktop.

Table 3.6 summarizes the key characteristics of Fast Ethernet configurations used within switched LANs.

3.5.4 Ethernet Abbreviations

Each LAN technology comes with its own baggage of technology; Ethernet, unlike many of the other technologies, has a small bag. Table 3.7 shows terms specific to Ethernet.

3.5.5 Ethernet Management

Unlike many of the other technologies, Ethernet does not have any built-in management features. The technology's simple nature significantly reduces the amount of management necessary; this is a key advantage of Ethernet. The following sections discuss key management areas for performance, configuration, and fault management of switched Ethernet connections.

Table 3.6 Key Fast Ethernet Characteristics

Fast Ethernet Technology	Ethernet (100BASE-T)	Ethernet (100BASE-FX)
Standard	802.3u	802.3u
Speed	100 Mbps	1000 Mbps
Important MIB(s)	Ethernet MIB, MIB-2, RMON	(same)
Medium	2-pair Category 5 Unshielded Twisted Pair (100BASE-TX) 4-pair Category 3/4/5 Twisted Pair (100BASE-T4)	multimode/ single-mode fiber
Segment Length	100 m 2-pair Category 5 or 4-pair Category 3/4/5 (1024 stations per segment)	2000 m (multimode) 10 km (single-mode)
Frame Size	64 to 1518 8-bit bytes	64 to 1518 8-bit bytes
Physical Topology	Star	Star

Table 3.7 Ethernet Abbreviations

Ethernet Acronyms	Meanings
CSMA/CD	Carrier Sense Multiple Access with Collision Detection
FCS	Frame Check Sequence (same as Cyclic Redundancy Check)

3.5.5.1 Performance Management

Performance is managed by taking periodic "snapshots" of each switched port's utilization. Typically for switched networks you like to see average utilization of 30 percent or less of the available utilization, giving plenty of room for bursts of traffic.

Utilization is calculated using standard MIB-2 counters across two samples, taken first at time A, then at time B.

$$\text{Ethernet Port Utilization} = ((\Delta\ \text{ifInOctets} + \Delta\ \text{ifOutOctets}) * 8\ \text{bits per octet})/((\text{time B} - \text{time A}) * \text{ifSpeed}))$$

where Δ implies delta or "change in values over time interval."

If you find traffic is consistently greater than 30 percent and the port is shared among several network devices, you may move one or more of the devices to another port. If the port is dedicated, you may want to move the network device to a higher-speed technology such as 100 Mbps Ethernet or to full-duplex Ethernet. Typically database servers and file servers are placed on their own port to ensure best performance.

Since Ethernet performance denigrates rapidly as the number of collisions increases, it is very important that you keep an eye on utilization. If you have the luxury and can spare the expense, set up each user with his or her own Ethernet switched port. This will restrict the collision domain to a single user, giving a full 10 Mbps (20 Mbps if running full-duplex) communication channel. We all know how enjoyable it is to be in the commuter lane when the other three lanes are backed up for miles.

A S I D E . . .

RMON will detect the top 10 talkers and guide you to the users who should have their own switched port.

There is a significant correlation between frame size and utilization; more frames sent "simultaneously" result in more collisions. Table 3.8 provides a rough correlation of frame size, utilization, and performance for Ethernet.

A n o t h e r A S I D E . . .

It is difficult to give an exact rule of thumb as to when utilization is too high. The two factors to monitor are the number of collisions and the size of frames (viewable via RMON). If you have mostly small frames and lots of collisions, 30 percent may be your "I've got a problem" point; if you have mostly large frames and virtually no collisions, 80 percent may be your "I've got a problem" point. Unfortunately frame sizes are variable and so are collision rates. The best advice is to monitor your utilization and collisions over time and look for trends in your own switched LAN.

Table 3.8 Ethernet Frame Size, Utlization, and Performance

Utilization	64-byte frames	512-byte frames	1500-byte frames
10%	Performance is okay.	Performance is better.	Performance is best.
30%	Performance is bad.	Performance is marginal.	Performance is average.
60%	"Am I still connected to the network?"	"The data should get there today."	Performance is okay.

3.5.5.2 Configuration Management

Switched Ethernet is truly "plug-and-play." From the desktop the only configuration is with the NIC to ensure that your workstation or PC can communicate with the NIC; there aren't any Ethernet parameters to set. The following represents the typical steps taken to attach an end station to an Ethernet switched LAN:

1. You buy a Network Interface Card (NIC) or use the network interface found on the mother board of your workstation/PC.
2. You connect a length of 2-pair Category 3 Twisted Pair (< 100 m) from your switch Ethernet port to your workstation/PC.
3. You observe link status on both sides of the connection by ensuring that the LED is illuminated.
4. You install the appropriate network driver for your NIC and reboot your end station.
5. Voilá! You are networked at the physical layer.

A S I D E . . .

If you fan out a port to several users by introducing a hub (also known as a repeater) between your end nodes and your switch, make certain you have link status between the switch port and the hub and between the hub and the desktop.

A n o t h e r A S I D E . . .

If you connect a desktop to Fast Ethernet, ensure that you have the correct cabling and 100 Mbps NIC at the desktop.

Y e t A n o t h e r A S I D E . . .

For Ethernet interconnections (switch-to-switch) make certain you connect 10 Mbps to 10 Mbps, 100 Mbps to 100 Mbps, and so on. Also check link status at both ends. If you connect 10 Mbps to 100 Mbps the connection will "fall back" to 10 Mbps, through autonegotiation; make certain that this is what you intend. Also note that some vendors' Fast Ethernet implementations do not support autonegotiation.

> ### Last A S I D E . . .
>
> Sometimes getting the network drivers to match your hardware and picking an interrupt to satisfy your O/S can be painful. Device configuration has come a long way though with plug-and-play standards; there is, however, room for improvement . . .

3.5.5.3 Fault Management

There are only a few Ethernet faults that need to be managed. For each switched Ethernet port, it is important periodically to monitor the following five fault conditions:

1. **Link status:** You will impress your users if you detect that their network connection is severed before they detect it. Backbone links should obviously be monitored more frequently.

2. **Excessive number of invalid frames:** Ethernet frames are invalid if they:
   - are too short (less than 64 bytes in length), often called a *runt*.
   - are too long (greater than 1518 bytes in length), often called a *jabber*.
   - are misaligned (cannot be reconstructed at the other end of the communication and usually have an FCS error).
   - have a bad FCS (see the following).

3. **Excessive number of bad FCSs:** The checksum calculated at the receiver end does not match the checksum in the frame.

4. **Excessive collisions:** There are many collisions on a given segment. Excessive collisions happen when there are too many nodes contending for access to the wire; that is, many nodes are attempting to "speak at once." In a switched environment an easy solution is to distribute the load of a port experiencing excessive collisions over several ports—ideally one node per port.

5. **Late collisions:** Collisions are late (indicative of exceeding the 100 m segment length), resulting in many retransmissions and poor response times.

Fault conditions 1, 2, and 3 can be monitored using periodic polling of MIB-2 objects and calculating rates. See Table 3.9 for counters such as `dot3Stats-FCSErrors-dot3StatsExcessiveCollisions`. Also look at RMON objects found in the `etherHistoryTable` (for example, `etherHistory` or `CRCAlign Errors`, `etherHistoryUndersizedPkts`).

3.5.5.4 Important MIB variables

Ethernet is managed through MIB-2 (RFC 1213), RMON (RFC 1757), and the Ethernet (RFC 1398) MIBs. Table 3.9 illustrates some of the most important objects used for monitoring Ethernet switched ports. Note that I did not list all of the RMON statistics because of space constraints and because, to date, even if you have RMON on your switched ports, it is often disabled due to overall switch performance. Many vendors employ sampling techniques for RMON to address the problem of burdening switch performance.

Table 3.9 Objects Used to Monitor Ethernet Switched Ports

Object	MIB	Description from MIB
dot3StatsAlignmentErrors	Ethernet	A count of frames received on a particular interface that are not an integral number of octets in length and do not pass the FCS check. The count represented by an instance of this object is incremented when the alignmentError status is returned by the MAC service to the LLC (or other MAC user). Received frames for which multiple error conditions obtain, per the conventions of IEEE 802.3 Layer Management, are counted exclusively according to the error status presented to the LLC.
dot3StatsFCSErrors	Ethernet	A count of frames received on a particular interface that are an integral number of octets in length but do not pass the FCS check. The count represented by an instance of this object is incremented when the frameCheckError status is returned by the MAC service to the LLC (or other MAC user). Received frames for which multiple error conditions obtain, per the conventions of IEEE 802.3 Layer Management, are counted exclusively according to the error status presented to the LLC.

Continued

Table 3.9 Objects Used to Monitor Ethernet Switched Ports (*Continued*)

Object	MIB	Description from MIB
dot3StatsExcessiveCollisions	Ethernet	A count of frames for which transmission on a particular interface fails due to excessive collisions.
IfOperStatus	MIB-2	The current operational state of the interface, including: • up (1): ready to pass packets • down (2) • testing (3): in some test mode The testing (3) state indicates that no operational packets can be passed.
ifAdminStatus	MIB-2	The desired state of the interface, including: • up (1): ready to pass packets • down (2) • testing (3): in some test mode The testing (3) state indicates that no operational packets can be passed.
ifInErrors	MIB-2	The number of inbound packets that contained errors preventing them from being deliverable to a higher-layer protocol.
ifInUcastPkts	MIB-2	The number of subnetwork-unicast packets delivered to a higher-layer protocol.
ifInNUcastPkts	MIB-2	The number of non-unicast (i.e., subnetwork-broadcast or subnetwork-multicast) packets delivered to a higher-layer protocol.
ifInDiscards	MIB-2	The number of inbound packets chosen to be discarded, even though no errors had been detected, to prevent their being delivered to a higher-layer protocol. One possible reason for discarding such a packet could be to free up buffer space.

Continued

Table 3.9 Objects Used to Monitor Ethernet Switched Ports (*Continued*)

Object	MIB	Description from MIB
ifInOctets	MIB-2	The total number of octets received on the interface, including framing characters.
ifOutErrors	MIB-2	The number of outbound packets that could not be transmitted because of errors.
ifOutUcastPkts	MIB-2	The total number of packets that higher-level protocols requested be transmitted to a subnetwork-unicast address, including those that were discarded or not sent.
ifOutNUcastPkts	MIB-2	The total number of packets that higher-level protocols requested be transmitted to a non-unicast (i.e., a subnetwork-broadcast or subnetwork-multicast) address, including those that were discarded or not sent.
ifOutDiscards	MIB-2	The number of outbound packets chosen to be discarded, even though no errors had been detected, to prevent their being transmitted. One possible reason for discarding such a packet could be to free up buffer space.
ifOutOctets	MIB-2	The total number of octets transmitted out of the interface, including framing characters.
ifSpeed	MIB-2	An estimate of the interface's current bandwidth in bits per second. For interfaces that do not vary in bandwidth or for those where no accurate estimation can be made, this object should contain the nominal bandwidth.
ether	RMON	Various Ethernet MIB objects.

3.6 FDDI

Fiber Distributed Data Interface (FDDI) is a mature backbone technology that provides 100 Mbps communication. Table 3.10 summarizes the key characteristics of FDDI. Unlike Ethernet, FDDI provides fault tolerance by incorporating a dual communication path scheme. This scheme includes two separate communication media (primary and secondary rings) that are run between devices. FDDI guarantees access by using a token passing-access method and contains built-in network management. These features have made FDDI well suited for (and very popular as) a backbone technology. FDDI is, however, much more expensive and significantly more complex to manage, and hence it is not widely deployed to the desktop.

A S I D E . . .

Although FDDI's speed is limited to 100 Mbps, FDDI switching can easily be used to extend this capacity and still benefit from the integrated management and overall fault tolerance of FDDI. The technique is simple—simply divide an FDDI ring among two or more separate rings and switch the rings together. This results in several FDDI rings, each with 100 Mbps, fewer network devices to service, and hence more bandwidth.

Table 3.10 Key FDDI Characteristics

Technology	FDDI
Standard	ANSI X3T9.5
Important MIB(s)	FDDI-SMT73 MIB (RFC 1512) Optional SMT MIB for FDDI traps
Speed	100 Mbps
Medium	Multi- or Single-mode fiber or Twisted Pair (copper)
Segment Length (between neighbors)	60 km for single-mode fiber, 2 km for multi-mode fiber, 100 m for twisted pair
Frame Size	4500 8-bit bytes
Physical Topology	Star (though logically a Ring)

3.6.1 Physical Topology

FDDI networks are in the form of a ring that is constructed of fiber or copper (then called CDDI). The greater the distance, the more expensive the cable required. The least expensive cable is copper, then multimode fiber; the most expensive is single-mode fiber. FDDI cabling has two paths—often represented as A and B. Typically one of the two paths is in standby mode for fault tolerance if a break in the other path occurs. A ring can be up to 200 km in length (100 km for each cable if you use the fault-tolerance feature) and can support up to 500 stations where each station may be up to 2 km apart.

FDDI supports a variety of connection options for connecting stations and FDDI concentrators. Concentrators are logically equivalent to repeaters.

- **Single Attached Station/Concentrator (SAS, SAC)**: A station or concentrator is attached to the FDDI network by one path only.

- **Dual Attached Station/Concentrator (DAS, DAC)**: A station or concentrator is attached to the FDDI network by two paths; one path is in standby mode.

- **Ring of Trees**: One or more FDDI concentrators are attached to FDDI concentrators, providing a tree of attachments.

By dual attaching stations or concentrators, you provide fault tolerance if a single break in one of the cables occurs. A break in the ring can automatically reconnect by using the other cable that is in standby mode. When a ring reconnects, it is said to have "wrapped" or to be in a "wrapped" state. Note that once wrapped, a subsequent break will not be automatically repairable; there can be only one break in a dual attached setup for this reconnection to work. A subsequent break will result in more than one ring with stations segmented.

Often stations are dual-homed to two separate FDDI concentrators for fault tolerance. In this case, the station is single-attached to each concentrator. Concentrators can span switches for maximum fault tolerance; if one switch goes down, the FDDI station falls back to the other connection which is in standby mode. Although dual homing eliminates the FDDI fault tolerance of being resilient to a single break in the cable, the fault tolerance gained with dual homing is considered to be more important. For example if one switch goes down, your FDDI network switches to the other switch and stays up. Dual homing is often instrumental in situations where the network cannot be brought down (not at all uncommon in the backbone) and switch reconfiguration or agent software upgrade is needed. The network manager can switch to the other concentrator temporarily when the other device is brought down and backed up for reconfiguration. Refer to Figure 3.3.

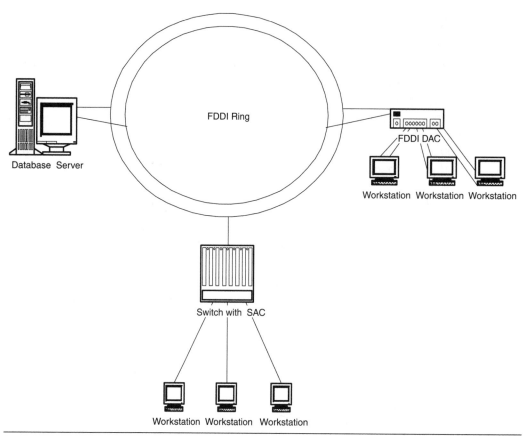

Figure 3.3 Figure showing database server (DAS), FDDI SAC in switch with SASs, and FDDI DAC with DASs

A S I D E . . .

When dual homing with an FDDI DAS, the B port has precedence. If B fails then A takes over.

3.6.2 Operation

FDDI uses a token to arbitrate communication. Essentially a token is created during ring initialization, and it continuously circulates around the ring. A station must grab the token to communicate. Once it acquires the token, it puts an FDDI frame on the ring and reclaims it when it comes back to the station. By using a token-passing mechanism for communication, FDDI is able to provide a guaranteed bounded waiting time for transmission. This makes the technology more suitable than Ethernet for multimedia, since it can guarantee bandwidth for voice and video. Some argue the applicability of FDDI for multimedia, especially ATM proponents.

On the ring, adjacent stations and concentrators are called neighbors. Each neighbor has an upstream neighbor and a downstream neighbor. In the rare case of only two stations on a ring, the upstream and downstream neighbors for each of the stations would be the same.

FDDI is considered to be very reliable and have low error rates. In addition to the flexibility of fault-tolerance attachments discussed in the previous section, FDDI provides a significant amount of self-management to achieve its reliability. For example, FDDI has a formal process for managing the token. This includes an arbitration process for creating the token and a token rotation timer (TRT) to ensure that the ring is resilient to token loss. FDDI provides extensive station management (SMT) that includes a test for link quality (LCT) when a station attaches to the ring and periodic monitoring of the link quality (LEM) of each station. FDDI uses a beacon protocol to beacon or "shout out" faults.

A S I D E . . .

The TRT is really used to ensure that each station sees the token when needed. During insertion the arbitration process sets the TRT to the minimum value asked for by the stations. For example, station A may ask for 8 milliseconds (ms), station B for 20 ms, and station C for 60 ms; in this case 8 ms will be used. Beware of stations that come into the ring asking for strange TRTs; in particular some FDDI NICs in Windows/NT ask for 165 ms, and that can cause problems.

3.6.3 FDDI Abbreviations

FDDI is plagued by many abbreviations. Table 3.11 show the ones that appear most frequently.

3.6.4 FDDI Management

One of FDDI's greatest strengths is the rich amount of management built into it. FDDI's Station Management (SMT) is capable of detecting and automatically correcting many communication faults.

At the MAC layer SMT provides both beaconing and token rotation management. Beaconing is a technique used by a station to alert of a fault; for example, a ring beacons when there is a break in the ring. Since the token is fundamental to communication, all stations monitor the time between the last

Table 3.11 FDDI Abbreviations

CDDI	Copper Distributed Data Interface
DAC	Dual-Attachment Concentrator
DAS	Dual-Attachment Station
DNA	Downstream Neighbor Address
ECF	Echo Frame
FDDI	Fiber Distributed Data Interface
FS	Frame Status
LCT	Link Confidence Test
LEM	Link Error Monitor
LER	Link Error Rate
NAC	Null-Attachment Concentrator
NIF	Neighbor Information Frame
NSA	Next Station Addressing
RMT	Ring Management
SAC	Single-Attachment Concentrator
SAS	Single-Attachment Station
SIF	Status Information Frame
SMT	Station Management
SRF	Status Report Frame
THT	Token Holding Timer
TRT	Token Rotation Timer
TTRT	Target Token Rotation Time
UNA	Upstream Neighbor Address

and next time it sees the token. The stations will go into the token claim process to regenerate a token if it is lost for a time greater than a target token-rotation time (TTRT).

SMT uses several frame types to perform traffic and error monitoring, ring initialization, and link testing. A Neighbor Information Frame (NIF) is used by a station to announce its address; this is useful for determining the ring's logical topology. Configuration Station Information Frames (SIFs) find out dynamic- and static-configuration information about a station's configuration. SIFs are used to find out whether a station is wrapped, to identify the up- and downstream neighbors, to determine if errors have been detected, or to get information on dropped frames. SIFs can also be used to determine whether a station is a concentrator or an end station. Status Report Frames (SRFs) are used to report on abnormal conditions such as high-frame error rate or high-frame loss. Parameter Management Frames (PMFs) alert one of configuration change.

SMT identifies three important areas of management:

Ring Management (RMT) includes token monitoring, beaconing, and duplicate address detection. Ring Management is on a per-MAC basis.

Configuration Management (CFM) includes access to defining the path a station is on (primary, secondary, local, isolated, or none), the state of the port (thru or concatenated; primary and secondary are joined). Configuration Management is on a per station basis.

Physical Connection Management (PCM) manages the physical port connection. FDDI concentrators have as many PCMs as they have ports.

Link status (that is, connection to network), part of Physical Connection Management, is taken very seriously by FDDI—not surprisingly because a bad link can result in being cut off entirely from the network as well as being disruptive to others on the network. During initialization of the ring a link confidence test (LCT) is performed. Only interfaces that pass the LCT are allowed onto the ring. Then SMT does periodic link error monitoring (LEM). A counter is maintained for the number of times an interface is brought down due to link errors (from the FDDI MIB, see `fddimibPORTLemRejectCts`). When this reject count exceeds a certain threshold (`fddimibPORTLerAlarm`), an SNMP trap is sent out. When this reject count exceeds another configurable cutoff value (`fddimibPORTLerCutoff`), the interface is taken off line.

Configuration Management provides indication of a twisted ring where the primary and secondary paths cross. When a ring is twisted and the primary and secondary paths cross, it is unclear which path is the primary. Correcting this problem is usually quite simple; you just need to ensure that when you connect two interfaces you invert the A and B connections. That is, A must connect to B and B to A, because the primary path always enters A and exits B and the secondary always enters B and exits A. A ring is in a "thru" (or normal) state when both secondary and primary paths are separate.

Ring scrubbing ensures that all of a station's frames are off the ring prior to leaving the ring. If a station issues claim frames for the length of time equal to the ring latency (time to traverse the ring) and discards all of these frames, the station can safely leave the ring knowing it is clean. Sometimes a station can leave the ring rather abruptly, in which case there was no opportunity to scrub the ring. Using void frames, many vendor FDDI implementations do ring purging. Essentially a series of void frames are transmitted upon receipt of a token, and everything received between the void frames is removed from the ring. This makes certain that frames go around the ring only once.

In *FDDI Handbook,* (p. 211), Raj Jain identifies many FDDI management scenarios that can be automatically detected and corrected by FDDI. He says:

- *A short or open electrical path occurs within a station.* TVX expires. The claim fails. The station downstream from the fault is stuck beaconing. It uses direct beacons to announce the fault and starts a PC trace to locate the failed component. After the trace completes, the ring is reconfigured without the failed component.

- *A cable or connector breaks.* No light is received. The physical connection management (PCM) detects the problem and takes the link off the ring.

- *A connector becomes loose.* A high error rate results in a failure of the link error monitor (LEM). The network manger is notified. The failed link is reinitialized by PCM, which conducts a link confidence test (LCT). If the link fails the LCT, it is taken off the ring. The link remains off the ring until it passes the LCT.

- *A user connects wrong ports with a cable.* Topology rules will not allow that cable to become part of the ring. If included in the ring, the error is reported to SMT.

- *The token is lost.* No frames or tokens are seen. TVX at one or more stations expires. The claim process is used to regenerate a token.

- *An extra token is created.* Frames generated by one token holder are stripped by the other token holder, resulting in a high frame lost rate. In some implementations, a MAC can detect a duplicate token when it receives a token while already holding one. In any case, the token is eventually stripped by a transmitting station.

- *A station stops stripping its frames.* The frames will be removed when they meet a transmitting station. A ring purger, if used, will remove the frames.

- *The source address of a frame becomes in error.* The frame will be removed when it meets a transmitting station. A ring purger, if used, will remove the no-owner frame.

- *A station is unable to receive frames although it can transmit.* No frames are received at this station and the TVX expires. The claim process fails because the station receives neither its own nor other stations' claim frames. The beacon process begins. The station is stuck beaconing, PC trace occurs, path test detects the failure by means of an internal loopback test, and the station removes itself from the ring.

FDDI management is a bit more involved than Ethernet, due to the complexity of the technology. The following sections discuss key management areas for performance, configuration, and fault management of switched FDDI connections.

A S I D E . . .

In a switched LAN, you may have several interfaces attached to the same FDDI path, that is, to the same physical ring. Certain calculations, like utilization, are on a path basis. Therefore you need only to calculate the utilization for one interface on a path; this one value is applicable to all interfaces on the path.

3.6.4.1 Performance Management

As with all technologies, you need to monitor utilization. FDDI utilization is calculated using the following formula on a path basis. Like Ethernet and all utilization calculations, you need to take two samples at time A and time B.

```
FDDI Path Utilization = (1 - ring latency/average
                        TRT)*100
```

$$\text{FDDI Path Utilization} = (1 - \Delta\, \text{fddimibMACTokenCts} * \text{Latency}/(\text{Time B} - \text{Time A})) * 100$$

```
where Δ implies delta or "change in values over time
                    interval."
```

A S I D E . . .

It is difficult to say what a "good" target utilization for FDDI is, since it is largely environment-dependent. It is recommended that you monitor your rings over time, converge on what is normal, and then establish an upper threshold upon which you "alarm."

3.6.4.2 Configuration Management

Make certain that your paths are configured correctly, that your rings are not twisted, that your A and B paths are not wrapped, and that FDDI stations are not isolated. If you use dual homing, make certain that your fall back to the standby concentrator works properly. The `fddimibSMTCFState` will tell whether your station is thru (normal), wrapped, or isolated. `FddimibSMTPeerWrapFlag` will simply tell you if they are wrapped.

Set your `fddimibPORTLerAlarm` (the link error rate estimate at which a link connection will generate an alarm) for each FDDI port. Set your `fddimibPORTLerCutoff` (the link error rate estimate at which a link connection will be broken) for each FDDI port. It is important to configure your switch to send the LER traps to your management station(s).

A S I D E . . .

A management station will receive a particular trap from a switch only if you have previously configured the switch to send the trap to the management station. Typically a switch will maintain a table of destination addresses and trap numbers that will be sent to each destination address.

3.6.4.3 Fault Management

There are quite a few FDDI fault conditions to monitor. For each FDDI interface, it is important to:

1. Monitor some of the optional FDDI traps that are supported by your network device, and you will find that some traps occur too frequently and are not worth monitoring. Some of the traps, however, can be used to complement standard FDDI counters so that you don't need to spend all of your time polling. Track the number and frequency of these events. Some devices support generation of an event when:

   - there are port LER errors (indicative of link breakdown).
   - a peer-wrapped condition is encountered.
   - a duplicate FDDI MAC is detected (rare, as vendors tend to keep these unique, although they will cause havoc).
   - a ring is put in the hold state (rare, because in most cases it is desirable to wrap if one ring fails).

- there is an Elasticity Buffer error (indicative of link breakdown or a transmission failure).

2. **Monitor link errors.** High-link errors may be indicative of a loose or bad connector. Since the connector is the attachment to the ring, a bad connector can mean that communication will be cut off—not a great situation when the big boss is trying to get to a file server (probably containing a slide presentation that he is about to give) that is connected to the FDDI ring with a flaky connector. `fddimibPORTLerEstimate`, `fddimibPORTLemRejectCts`, and `fddimibPORTLemCts` can be used to monitor link errors. Note that you can configure your `fddimibPORTLerCutoff` and `fddimibPORTLerAlarm` as defined earlier in the configuration section.

3. **Monitor amount of SMT beaconing.** Stations beacon only when there are problems on the ring. Lots of SMT beaconing often indicates network instability.

4. **Monitor for peer-wrap condition.** If your network becomes wrapped, you should fix the problem as a network can withstand only one wrap—the next wrap attempt will cause isolation.

5. **Monitor when SMT is put into a ring hold state.** Usually this state is abnormal as wrapping a ring in the event of failure is desirable.

6. **Monitor the number of ring operation reports over time.** Ring operation reports include such events as neighbor changes, station inserts, and station deletes. If you have a high number of ring operation reports, stations may be going online and offline indicating your ring is unstable. `fddimibMACRingOpCts` is the MIB variable to monitor.

7. **Monitor the level of frame errors such as elasticity buffer errors and frame errors.** For example, if the `fddimibMACFrameError-Flag` is set to TRUE, your MAC has experienced errors.

8. **Monitor for duplicate addresses.** Although this condition should be very rare, a duplicate address will cause havoc on your network. Use the duplicate address flag (`fddimibMACDaFlag`) and upstream neighbor duplicate address flag (`fddimibMACUnaDaFlag`).

9. **Monitor the level of dropped frames.** `fddimibMACNot-CopiedCts` is the number of frames that were addressed to this MAC but were not copied into its receive buffers. If this is high, it indicates that lots of frames are being dropped by the MAC layer.

10. **Monitor the level of lost tokens.** Track the count of how often a valid transmission timer (TVX) expires on an FDDI MAC (`fddimibMACTvxExpiredCts`).

3.6.4.4 Important MIB variables

FDDI-SMT73 MIB (RFC 1512) is the main MIB for FDDI management. There is also an optional SMT MIB that defines many FDDI traps. The FDDI-SMT73 MIB divides management into 5 groups that are interconnected through indexes. These relationships are illustrated in Figure 3.4.

At the heart of all the tables is the `fddimibMAC` Group. The MAC Group has many objects including error counts, the current path, and a useful frame error ratio (`fddimibMACFrameErrorRatio`) and contains all the indexing to the other tables. It also contains a `fddimibMACIfIndex` that gets you back to the MIB-2 Interfaces table and a `fddimibMACSMTIndex` that gets you to the `fddimibSMT` table and to the `fddimibMACCounters` table.

The `fddimibSMT` table contains useful information like the `fddimibSMTCFState`, the connection state of the SMT. This tells you whether the station is isolated, wrapped, local, or thru. The `fddimibSMTPeerWrapFlag` tells you specifically if the station is wrapped. (See Table 3.12 for FDDI state terminology.)

The `fddimibMACCounters` (MAC Counters Table) provides `fddimibMACTvxExpiredCts`—the number of times the valid transmission timer (TVX) has expired. If the number is high, it means that the token is getting lost and time is being spent reclaiming the token. The `fddimib-`

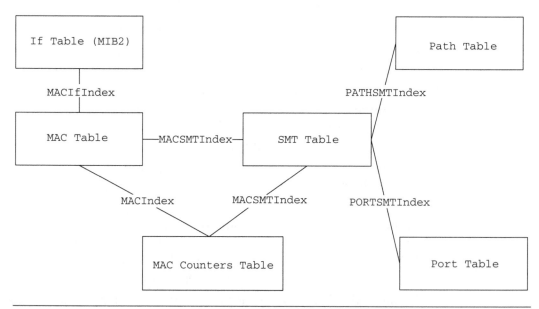

Figure 3.4 Relationship between various FDDI-SMT3 MIB tables

Table 3.12 FDDI State Terminology

FDDI states	Meaning
isolated	Station not attached to any path.
wrapped	Primary and secondary paths of station are joined, that is, concatenated.
local	Station is attached to local path.
thru	Primary and secondary paths of station remain separate.

MACRingOpCts is also within the MAC Counters Group. If this value is high over time, it may indicate that a port is transitioning from state to state frequently (online, offline, and so on), indicating that the port is bad.

Both the Port Group and Path Groups are indexed by the SMT index. The Port Group contains important objects like the fddimib-PORTLemRejectCts, fddimibPORTLemCts, fddimibPORTLerCutoff, fddimibPORTAlarm, and fddimibPORTConnectState. These objects provide information for monitoring the number of link error rates on a port. The Connect State gives an indication as to whether a port is active, in standby, connecting, or disabled. The connecting state is somewhat ambigious as ports that are not connected to anything but are not disabled are in a connecting state. This state is also used when a port is "coming up," that is initially coming online.

The Path Group contains a list of path entries, one for each FDDI path. The object, fddimibPATHConfigCurrentPath, will tell you whether your path is isolated, local, secondary, primary, concatenated (wrapped), or thru.

As shown in Table 3.13, the following MIB variables (all from the FDDI-SMT73 MIB, RFC 1512) are some of the most important ones used for monitoring FDDI switched ports and FDDI paths.

3.7 Token Ring

Token Ring is a widely deployed LAN technology, especially in networks with lots of PCs. Token Ring predates FDDI as a ring technology. Since FDDI had Token Ring to learn from when it was being developed, there are a lot of similarities between the two technologies. Table 3.14 on p. 102 summarizes the key characteristics of Token Ring.

Table 3.13 MIB Variables

Variable	Description from MIB
fddimibPORTLCTFailCtr	The count of the consecutive times the link confidence test (LCT) has failed during connection management (refer to ANSI 9.4.1).
fddimibPORTLerEstimate	A long-term average link error rate. It ranges from 10^{-4} to 10^{-15} and is reported as the absolute value of the base 10 logarithm (refer to ANSI SMT 9.4.7.5.).
fddimibPORTLemRejectCts	A link error monitoring count of the times that a link has been rejected.
fddimibPORTLemCts	The aggregate link error/monitor error count, set to zero, only on station initialization.
fddimibPORTLerAlarm	The link error rate estimate at which a link connection will generate an alarm. It ranges from 10^{-4} to 10^{-15} and is reported as the absolute value of the base 10 logarithm of the estimate (default of 8).
fddimibPORTLerCutoff	The link error rate estimate at which a link connection will be broken. It ranges from 10^{-4} to 10^{-15} and is reported as the absolute value of the base 10 logarithm (default of 7).
fddimibPORTLerFlag	The condition becomes active when the value of fddiPORTLerEstimate is less than or equal to fddiPORTLerAlarm. This will be reported with the Status Report Frames (SRF) (refer to ANSI SMT 7.2.7 and 8.3).
fddimibMACFrameCts	A count of the number of frames received by this MAC (refer to ANSI MAC 7.5.1).
fddimibMACCopiedCts	A count that should match as closely as possible the number of frames addressed to (A bit set) and successfully copied into the station's receive buffers (C bit set) by this MAC (refer to ANSI MAC 7.5). Note that this count does not include MAC frames.

Continued

Table 3.13 MIB Variables (*Continued*)

Variable	Description from MIB
fddimibMacErrorCts	A count of the number of frames that were detected in error by this MAC but that had not been detected in error by another MAC (refer to ANSI MAC 7.5.2).
fddimibMACLostCts	A count of the number of instances that this MAC detected a format error during frame reception such that the frame was stripped (refer to MAC 7.5.3).
fddimibMACTvxExpiredCts	A count that should match as closely as possible the number of times that TVX has expired.
fddimibMACLateCts	A count that should match as closely as possible the number of TRT expirations since this MAC was reset or a token was received (refer to ANSI MAC 7.4.5).
fddimibMACFrameErrorRatio	This variable is the value of the ratio, ((delta `fddiMACLostCts` + delta `fddiMACErrorCts`)/(delta `fddiMACFrameCts` + delta `fddiMACLostCts`)) $\circ$ 2^{16}
fddimibMACTokenCts	A count that should match as closely as possible the number of times the station has received a token (total of nonrestricted and restricted) on this MAC (see ANSI MAC 7.4). This count is valuable for determination of network load.
fddimibMACNotCopiedCts	A count that should match as closely as possible the number of frames that were addressed to this MAC but were not copied into its receive buffers (see ANSI MAC 7.5). For example, this might occur due to local buffer congestion. Because of implementation considerations, this count may not match the actual number of frames not copied; it is required that this count be exact. Note that this count does not include MAC frames.

Continued

Table 3.13 MIB Variables (*Continued*)

Variable	Description from MIB
`fddimibMACRingOpCts`	The count of the number of times the ring has entered the 'Ring_Operational' state from the 'Ring_Not_Operational' state. This count is updated when a SM_MA_STATUS indication of a change in the Ring_Operational status occurs (refer to ANSI 6.1.4). Because of implementation considerations, this count may be less than the actual RingOp_Ct. It is not a requirement that this count be exact.

Table 3.14 Key Token Ring Characteristics

Technology	Token Ring
Standard	802.5
Important MIB(s)	Token Ring MIB (RFC 1743) Token Ring Extensions to RMON
Speed	4 Mbps 16 Mbps (Speeds on a single ring cannot be mixed.)
Medium	Shielded Twisted Pair (STP) Unshielded Twisted Pair (UTP)
Segment Length (between neighbors)	100 m for STP 45 m for UTP
Frame Size[4]	4511[5] 8-bit bytes at 4 Mbps 17839[5] 8-bit bytes at 16 Mbps
Physical Topology	Star (although logically a ring with a maximum of 260 stations per ring)
Priority Levels	7

4. In the strictest sense, the Token Ring specification does not specify a maximum or minimum frame size. The frame sizes are calculated based on the token holding timer. Use these sizes for technology comparison purposes only.

5. Original implementation of a 4-Mbps Token Ring is limited to 2091 bytes.

3.7.1 Physical Topology

Token Ring networks are in the form of a ring. A Token Ring can be constructed of either Shielded Twisted Pair (STP) or Unshielded Twisted Pair (UTP). STP offers Token Ring a range of 100 m between neighbors; UTP has a limit of 45 m between neighbors. The wires connecting a Token Ring station are typically called *lobes*—Token Ring neighbors are often referred to as lobes.

In a switched environment, Token Ring boxes come in two varieties: a Multistation Access Unit (MAU) or a Token Ring switch. A MAU is logically equivalent to an Ethernet hub or repeater and usually contains eight or more ports when used to connect stations into a single ring. MAUs have RING IN and RING OUT connectors that allow you to extend the ring to another MAU. Likewise, each station is connected to the MAU with a RING IN and RING OUT, although this is often a single cable. Like FDDI where A must be connected to B, RING OUT must be connected to RING IN, and RING IN must be connected to RING OUT in two adjacent MAUs. On a MAU (which essentially is a single ring) you *cannot* mix port speeds—they must be either all 4 Mbps or all 16 Mbps.

A Token Ring switch may be a stand-alone box or a module that plugs into a slot on a multitechnology chassis. Token Ring switching models typically contain 8 or more ports which are switched together as 8 or more Token Rings. Each ring is independent and hence can have its own speed—4 Mbps or 16 Mbps. Many Token Ring switches switch "up" to a faster technology like FDDI to connect with the backbone. See Figure 3.5 for an example of token ring switching.

3.7.2 Operation

Like FDDI, Token Ring communication is controlled by a token. When a station needs to communicate, it seizes the token as it passes by. Token Ring transforms the frame containing the token into a communication frame and sends it off. When the frame returns, the frame is removed from the ring and generates either another communication frame, if there is more to communicate, or a token frame, if it is finished. To ensure that the token is shared, there is a maximum holding timer.

Token Ring is often compared to Ethernet because like Ethernet it is largely deployed at the desktop. It is used extensively for transaction systems used by banks and airlines. The main advantage of Token Ring over Ethernet is that communication is fair and efficient, even when there are many users. The token facilitates fair communication without contention. Token Ring has a priority and a reservation scheme, and like FDDI, it must properly manage its token, since without it communication ceases.

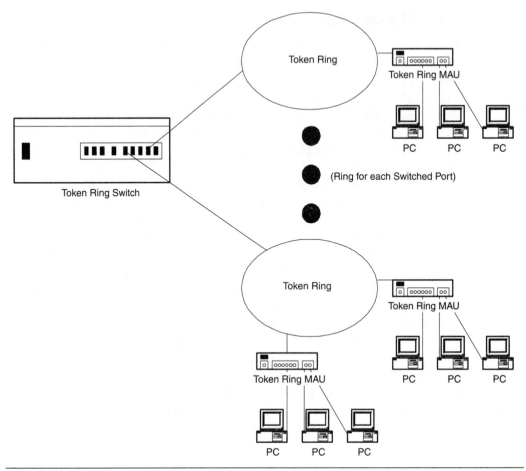

Figure 3.5 Token Ring switch with attached Token Ring MAUs

3.7.3 Token Ring Abbreviations

Table 3.15 provides Token Ring abbreviations.

3.7.4 Token Ring Management

Like FDDI, Token Ring has many special MAC frames used for management. Special interest management frames are used for ring initialization (for example, station attachment, election of an active monitor, management by the active monitor), as well as neighbor notification and beacon frames used to ensure that the ring's logical topology remains intact and reports neighbor faults respectively.

Table 3.15 Token Ring Abbreviations

LRM	LAN Reporting Mechanism
MAU	Multistation Access Unit
NAUN	Next Addressable Upstream Neighbor Frame (like FDDI NIF)
REM	Ring Error Monitor
SMP	Standby Monitor Present (Frame)
SR	Source Routing
STM	Station Manager

When a station attaches to the ring initially, it goes through a series of steps to ensure communications are operational:

1. **Performs lobe test.** The station sends a series of frames to ensure that the attachment cable (the lobe) provides adequate communication to the ring.

2. **Does active monitor check.** The station validates whether it sees a monitor frame (for example, active/standby monitor present, ring purge MAC) within a certain time interval. If the timer expires and nothing has been seen, the station initiates the token claim process.

3. **Does duplicate address check.** The station uses a duplicate address frame to verify that its address is unique.

4. **Determines neighbor status.** The station learns its upstream neighbors and finds out whether beaconing is occurring or needs to occur.

In order to ensure ring health, Token Ring uses an active monitor. Any of the stations on the ring can be the active monitor, and, if the active monitor leaves the ring for some reason, other stations (all of which are standby monitors) automatically detect this and go into a claim phase to elect a new active monitor. The active monitor recovers the token if lost, provides clock synchronization, initiates and monitors the neighbor notification process, and normally clears the ring of data if there is an error. It also adds a 24-bit delay in the ring ensuring that the ring is large enough to hold the token. Adding the 24-bit delay is necessary for rings with too few stations to hold the token.

One or more Ring Error Monitors (REMs) is used to roll up errors. Each REM collects and analyzes error frames and selectively "rolls up" information to the management station. For example, beaconing is used to alert neighbors on the ring of ring problems. When a station issues a beacon frame, the ring error monitor detects the frame and sets a timer. If the error is not corrected within the allotted time period, an error is sent to the network management station indicating that automatic recovery has failed.

Like FDDI, Token Ring has separate MAC frames for reporting errors and station states. Excessive numbers of MAC frames may be indicative of a pending or existing ring failure. The key word is *excessive* because MAC frames are used to perform normal operations like adding a new station to the ring.

If available, I recommend using RMON to monitor Token Ring. In addition to providing statistics for all errors, including beacons, lost frames, and congestion errors, Token Ring RMON gives you counts on broadcast and multicast frames and frame-size distributions. The History Group can be used to observe these counters over time. As with Ethernet, however, RMON may significantly impact switch performance. If this is the case for your switch, you may want to turn on RMON collection based on some other event, such as utilization exceeding a threshold.

3.7.4.1 Performance Management

Like all the other technologies, monitoring Token Ring utilization is fundamental to performance management. Unlike Ethernet, Token Ring can run at much higher utilization rates (approaching 100 percent) without degradation of performance because Token Ring does not use CSMA/CD.

Token Ring utilization is calculated with the formula. It is the same as Ethernet with different speed.

$$\text{Token Ring Port Utilization} =$$
$$((\Delta \text{ifInOctets} + \Delta \text{ifOutOctets}) * 8 \text{ bits per}$$
$$\text{octet})/((\text{time B} - \text{time A}) * \text{ifSpeed})$$

where Δ implies delta or "change in values over time interval."

3.7.4.2 Configuration Management

Ring speed and ring IDs are the primary configuration considerations.

- Be sure that you do not mix 4- and 16-Mbps rates on ports within the same ring; doing so will cause havoc. Each port on a Token Ring switch is a separate ring, so it is okay to mix 4 and 16 Mbps across different switched ports.
- If you use source routing (discussed in the next chapter), make certain that your ring IDs are unique across your rings.

3.7.4.3 Fault Management

Token Ring has many faults that you should monitor.

- Monitor error rate frequency and types of errors. Use Token Ring RMON, if available.

- Monitor jitter, a fancy word for loss of synchronization. Token Ring jitter is common in environments where the Token Ring specifications are exceeded, for example, going too far with a cable. Jitter is observed indirectly through high error counts, "network is slow" reports, or "network is periodically dead" reports. Jitter is more of a problem on high-speed Token Ring installations than on low-speed Token Ring installations.

- Monitor both hard and soft Token Ring errors.

Token Ring errors are divided into two groups: hard and soft errors. Hard errors normally result in a station being disconnected from the ring, whereas there are many soft errors that are normal. In *How to Manage Your Network Using SNMP* (p. 257) by Marshall T. Rose and Keith McCloghrie, the authors give examples of two errors that are normal—line errors (FCS errors or coding violations) and burst errors (a momentary disconnection from the ring). They explain, however, that A/C Errors, Internal Errors, and Abort Delimiter Transmitted indicate that the interface is faulty and should be replaced. These errors are called *isolating errors* as they can pinpoint the station at fault.

Rose and McCloghrie continue on page 258 with definitions of important *nonisolating errors:*

Receiver Congestion: a station recognized its address as the destination of a frame but did not have sufficient unused buffer space to receive it. This typically occurs because a file server or bridge is temporarily overloaded.

Lost Frame Error: the station transmitted a frame onto the ring, but did not receive it back. This often happens when a station is inserted/removed from the ring, because of the momentary break in ring connectivity.

Token Error: the active Monitor did not see a valid token within the required time interval. This can also happen when a station is inserted/removed from the ring.

Frequency Error: the signal received by the Active Monitor differs too much from its own internal clock. One cause of this error is exceeding the limit of the number of stations on the ring (e.g., 72 stations for UTP cabling).

Frame Copied Error: a station recognized its own address in the destination address of the frame, but the frame already has its A bit set. This can be caused by having multiple stations with the same address on the ring, or by a line hit on the Frame Status field.

Beacon frames are indicative of hard errors. When a station beacons, it indicates that the station is not receiving a valid ring signal. The beacon frame contains the address of the upstream neighbor, the suspect station. If the suspect station does not remove itself within a specified time interval, the beaconing station will remove itself from the ring.

A S I D E . . .

When choosing a protocol analyzer for Token Ring it is a good idea to look for one that can "enter a beaconing ring." Not all analyzers can do this.

3.7.4.4 Important MIB variables

The information provided in Table 3.16, taken from *How to Manage Your Network Using SNMP* by Marshall T. Rose and Keith McCloghrie (pp. 303–304), illustrates some of the most important MIB variables used for monitoring Token Ring switched ports. All variables and MIB definitions (except for those prefixed with Token Ring° which comes from the Token Ring extensions to the RMON MIB, RFC 1513) are from the Token Ring MIB, RFC 1231.

Table 3.16 MIB Variables

Variable	Description from MIB
dot5StatsLineErrors	This counter is incremented when a frame or token is copied or repeated by a station. The E bit is zero in the frame or token, and one of the following conditions exists: 1) there is a nondata bit (J or K bit) between the SD and the ED of the frame or token, or 2) there is an FCS error in the frame.
dot5StatsBurstErrors	This counter is incremented when a station detects the absence of transitions for five half-bit timers (burst-five error).
dot5StatsACErrors	This counter is incremented when a station receives an AMP or SMP frame in which A is equal to C is equal to 0. The station then receives another SMP frame in which A is equal to C is equal to 0 without first receiving an AMP frame. It denotes a station that cannot set the AC bits properly.

Continued

Table 3.16 MIB Variables (*Continued*)

Variable	Description from MIB
dot5StatsAbortTransErrors	This counter is incremented when a station transmits an abort delimiter while transmitting.
dot5StatsInternalErrors	This counter is incremented when a station recognizes an internal error.
dot5LostFrameErrors	This counter is incremented when a station is transmitting and its TRR timer expires. This condition denotes a condition where a transmitting station in strip mode does not receive the trailer of the frame before the TRR timer goes off.
dot5StatsReceiveCongestions	This counter is incremented when a station recognizes a frame addressed to its specific address but has no buffer space indicating that the station is congested.
dot5StatsFrameCopiedErrors	This counter is incremented when a station recognizes a frame addressed to its specific address and detects that the field A bits are set to 1, indicating a possible line hit or duplicate address.
dot5StatsTokenErrors	This counter is incremented when a station acting as the active monitor recognizes an error condition that needs a token transmitted.
dot5StatsSoftErrors	The number of Soft Errors the interface has detected. It directly corresponds to the number of Report Error MAC frames that this interface has transmitted. Soft Errors are those that are recoverable by the MAC layer protocols.
dot5StatsHardErrors	The number of times this interface has detected an immediately recoverable fatal error. It denotes the number of times this interface is either transmitting or receiving beacon frames.

Continued

Table 3.16 MIB Variables (*Continued*)

Variable	Description from MIB
dot5StatsSignalLoss	The number of times this interface has detected the loss of signal condition from the ring.
dot5StatsTransmitBeacons	The number of times this interface has transmitted a beacon frame.
dot5StatsRecoverys	The number of Claim Token MAC frames received or transmitted after the interface has received a Ring Purge MAC frame. This counter signifies the number of times the ring has been purged and is being recovered into a normal operating state.
dot5StatsLobeWires	The number of times the interface has detected an open or short circuit in the lobe data path. The adapter will be closed and dot5RingState will signify condition.
dot5StatsRemoves	The number of times the interface received a Remove Ring Station MAC frame request. When this frame is received, the interface will enter the close state and dot5RingState will signify this condition.
dot5StatsSingles	The number of times the interface has sensed that it is the only station on the ring. This will happen if the interface is the first one up on a ring or if there is a hardware problem.
dot5StatsFreqErrors	The number of times the interface has detected that the frequency of the incoming signal differs from the expected frequency by more than that specified by the IEEE 802.5 standard. See chapter 7 in Token Ring Access Method and Physical Layer Specifications, IEEE Standard 802.5-1989.
tokenring	Various objects from Token Ring extension to the RMON MIB.

3.8 ATM

Asynchronous Transfer Mode (ATM) provides a common communication medium that simultaneously supports multiple types of data (multimedia such as voice, video, text) at high transmission across switched WAN or LAN backbones. Unlike other LAN technologies, ATM is not a shared medium. The performance does not degrade as the number of users increases as with Ethernet. ATM is connection-oriented, meaning that an end-to-end connection is set up prior to communication, enabling ATM to provide a way to guarantee delivery with a negotiated set of parameters. This important feature is called Quality of Service (QoS). Table 3.17 summarizes the key characteristics of ATM.

ATM runs at many different speeds across all the popular media. Three popular LAN speeds are 25 Mbps, 155.52 Mbps (OC-3), and 622 Mbps (OC-12). UTP and STP are typically used at the desktop whereas fiber is used in the backbone.

ATM uses the notion of Permanent and Switched Virtual Circuits (PVCs and SVCs) to define communication paths within the LAN. Permanent Virtual

Table 3.17 Key ATM Characteristics

Standard	Several B-ISDN/ATM Standards
Important MIBs	Classical IP and ARP over ATM (RFC 1577) ATM MIB (RFC 1695) ATM signaling support for IP over ATM (RFC 1755) IP over ATM (RFC 1932) MIB-2 (with high capacity interface extensions)
Speed	25 Mbps 51.84 Mbps 100 Mbps 155 Mbps 622 Mbps
Medium	Unshielded Twisted Pair (UTP) for 25.6 and 51.84 Mbps Multi-single-mode fiber primarily for 100+ Mbps[6]
Segment Length	N/A
Cell Size	53 bytes including 5-byte header
Physical Topology	Star

6. Category 5 UTP and Category 1 STP may be used for higher speeds.

Circuits are statically configured by the network manager for commonly used communication paths such as a highly used backbone. Switched Virtual Circuits are set up dynamically on an as-needed basis. SVCs are set up and torn down and maintained via a signaling protocol. When a user wishes to establish a connection with another node, the user sends a message specifying the desired bandwidth and QoS desired. Simply stated, the signaling protocol "walks" through the network keeping track of its path to the desired destination. If the destination is successfully reached and the path satisfies the QoS parameters given, the switched connection is established and ready for use. There is a fair amount of overhead with setting up a switched virtual circuit, one disadvantage of a connection-oriented protocol, especially when the connection will carry data for only a short period of time.

3.8.1 ATM LANE

LAN Emulation (LANE) was defined to incorporate ATM in existing networks consisting of Ethernet and Token Ring. LANE provides the normal connectionless service and multicast service characteristic of traditional LANs. LANE emulates the media access control (MAC) protocol used by the connectionless technologies, enabling you to support legacy LAN technologies over ATM. FDDI and Fast Ethernet over LANE require translational bridging. LANE is commonly used to define an ATM pipe to bridge two LANs—the systems that participate in this emulated LAN across legacy LANs are said to be part of a designated Emulated LAN (ELAN). Often Virtual LANs (VLANs) are defined to overlap with ELANs. We will talk in-depth about VLANS in Chapter 4, since VLANs are not just for ATM.

As you probably just noticed, LANE like ATM includes a plethora of new, esoteric abbreviations. Unfortunately the ATM community talks in these terms. I've heard entire sentences spoken by ATM gurus with as few as two recognizable words. So as painful as it might be, we'll go through the terms that you should know for ATM management (Table 3.18). To put things into perspective, though, we will discuss LANE in the section on physical topology, since it is best illustrated with a picture of the design of a network.

A S I D E . . .

Multiprotocol over ATM (MPOA) is a future standard that goes beyond LANE. MPOA addresses the limitations of LANE such as the distributed nature of required servers, that is, what happens to your LANE if the Broadcast and Unknown Server (BUS) becomes inaccessible, and BUS bumps up support to Layer 3.

Table 3.18 ATM Abbreviations

ATM Acronym	
AAL	ATM Adaption Layer
ATM	Asynchronous Transfer Mode
BER	Bit Error Rate
B-ISDN	Broadband-Integrated Services Digital Network
BUS	Broadcast and Unknown Server
CBR	Constant Bit Rate
CIR	Cell Insertion Ratio
CL	Connectionless Service
CLP	Cell Loss Priority
CLR	Cell Loss Ratio
CO	Connection-Oriented Service
CRC	Cyclic Redundancy Check
GFC	Generic Flow Control
HEC	Header Error Control
LEC	LAN Emulation Client
LES	LAN Emulation Server
MARS	Multicast Address Resolution Server
MTU	Maximum Transmission Unit
NNI	Network Node Interface
QoS	Quality of Service
UNI	User Network Interface

Continued

Table 3.18 ATM Abbreviations (*Continued*)

ATM Acronym	
VBR	Variable-Bit Rate
VC	Virtual Channel
VCC	Virtual Channel Connection
VCI	Virtual Channel Identifier
VCL	Virtual Channel Link
VP	Virtual Path
VPC	Virtual Path Connection
VPI	Virtual Path Identifier
VPL	Virtual Path Link

3.8.2 Physical Topology

There are lots of ways to utilize ATM in both the WAN and the LAN. There is only one way that I believe is (and will be) the most common in the LAN—LAN Emulation, where ATM is used as a backbone trunk or pipe. I will focus on this physical topology.

LANE revolves around the concepts of LECs (LAN Emulation Clients), LESs (LAN Emulation Servers), LECS (LAN Emulation Configuration Servers), BUSs (Broadcast and Unknown Servers), LUNI (LAN Emulation User-to-Network Interface), and LNNI (LAN Emulation Network to Network Interfaces). An ELAN (Emulated LAN) contains many LECs, a single LECS (shared with the entire ATM network), a LES, and a BUS.

LECs refer to the software that connect end node devices such as database servers, PCs, or workstations to the ATM network. A LEC's interface into the network is provided by the LUNI. Internetwork connections use a LNNI. The LES provides such functionality as MAC to ATM address resolution (ATM uses 20-byte addressing, whereas traditional LANs use the 48-bit MAC address) and client registration to LECs. The BUS is used to process all broadcast, multicast, and unknown traffic into the emulated LAN—remember, since ATM is point-to-point it has no built-in knowledge on how to process broadcast and multicast traffic. When you have many ELANs, you must have a single LEC that identifies each ELAN and its LES location.

A S I D E . . .

Unlike Ethernet or Fast Ethernet there can be more than one LEC associated with an ATM switched port; this allows clients to be part of more than one Emulated LAN. However, there is generally a vendor-specific physical limitation on the number of PVCs that a given switch may support. This, in turn, limits the number of LECs that can be supported.

An ATM trunk is a high-speed (often 622 Mbps (OC-12)), permanent, virtual circuit link between two switches in your network. This trunk line may be used by traditional (non-ATM) LANs via LANE or in a pure ATM network where ATM goes out to the desktop. If LANE is employed, the P-to-C/C-to-P (packet to cell/cell to packet) conversions will happen inside of each switch on alternate sides of the trunk. Sometimes this trunk line is called a *pipe*. Because this trunk line is permanent, it is statically configured without the need to go through the signaling protocol. (This isn't to say that channels within the static paths may not come and go and be setup via signaling.) This is a popular use of ATM today in the LAN (see Figure 3.6) because there is not another technology (albeit fiber channel that isn't well known) that comes close to the available bandwidth of 622 Mbps; Gigabit Ethernet, though, is on the horizon . . .

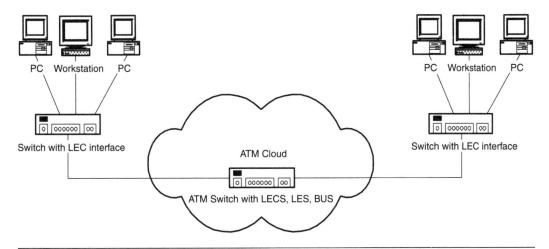

Figure 3.6 LAN with ATM trunk via LANE

3.8.3 Operation

It is important to note a few key distinctions that distinguish the operation of ATM from the other technologies:

- ATM is connection-oriented; either an ATM circuit is setup permanently or it is set up as needed via signaling.

- Because ATM is connection-oriented, ATM can provide quality of service (QoS). This means ATM can guarantee delivery of data based on a negotiation up front. This guarantee is absolutely critical for time-sensitive data like multimedia. As an example, can you imagine how awful it is to see one of those foreign movies where the sound is out of synch with the picture? Well, ATM via QoS is a powerful solution to guarantee that the sound arrives when the picture arrives. QoS (coupled with bandwidth) is the most important feature of ATM within a LAN environment; currently if you need jitter-free multimedia, you need ATM, end-to-end.

- ATM cells do not contain 48-byte MAC addresses (also known as LAN addresses), rather they contain path and circuit identifiers. LANE is used to map these path and circuit identifiers to MAC addresses.

- ATM works by literally pumping cells through a predefined mesh. Once a path is set up, ATM leverages switching to move data from source to destination at wire speeds. Switches use high-speed *switching fabrics* to route data. (Switching fabrics refers to the hardware and software design of the switch, and *fabrics* are comprised of intricate, parallel interconnections built using very advanced application-specific integrated circuit (ASIC) technologies.)

3.8.4 ATM Abbreviations

I'm certain that ATM wins the award for the most abbreviations among the technologies. In Table 3.18 I present a subset of the ones I've seen most often.

3.8.5 ATM Management

There are lots of ATM MIBs and RFCs. They are necessary to satisfy the rich management requirements needed to manage the signaling process used to set up Virtual Circuits within the WAN or within a "pure" (ATM going end-to-end) ATM LAN (currently not all that common).

Again, I focus on what is most common in a LAN; that is, ATM trunks use LANE. This greatly simplifies and reduces the scope of our discussion.

(Perhaps if pure ATM takes off in the LAN, I will go into the gory details in a future book revision). Given an ATM trunk, you can manage it pretty well with just the ATM MIB and MIB-2.

3.8.5.1 Performance Management

You guessed it—utilization! Again, ATM utilization is similar to Ethernet Utilization calculation where standard MIB-2 objects are used. Because it is often desirable to show both inbound and outbound ATM utilization, I show all three formulas. It may be necessary to use the new high-capacity counters if they are implemented.

```
          Total ATM Interface Utilization =
       ((Δ ifInOctets + Δ ifOutOctets) * 8 bits per
          octet)/((time B - time A) * ifSpeed)

          InBound ATM Interface Utilization =
    (Δ ifInOctets * 8 bits per octet)/((time B - time A)
                   * ifSpeed)

          OutBound ATM Interface Utilization =
   (Δ ifOutOctets * 8 bits per octet)/((time B - time A)
                   * ifSpeed)
      where Δ implies delta or "change in values over time
                   interval".
```

3.8.5.2 Configuration Management

Setting up a switched ATM trunk is usually limited to defining path and circuit identifiers (atmInterfaceIlmiVpi, atmInterfaceIlmiVci) at each end of the ATM interface. A read-only path and circuit numbers (atmInterfaceConfVpcs, atmInterfaceConfVccs) are associated with each path and circuit identifier. The ATM interface defines the actual number of paths and circuits.

3.8.5.3 Fault Management

As with Ethernet, you need to monitor MIB 2 objects at each end of your ATM trunk and the error rates of each ATM interface.

3.8.5.4 Important MIB variables

The MIB variables, shown in Table 3.19, are some of the most important ones used for monitoring ATM switched ports. They come from MIB-2 (RFC

Table 3.19 ATM MIB Variables

Variable	MIB	Description from MIB
ifOperStatus	MIB-2	(see description in Ethernet section)
ifAdminStatus	MIB-2	(see description in Ethernet section)
ifInErrors	MIB-2	(see description in Ethernet section)
ifInUcastPkts	MIB-2	(see description in Ethernet section)
ifInNUcastPkts	MIB-2	(see description in Ethernet section)
ifInDiscards	MIB-2	(see description in Ethernet section)
ifInOctets	MIB-2	(see description in Ethernet section)
ifOutErrors	MIB-2	(see description in Ethernet section)
ifOutUcastPkts	MIB-2	(see description in Ethernet section)
ifOutNUcastPkts	MIB-2	(see description in Ethernet section)
ifOutDiscards	MIB-2	(see description in Ethernet section)
ifOutNUcastPkts	MIB-2	(see description in Ethernet section)
ifOutOctets	MIB-2	(see description in Ethernet Section)
ifInMulticastPkts	MIB-2-Evol	The number of packets, delivered by this sublayer to a higher sublayer, which were addressed to a multicast address at this sublayer. For a MAC-layer protocol, this includes both Group and Functional addresses.
ifInBroadcastPkts	MIB-2-Evol	The number of packets, delivered by this sublayer to a higher sublayer, which were addressed to a broadcast address at this sublayer.

Continued

Table 3.19 ATM MIB Variables (*Continued*)

Variable	MIB	Description from MIB
ifOutMulticastPkts	MIB-2-Evol	The total number of packets that higher-protocols requested be transmitted, and which were addressed to a multicast address at this sublayer, including those that were discarded or not sent. For a MAC-layer protocol, this includes both Group and Functional addresses.
ifOutBroadcastPkts	MIB-2-Evol	The total number of packets that higher-level protocols requested be transmitted and which were addressed to a broadcast address at this sublayer, including those that were discarded or not sent.
ifHCInOctets	MIB-2	64-bit version of ifInOctets.
ifHCInUcastPkts	MIB-2	64-bit version of InUcastPkts.
ifHCInMulticastPkts	MIB-2	64-bit version of MulticastPkts.
ifHCInBroadcastPkts	MIB-2	64-bit version of InBroadcastPkts.
ifHCOutOctets	MIB-2	64-bit version of OutOctets.
ifHCOutUcastPkts	MIB-2	64-bit version of OutUcastPkts.
ifHCOutMulticastPkts	MIB-2	64-bit version of OutMulticastPkts.
ifHCOutBroadcastPkts	MIB-2	64-bit version of OutBroadcastPkts.
ifHighSpeed	MIB-2	An estimate of the interface's current bandwidth in units of 1,000,000 bits per second. If this object reports a value of 'n,' then the speed of the interface is somewhere in the range of 'n-500,000' to 'n+499,999'. For interfaces that do not vary in bandwidth or for those where no accurate estimation can be made, this object should contain the nominal bandwidth. For a sublayer that has no concept of bandwidth, this object should be zero.

Continued

Table 3.19 ATM MIB Variables (*Continued*)

Variable	MIB	Description from MIB
`ifLinkUpDownTrapEnable`	MIB-2	Trap indicating that an interface has gone from an up-to-down state or from a down-to-up state.
`atmInterfaceIlmiVpi`	ATM	The VPI value of the VCC supporting the ILMI at this ATM interface. If the values of `atmInterfaceIlmiVpi` and `atmInterfaceIlmiVci` are both equal to zero, then the ILMI is supported at this ATM interface.
`atmInterfaceIlmiVci`	ATM	The VCI value of the VCC supporting the ILMI at this ATM interface. If the values of `atmInterfaceIlmiVpi` and `atmInterfaceIlmiVci` are both equal to zero, then the ILMI is not supported at this ATM interface.
`atmInterfaceConfVpcs`	ATM	The number of VPCs (PVCs and SVCs) configured for use at this ATM interface. At the ATM UNI the configured number of VPCs (PVCs and SVCs) can range from 0 to 256 only.
`atmInterfaceConfVccs`	ATM	The number of VCCs (PVCs and SVCs) configured for use at the ATM interface.

1213), the Evolution of the Interfaces Group of MIB-2 (RFC 1573, MIB-2-Evol), and one of the ATM MIBs (RFC 1695).

Note the new high-capacity (HC) counters. They were introduced because with high-speed technologies like ATM, the 32-bit counters tend to wrap (go back to 0) too frequently. High-capacity counters have 64 bits of significance, greatly extending the amount of time between wrapping.

3.9 Summary

As the size of a LAN grows, so does the need for multiple layer 2 (data link) technologies. Small LANs get by with Ethernet or Token Ring. Larger LANs are typically constructed of two or more LAN technologies—Ethernet or Token Ring to the desktop and FDDI, Fast Ethernet, and ATM in the backbone.

One of the greatest benefits of switching is that it enables you to plug in new technologies quite easily, without major network disruption. As you outgrow your FDDI 100 Mbps backbone, you may decide to upgrade to an ATM 622 Mbps backbone. You can make this upgrade transparent to your end users. Likewise your 10 Mbps Ethernet connections to database servers can be upgraded to 100 Mbps Fast Ethernet connections without wholesale "forklift" (replace the box) requirements.

If I had to pick one thing to manage on a switched network, it would be utilization. Keeping tabs on utilization is indicative of the network health of your switched LAN. If utilization is 0 percent and normal utilization for that same time period is 10 percent, there is a good chance the network defined by that switched port is down. If utilization is too high on a Ethernet segment, chances are good that you have too many users on a single switched port, and you need to distribute the users to other ports or upgrade the connection to Fast Ethernet. Utilization is a metric that spans performance, configuration, and fault management: it is an important indicator of network service to the user(s) at the other end of each switched port.

With the ease of being able to swap technologies come the opportunity and requirement to learn the technologies and what is important to manage each of the them. Only by gaining a basic understanding of Ethernet, Fast Ethernet, FDDI, and ATM can you understand what to deploy and how to manage your deployment.

CHAPTER 4

LAN Switching and VLANs

4.1 Introduction

This chapter discusses how the fundamental layer-2 technologies introduced in Chapter 3 are applied in a switched-LAN environment. The chapter focuses on the following two areas:

- Aspects of switching that are required to manage a layer-2 switch, and
- virtual software-based LANs (VLANs) that are becoming increasingly popular in today's switched LAN environments.

Note that I purposely omit a detailed discussion of switching architectures and theory. Although this information is interesting to know, it is not prerequisite to managing a switch. If you are interested in these subjects, select a book listed in the bibliography. I recommend *Gigabit Networking* by Craig Partridge.

4.2 Bridging and Routing

All switches provide bridging functions within the network. Some switches also provide routing functions. Technically, switching is discrete from routing, but often the distinction is blurred by saying "layer-3 switch" or by indicating that a switch routes. Switching and routing are complementary technologies, and it is necessary to understand both when you build your switched LAN. Subsequently a quick survey of how each of these technologies works is presented in this section.

4.2.1 What is the Functionality of a Bridge?

Bridging is a fundamental technology used within LANs. Figure 4.1 provides a conceptual illustration of two bridges within a LAN.

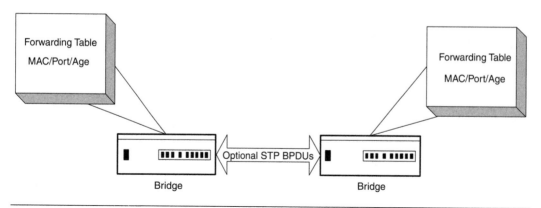

Figure 4.1 Conceptual representation of bridges within a LAN

- Bridges forward frames (FDDI, Token Ring, Ethernet, and so on) at the data link layer, layer 2.
- Bridges forward frames based on the contents of a "learned" forwarding table.
- Forwarding tables provides a "mapping" from a MAC address to a port on the bridge.
- Bridges "learn" where MAC addresses are by monitoring the source addresses within frames. For example, if a frame comes from port 2 with a *source MAC address* of 02-60-8C-00-09-83, subsequent frames with a *destination MAC address* of 02-60-8C-00-09-83 are forwarded to this port. See Figure 4.2.
- A bridge's forwarding table may also contain entries that are statically entered by the network administrator.
- If a bridge does not have an entry for a destination address, the bridge "floods" the frame to all ports except for the source port.
- If a bridge looks up the destination address and finds out that it maps to the same port as the source port, it drops the frame since it does not need to be bridged. This will happen if you have a number of devices attached to a concentrator or hub that plugs into the bridge port.
- Bridges "age out" addresses from their forwarding tables to eliminate stale information and to keep the table from overflowing over time. Typically a bridge forwarding table can hold only so many entries, for example 8K or 8192 entries. Aging is typically done by maintaining a counter for each entry indicating the time that the entry was last updated. When the counter exceeds a preconfigured value, the entry is

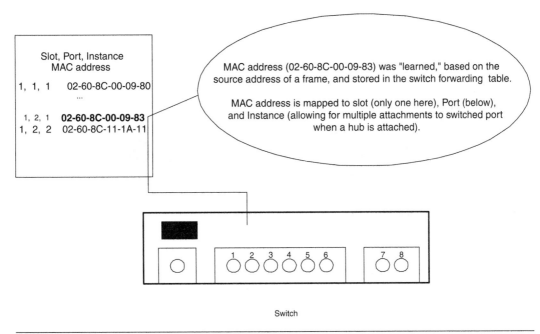

Figure 4.2 Figure showing relationship of MAC addresses and switch forwarding table. Note that the forwarding table is a conceptual view as it will differ depending on vendor.

deleted from the table. As subsequent frames come in, their associated table entries are refreshed; that is, the counters are reset.

- Optionally bridges implement the Spanning Tree Protocol (STP). This protocol provides a mechanism for bridges to communicate with one another and to ensure that only one path exists between any two bridges; STP eliminates bridge loops. Bridge Protocol Data Units (BPDUs) are used to communicate between bridges.

- One noteworthy disadvantage of large bridged networks is the proliferation of broadcast traffic. Broadcast traffic, unlike unicast (traffic destined to a single destination), must be "read" by all network devices (include PCs, UNIX workstations, and so on) on your switched LAN. Lots of broadcast traffic can place significant overhead on each network device on the switched LAN. In addition, a broadcast storm can be catastrophic (more on storms later in this chapter). Routers and VLANs (discussed later in this chapter) contain broadcast traffic.

4.2.2 What is the Functionality of a Router?

Routing is also key to LAN construction. Figure 4.3 presents a conceptual illustration of two routers within a LAN.

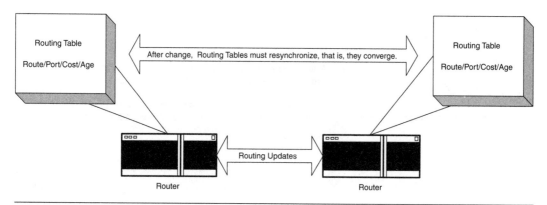

Figure 4.3   Conceptual representation of routers within a LAN

- Routers route packets at the network layer, layer 3.
- Routers route packets based on the contents of a routing table.
- Routers route based on protocol. Routing for three popular protocol families (AppleTalk, NetWare, and TCP/IP) is discussed in the next chapter.
- Routing tables contain a mapping of destination to a port. With each entry are one or more metrics providing some indication of "cost." Thus if two or more routes exist for an entry, the router will pick the "least expensive" route. Note also that some routers will load balance across multiple routes.
- Routers "learn" their routing table entries by communicating with their routing peers. Essentially each router has a set of preconfigured routes that it knows about. By exchanging information at periodic intervals, routing peers can learn other routes provided by these peers.
- There are many routing protocols used to implement routing, and these are discussed in the next chapter. For example, Open Shortest Path First (OSPF) and Routing Information Protocol (RIP) are particularly popular for TCP/IP implementations in LANs.
- Routers "age out" routes from their routing tables to eliminate stale information. Aging typically uses a similar algorithm as discussed earlier in the section on bridging.
- Each router is statically configured with the networks (subnets in TCP/IP terminology) to which it is directly attached. With bridges (and their respective forwarding tables) this is optional; with routers it is not. Preconfiguration is how routes are "seeded" for being "learned" by others. Somewhere in the network each route must be statically configured.

- Routers do not flood if they do not know where to forward a packet. Either the router will send the packet to a default route or the packet will be dropped. Packets have a built-in mechanism (for example, TCP/IP TTL [Time to Live]) that maintains the number of routers through which the packet has passed (also called hops); once TTL reaches a certain value, the packet is discarded, preventing the endless forwarding of "lost" packets.

- Certain protocols are not routable; for example, NetBIOS is not routable. We will discuss this more in the next chapter.

- Routers provide broadcast containment. Broadcast traffic is not typically routed. (Some routers can be configured to forward broadcast traffic, but forwarding, however, is not recommended. Some switches can also filter broadcasts.)

- The key to routing is prompt updating and quick routing-table convergence. If a route goes down, other routers must be notified and the tables need to converge as soon as possible. Certain routing protocols converge more quickly than others; for example, OSPF converges faster than RIP.

4.3 Switch Fundamentals

LAN switches are based on a very simple concept. LAN switches take frames from a source port and, based on the destination MAC address, *switch* the frame to the appropriate destination port at incredibly fast (line) speeds. LAN switching gets its roots from circuit switching done by telephone companies, which have been switching and multiplexing voice data across circuits for years.

Switching combines advanced microprocessor technology with the concept of a layer-2 bridge. Like a bridge, a switch reads header information in a frame and, based on source information, switches the frame to the appropriate port (or interface—I tend to use "interface" and "port" interchangeably although "interface" is more generic and "port" is somewhat Ethernet-centric). A switch also "learns" what source is where, based on the source address of incoming frames, and builds and maintains an address table. And finally a switch "floods" when it doesn't know where to send a frame. These are all characteristics of a bridge. *A switch, then, is really a high-speed multiport bridge.*

Switches come in many configurations. There are dedicated boxes with 16 switched 10 Mbps ports; there are cards with eight 100 Mbps ports. There are cards that switch from FDDI to FDDI; there are cards with a bunch of

Ethernet ports that switch to an FDDI ring. Nearly every useful combination has been made. Large switches often can be configured with several cards. Since each card may have several interfaces (16 or more), a large switch can easily have more than 100 discrete interfaces.

4.3.1 Types of Switches

There are three types of devices called switches:

1. **Port switches** is a fancy name for a repeater that does not really use switching technology. Essentially all ports share the same LAN segment. For example, given an 8-port Ethernet Port Switch, all 8 ports would be sharing the same 10 Mbps Ethernet segment. Given an 8-port Token Ring MAU, all stations are connected to the same ring and share the same 4-Mbps or 16-Mbps ring.

2. **Switches** are network devices that operate at layer 2 of the OSI model. They are also known as LAN multiport bridges where all ports are discrete LAN segments. For example, given an 8-port Ethernet Port Switch, all 8 ports have their own 10 Mbps segment. Given an 8-port Token Ring Switch, all ports are separate rings running at 4 Mbps or 16 Mbps. Ports bridged between each other provide communication among ports; typically one port provides a high-speed uplink (for example, FDDI or 100 Mbps Ethernet) to the backbone.

   Layer-2 switches leverage transparent bridging (as discussed in section 4.2.1) that connects networks at layer 2, transparent to high-level protocols. This means that packets from TCP/IP, IPX, and AppleTalk can all be bridged together.

3. **Layer 3 Switches** are also known as multilayer switches (layers 2 and 3 of the OSI model—datalink and networking). They have the same layer-2 switch properties as a switch but also include some layer-3 capabilities, that is, routing capabilities—although often more limited than those of a dedicated router. For example, you could assign ports to a certain IP subnet and a port to be the "default route" when packets need to be routed to a different subnet. I've often heard that these types of devices follow the philosophy "Switch (bridge) where you can; route where you must." This concept focuses attention around speed since the routing logic, which is significantly more complex than switching logic, is what slows down the process of routing packets. The amount of packet reading that must be done to route is far more than what must be read to switch frames.

A S I D E . . .

When using a layer 3 switch as a router, make certain you understand what the switch will do with a packet that it cannot route. Will it be bridged, or will it be dropped?

4.3.2 Inside a Switch

LAN switches vary greatly among switch vendors. Generally speaking LAN switches leverage Application Specific Integrated Circuits (ASIC) to implement a switching "fabric" that is capable of moving large volumes of data quickly. As mentioned in Chapter 3, switching fabric refers to the hardware and software design of the switch; fabrics are usually comprised of intricate, parallel interconnections.

Digital Signal Processors (DSPs) offer an alternative to ASICs. Typically ASICs are used at the high end of switching, whereas DSPs are used at the low end. Switches tend to have several ports or interfaces to move data

- from a higher-speed technology to a lower-speed technology (FDDI to Ethernet).

- among similar technologies (FDDI to FDDI or Ethernet to Ethernet).

- among many technologies (FDDI to Ethernet or Fast Ethernet).

As shown in Figure 4.4, the combinations are vendor-specific and many.

Switches use a variety of switching techniques to implement their switching fabric. Cross-point switches create a "path" from the incoming port to the outgoing port based on destination address. Cross-point switches are often advertised to switch at line speed, meaning there is no latency in moving frames across the switch.

Switching designs may be "cut-through" where a subset of the data (frame header with source and destination MAC addresses) is read and switched without temporarily buffering data when "switching" data from the input interface to the output interface. Modified cut-through does not forward runts (packets that are too short because of collisions); it reads 64 bytes, buffers, and then forwards. The disadvantage of cut-through switching is that good as well as bad frames are switched, since there is no way to verify the checksum of each frame. Although the advantage of cut-through designs is speed, expect more FCS errors with cut-through switching.

"Store-and-forward" switches buffer data temporarily. They check the entire frame for cyclic redundancy check (CRC) errors as well as filter out frames

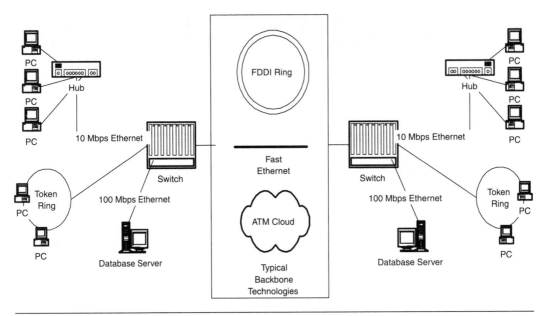

Figure 4.4 Sparsely populated switch environment switching to/from a variety of technologies

that are too short or too long. After error checking, store-and-forward switches create the cross-connection. Latency comes with storing.

Switches may have a "blocking" or "nonblocking" architecture. Blocking refers to having to wait when a particular data path is busy; nonblocking architectures handle moving data from input interfaces to output interfaces without delay. Nonblocking switches are able to switch at line speed since they can forward data at the same rate as their input paths. Generally speaking, a nonblocking architecture is significantly better than a blocking one because blocking can kill performance by dropping frames when the switch cannot keep up.

There are not any rules as to which techniques a switch uses; a switch may use both cut-through and store-and-forward techniques in its implementation. Fundamental to switching is performance, and there are many creative buffering schemes and hardware designs employed that enable products to switch at line speed or as close to line speed as possible.

Pay very careful attention to the internal capacity of a switch (also known as the backplane speed) and the amount of memory used for buffering of data. The internal capacity of a switch must exceed the summation of all the port capacities, or there is going to be some blocking and frame dropping. Likewise a memory-poor implementation may have to drop frames when traffic becomes heavy. These factors are particularly important when evaluating chassis architectures. A chassis with a low-capacity backplane architecture and/or minimal buffer space discounts the flexibility of swapping in new switching modules as the internal capacity and/or memory of the switch becomes quickly exceeded.

A S I D E . . .

When evaluating switches, make certain the frames-per-second rates (or packets per second used with switch routes) are reflective of *actual* networks in which frame and packet sizes vary dramatically. Impressive statistics based on purely minimal frame/packet size will not be so impressive when you introduce the switch into the real world where frame/packet sizes vary greatly. Large file transfers, which use maximum packet size, may seriously degrade performance.

4.3.3 Switches Provide a "Map" of Your LAN

As mentioned previously, the concept of bridging is fundamental to switching because switches operate at layer 2. Switches are really multiport bridges that move data among many ports based on the MAC destination address. Like bridges, switches maintain a forwarding table that tells the switch which MAC address(es) are out at each port. Entries in forwarding tables are generally dynamically learned, although many bridges allow for configuration of static entries. A bridge learns where things are by monitoring source addresses in frames and storing an entry for each slot/port/MAC address in its bridge table. In order to keep the information up-to-date, addresses are purged after a given period of time when no data are seen from a given address.

A S I D E . . .

Although the standard bridge MIB (RFC 1286) contains a forwarding table (`dot1dTpFdbTable`), you may have to go to a vendor's proprietary MIB to get the slot/port granularity that you need for locating the exact mapping of MAC addresses to slot/port on a switch.

One interesting thing here is that by dumping out your bridge tables on your switches across your network, you can map network devices (end nodes, other switches, and so on) to the switch, slot, and port to which they are attached. Since MAC addresses are unique and are "burned" into NICs, the bridge tables will tell you where each of your devices is and whether it is active. Remember inactive MACs will be purged from the bridge table after a configurable period of time.

Even more interesting is that by using a network management platform or the MIB-2 `ipNetToMedia` table you can determine the layer-3 network address associated with some of the MACs. (Note that some MACs will not have a layer-3 network address since not all packets are routed.) Typically network management platforms provide both the MAC and network (IP or IPX address) and a way to map one to the other. The `ipNetToMedia` table maps IP addresses to their physical MAC address.

Note though in environments where switches are cascaded, that is, where a switch is connected to another switch, you will see MACs assigned to several device/slot/port combinations. Generally speaking, the device/slot/port combination with the fewer other MAC addresses will be the true location of a MAC source, hence the network device. This is in contrast to high-speed ports that provide switch-to-switch connections that have many bridge table entries for the many MACs that pass through the port. In essence, the bridge table provides you with a primitive inventory of what's where. This can be very useful when trying to address layer-2 problems across many switched ports.

If a switch is not able to "map" a destination address to a slot/port/MAC entry within its table, it must flood the frame to all ports except for the source port. Since flooding can create lots of traffic, there are some vendor-specific optimizations that reduce the amount of flooding performed. One example is explicitly not to flood. In this case communication is dependent on either statically configuring entries in the bridge table or waiting until destination addresses are learned before communicating to these destinations (destinations must speak before they are spoken to). VLANs (discussed later) can also be used to limit the scope of flooding.

4.3.4 Spanning Tree Algorithm

One common problem in switched networks is the accidental creation of a bridge loop. Bridge loops can cause frames to circulate endlessly, resulting in lots of unnecessary traffic. A bridge loop is created when two ports on a switch are connected to the same frame source. For example, if you take an 8-port Ethernet switch and connect two of the ports to two ports on another 8-port Ethernet hub, you have created a bridge loop. This may seem like a silly thing to do, but if the switch and hub are in separate wiring closets, it isn't all that uncommon. Frames destined for a device off the Ethernet hub will come back to the switch as well, looping and consuming the switch. You can only imagine what kind of havoc this causes if you create a loop in your backbone. See Figure 4.5.

The Spanning Tree Algorithm, invented by Radia Perlman, eliminates bridging loops and also allows for redundant (standby) links in a network. Another benefit of the Spanning Tree Algorithm is that it constructs a tree of your network and enables topology applications to construct a map of your

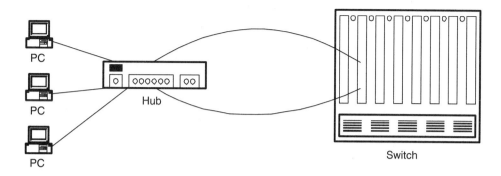

Figure 4.5 Simple example of bridge Loop (two hub ports connected to the same backbone bridge)

layer-2 network backbone. Without a spanning tree, topology applications have to make educated guesses as to your layer-2 network tree based on such heuristics as the frequency of MAC addresses per port and the number of MAC addresses within the bridge tables.

Essentially the Spanning Tree Algorithm works by having each of the bridges participate in a configuration protocol where designated bridges (those closest to a root bridge) are picked and maintained by sending configuration messages periodically. If a designated link goes down, the periodic configuration messages (Bridge PDUs) determine this and a standby link is opened up.

Several configurable standard bridge SNMP objects are available to set up and manage how the Spanning Tree Protocol works. All of these objects are found in the bridge MIB (RFC 1493). The following objects are important to managing your spanning tree:

- `dot1dStpPortPathCost` and `dot1dStpPortPriority` determine the path chosen by the spanning tree and influence the determination of the root bridge respectively. 802.1D-1990 recommends that the default value of the `dot1dStpPortPathCost` be in inverse proportion to the speed of the attached LAN.

- `dot1dStpMaxAge` (age in hundredths of a second) sets the frequency of when spanning tree information is discarded and recalculated.

- `dot1dStpHelloTime` (time in hundredths of a second) sets the time between bridge configuration PDUs.

- `dot1dStpForwardDelay` determines how fast a port changes in the various spanning tree states. Its use eases state transitions and reduces the chance of loops.

If you do implement STP, it is recommended that you adhere to the following:

- Avoid a mixed environment. On most bridges, spanning tree is optional—even on a port-by-port basis. It is extra work to manage an environment where some network devices and/or ports participate in the spanning tree and some don't. If you choose a mixed environment, make certain that your set up is clearly documented so that bridge loops (intended spanning tree redundant links) are not accidentally introduced.

- Ensure that your high-speed ports are configured to have a lower cost than lower-speed ports. Often you will have a low-speed port as a backup—don't reverse the primary and the backup.

- Ensure that the spanning tree is not constantly being reconfigured, causing excess traffic on your network. Monitor the MIB object, `dot1dStpTimeSinceTopologyChange` (the time, in hundredths of a second, since the last time a topology change was detected by the bridge entity) over time. If updates are excessive, you may need to adjust your `dot1dStpHelloTime` and/or your `dot1dStpMaxAge`. Also monitor error rates of network devices around the switches participating in STP. If STP transmissions fail this can cause reconfiguration. Always go back to the manufacturer's defaults initially and then "tune" from there.

For more detailed information on the Spanning Tree Protocol, refer to Radia Perlman's book, *Interconnections*.

4.3.5 Source Routing Bridging

An important part of the 802.5 Token Ring standard is source routing. With source routing the packet header includes the actual route that the packet must use to reach its destination. The embedded route is learned by sending out an initial "discovery" packet and then inserting the learned route into each subsequent packet. The end node is responsible for discovering and inserting the route into the packet. Normally routing is done at layer 3, not by layer-2 bridges. Layer-2 bridges that do source routing are called *source routing bridges.*

Source routing provides a mechanism for Token Ring to link up multiple rings in a LAN. This solution is very effective for LANs with many rings and is characteristic of switched Token Rings where several Token Rings are brought together via Token Ring switching. Essentially routing information is inserted in the standard packet directly after the source address. This routing information is "learned" while communication is established by a Token Ring path discovery process or is based on a previous route discovery stored by the bridge.

The alternate-source routing-packet format is flagged by setting the first bit in the source address to 1; normally as with nonsource routed packages, this bit retains a value of zero. The routing information contained within this second portion of the packet includes a series of routing pairs; each pair contains a ring number followed by a bridge number. This information enables Token Ring packets to travel along predetermined paths, as well as to allow the clever network manager to diagnose the network path that the packets are taking. This feature is not possible in traditionally bridged packets. The ability to determine paths taken at layer 2 is particularly useful to diagnose path problems such as congestion and communication failure. In a switched LAN, which by definition is a bridged layer-2 network, this is a particularly important feature.

Source routing also allows you to set up multiple bridged paths for Token Ring without worrying about bridge loops. This is possible because the routing decision for source-routed packets is in the node (and contained within the packets), not in the bridges. There are a few important restrictions with source routing: Source routing is limited to a maximum of 13 hops or 14 bridges, and if you use source routing, each Token Ring (that is, each Token Ring port) must have its own unique ring number. The SNMP variable, dot1SrPortLocalSegment, is used to set the source-routing ring number. Bridges also have their own ID, dot1SrPortBridgeNum.

A S I D E . . .

Typically all ports on a Token Ring switch share the *same* bridge number. Likewise ports that are on the same ring (as when ports are defined to be attached to a backplane ring that is used to interconnect multiple Token Ring modules with a chassis) all share a ring ID. Note bridge-number and ring-number administration is vendor-specific.

Another A S I D E . . .

With switched Ethernet you cannot set up more than one redundant *active* path. In fact, as noted earlier, unless you implement the Spanning Tree Protocol in your network, connecting multiple paths will result in bridge loops—a serious network management problem.

4.4 Switch Management Considerations

With switching comes additional management considerations. This section explores some important switch features/issues and presents considerations for each.

4.4.1 Filtering Features

One nice attribute of many switch implementations that you do not get with traditional bridging is the ability to filter traffic (forward traffic conditionally) based on reading a portion of the frame, say the first 48 bytes or so. Traditional bridges *do not interpret* the frame beyond the source and destination addresses; further interpretation is functionality left for layer-3 devices, that is, routers. Filtering emphasizes the hybrid nature of switching with bridging *and* routing.

Port filters are widely used to reduce traffic and to provide security. Although the administration and formation of port filters are vendor-specific, the function is not. Filters can be created to filter out broadcast and multicast traffic and to allow only traffic from certain source MACs, or to filter out traffic from IP, AT, or IPX. The possibilities are endless. If your vendor provides filtering capabilities and you would like to reduce traffic flows or implement security, consider filtering.

One caveat: Make certain that your filters do what you think they are doing (verify them) and that it is clear to your management team what the filters do and where they are applied. Special care should be given to filtering on TCP/IP. These filters can be very complex and require a detailed understanding of the associated TCP/IP ports and services. For example, if you filter out all UDP traffic, access to NFS-mounted (network file system) file systems, SNMP-based management, and traceroute diagnostics will not work.

Also note that sometimes filters will result in performance degradation, which may not be acceptable. Finally, the last creation of filters, associated MAC address groups, port groups and management of filters are very vendor-specific.

A S I D E . . .

The emerging standard, 802.1p, extends the 802.1d standard to include standard and extended filtering. Vendor-specific port filtering may coexist with these filters. 802.1p is discussed in Chapter 6.

4.2.2 Managing Bridge Table Size

On most devices, the address table of a bridge is fixed in size. When a bridge table "runs out," a bridge typically accelerates its aging out process, where entries, oldest entries first, are aged out to prevent "stale" information from remaining in the table. "Aging out" refers to deleting an address from the table after the address' refresh timer expires. If the bridge is constantly exceeding its size, many entries will be deleted prematurely. The result is lots of flooding of frames because MAC addresses are often unknown (they age out as quickly as they go in.) Often there is a vendor-specific trap that tells you when a table size is exceeded or when it reaches some percentage of capacity. If this trap is frequent, you might want to buy an additional switch or move some of your network devices to another switch. Also note that, depending on the switch architecture, lots of entries in the forwarding table will cause "longer" lookups that may slow down the switch.

4.4.3 Using Port Labels

Switches by their nature result in lots of manageable ports. One nice feature of many switches is the ability to label the ports via SNMP. This can help you manage your network since you can store in the device customized labels that are retrievable by any tool via SNMP. Smart port labels can be particularly helpful in finding a port when your switched LAN has several hundred ports.

4.4.4 Setting Up Trap Destinations

In order for a management station to receive traps, the switch must be explicitly configured with the station's IP address and the traps desired. Although it is usually not desirable to "turn on" all traps (for example, there are many optional FDDI traps that happen frequently and may be unimportant for management), there are certain traps that are instrumental to management. Knowing when a link goes down is especially important. Often in a switched LAN a down port minimally means a user is out of service; if the port is part of the backbone, it may mean several users are without service.

Since switching by nature has many interfaces that need to be managed, trap-based polling is particularly desirable. Trap-directed polling reduces the frequency of polling intervals to points when "something is awry so start polling." Note, though, that traps are unreliable; you can miss one, so you may want to poll just the same but on less frequent intervals.

4.4.5 Beware of Oversubscription

Oversubscription refers to setting up a network configuration where the aggregate bandwidth at the leaves (or endpoints) exceeds that of the trunk. For example, if you have an 8-port Fast Ethernet switch, the last thing you want to do is to connect it to your backbone with a 10 Mbps connection. This is like having a dirt road off an eight-lane highway as the access to Disney World.

4.5 Switching Features and Key Management Problems

Clearly, switching exploits the power and advantages of bridging. With switching you get:

- **Protocol independence**: This is the ability to move data transparently from FDDI, Ethernet, or Token Ring, all of which conform to the same LLC IEEE 802 standard.
- **Exceptional performance**: This allows data to move at line speed.
- **Flexibility to move unrouted traffic**: Lots of LAN traffic comes from unroutable protocols such as Network Basic Input Output System (NetBIOS) or NetBIOS Extended User Interface (NetBEUI). NetBIOS and NetBEUI are fundamental to the operation of Microsoft Windows for Workgroups. Although this traffic cannot be routed, it can be bridged and hence move across a large LAN.

Switching also has its shortcomings:

- **Vulnerability to bridge loops**: It is simple to create a bridge loop accidentally. The Spanning Tree Protocol is an aid that eliminates bridge loop and allows for redundant standby links.
- **Susceptibility to broadcast storms**: A broadcast storm results from too many frames directed to a broadcast or multicast destination in too short a period of time. On a network that is highly loaded it is often difficult to detect which multicast/broadcast traffic is legitimate and which is not. Generally speaking by watching traffic over a period of time (5 or so minutes) and observing a common pattern or sequence of frames with the same source and/or destination address, you can detect the problem. Many network analyzers will automatically detect broadcast storms for you. Because bridges just forward frames, broadcast storms result in a flooding of the network with too many useless frames that can bring a network down.

A S I D E . . .

As a rule, a storm is often characterized by greater than 100 nonunicast frames per second.

- **Vulnerability to duplicate MAC addresses**: If MAC addresses are locally administered rather than used as is from the hardware NIC manufacture (highly recommended), it is possible to duplicate the MAC addresses. This clearly will cause havoc in a bridged network.

- **Inability to contain broadcasts**: With lots of network devices and a flat bridged network, you tend to end up with lots of broadcasts. By definition this creates a lot of (in many cases "extra") traffic that every network device must sift through. Since routers do not transmit broadcasts, routes can be used for broadcast containment. VLAN, discussed in the next section, can also be used.

Clearly, management tools that help to identify (and/or help solve) these problems are useful. (See Chapter 10 for more information on selecting tools to manage your switched LAN.)

4.6 VLANs

Without question, flattening a LAN by using layer 2 primarily improves overall network performance. At the same time, a large, flat network can be detrimental to performance due to excessive amounts of broadcasting and, of course, the classic problem of broadcast storms sweeping across your network. In the past your only option was to divide your network into smaller pieces and route, since routers typically do not route broadcasts. VLANs is another *emerging* alternative.

Why *emerging*? To date there is no VLAN standard (802.1q is an emerging VLAN standard that is discussed in Chapter 6.) VLANs are proprietary in nature and usually work with equipment across only a single vendor. Early on, the 802.10 (the "VLAN" standard) included an optional frame header to be used for VLAN security. This optional header was overloaded by some vendors for VLAN tagging purposes. Since then, there is the 802.1q proposed standard, a standard for frame tagging. There is hope that this standard will remove the proprietary nature of VLANs and make them work across many vendors.

VLANs enable you to create logical groups of network devices across your LAN. These logical groups may span one or more switches, or they may be done on a switch-by-switch basis. However, within these logical groups that are formed based on various VLAN techniques, you can contain broadcast traffic.

4.7 VLAN Creation Techniques

There are many techniques used to partition a flat bridged physical topology into a collection of VLANs across your network. These include the following:

MAC Address Grouping: VLAN membership is determined by the MAC address of the network device.

Port Grouping: VLAN is a collection of ports across one or more switches. Devices attached to ports within the VLAN collection are members of the VLAN.

Protocol Grouping: The group is based on protocol type (that is, IP, IPX, or AppleTalk) or on network address (that is, given an IP subnet mask).

Figures 4.6, 4.7, and 4.8 illustrate port-based, MAC-based, and protocol-based VLANs respectively.

I've also heard of IP Multicast grouping as the basis for VLAN construction. The problem with IP Multicast grouping is that it is IP-centric and IP Multicasts are transitory. Perhaps after we get statically defined VLANs down, we can entertain dynamic VLANs.

Each VLAN technique has its own set of strengths and weaknesses, as shown in Table 4.1.

4.7.1 VLAN Advantages

The biggest advantage of VLANs is broadcast containment. With a set of well-defined VLANs you can retain the speed of a flat bridged network while eliminating the broadcasts that slow the network. In addition, broadcast containment also reduces the impact of a broadcast storm. Because you retain your layer-2 network, you don't need to segment with routers to fix the broadcast problem, which introduces increased latency.

VLANs allow you to define your own private and secure networks across your switched LAN. If security is important, this may be a viable solution for your LAN.

VLANs are purported to reduce the effort of adds, moves, and changes that add significant overhead to network management. I can see how this might be true for VLANs based on protocol grouping, but it is not necessarily so for VLANs using the other techniques.

Table 4.1 VLAN Technique Strengths and Weaknesses

VLAN Technique	Strengths	Weaknesses
Port Grouping	• It is easy to understand and administer. • There is a common methodology across vendors.	• It must reconfigure the user when it moves a workstation to a new port. • It cannot have a single port in more than one VLAN.
MAC Address Grouping	• VLAN membership moves with a device that has MAC embedded, so there is no need to reconfigure.	• It has performance degradation on ports with several MACs on different VLANs. • VLAN membership is tied to network device—it cannot use any PC to attach to the network and be in your VLAN. • All users must be configured to be on at least one VLAN.
Protocol Grouping	• Partitioning by protocol type is allowed. • A single port can participate in multiple VLANs. • There is no need for frame tagging. • It is particularly good in conjunction with IP subnet masks (it can assign VLANs by subnet and eliminate granularity of assigning individual users to specific VLANs).	• It can be a performance hit. • It must read layer-3 addresses in packets. • It does not work with "unrouted" protocols like NetBIOS.

4.7.2 VLAN Disadvantages

Like filtering or any other management technique that restricts traffic flow, it is critical that you confirm that your VLAN actually works the way you think it is working. An invalid "secure" VLAN may have serious consequences.

It is important that you understand the performance before and after VLAN segmentation. If the VLANs are not properly defined, performance can actually be worse. Note this can be the case when you define too many VLANs

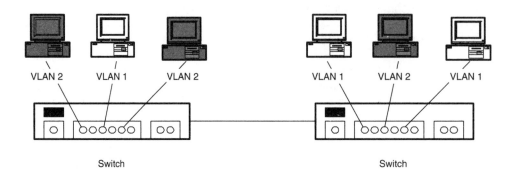

Figure 4.6 Two simple port-based VLANs

that need to communicate with each other. Because routers tend to slow traffic, ensure that you have the right amount of VLANs without becoming overly granular.

Having a mental picture of your network is a technique widely used to troubleshoot network problems. Obviously as your network becomes very big, you tend to rely on network management platforms to provide the majority of this picture.

With VLANs, you no longer can associate the physical layout of your network with its absolute operation. Just because you know the physical connectivity of a network device doesn't necessarily mean you know the logical network connectivity. Even if something is physically connected, it may not be logically connected. For example, if you have two VLANs and a user is on one of the VLANs and a printer is on the other (and then VLANs don't overlap), the user will not be able to send a print job to the printer, even though physically everything is connected to the same switch. This adds a level of abstraction to the network and increases the dependency on strong network management tools. VLANs add a software or "logical" view of your LAN that you must use in association with your "physical" view.

Since VLANs that span many devices depend on network connections for broadcast containment, VLANs add traffic to your network backbone. In a sense you are taking the traffic containment provided by a single switch in your network and spreading it out over your network to create a virtual switch. The result is additional traffic through your backbone. Make certain your backbone, which connects your VLANs, is sized appropriately to deal with the extra VLAN traffic.

Finally, VLANs are still largely proprietary. Most networks are made up of equipment from a variety of vendors, making it difficult to define viable VLANs.

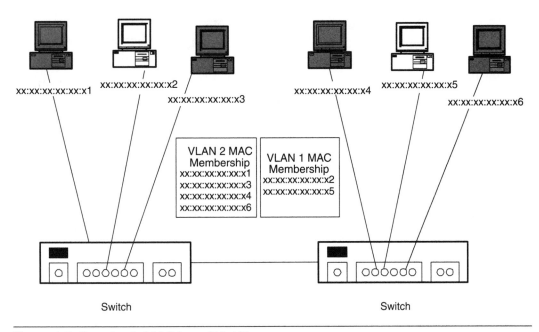

Figure 4.7 Two simple MAC-based VLANs

A S I D E . . .

One key to managing VLANs is the notion of open and closed VLANs. A closed VLAN is what you might expect—a VLAN that limits the broadcast domain to only elements within the VLAN definition. For example, if you define a port-based VLAN to contain ports 3, 4, and 8 on a switch and the VLAN is closed, only frames contained within this small port group (ports 3, 4, and 8) are switched together. Open VLANs may see additional traffic beyond the VLAN definition. This often happens when you have overlapping VLANs where a single port may be servicing more than one VLAN. Since ports on a switch often share a single bridge forwarding table, two or more VLANs, both containing the same port, will see frames from the other VLANs. Sometimes open VLANs are said to "leak."

4.8 Management Aspects of VLANs

Should you "virtualize" your network? If you primarily have a single-vendor solution with switches and layer-3 switches that feature VLANs that can be automatically created *and maintained* (hence greatly simplifying management of

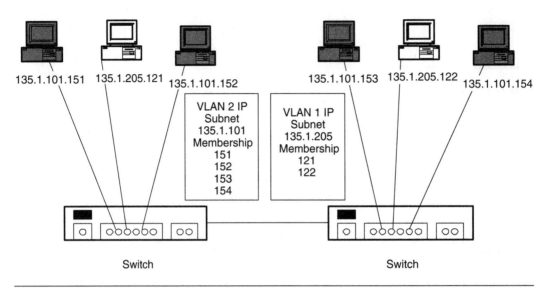

135.1.101.151 135.1.205.121 135.1.101.152   135.1.101.153 135.1.205.122 135.1.101.154

VLAN 2 IP
Subnet
135.1.101
Membership
151
152
153
154

VLAN 1 IP
Subnet
135.1.205
Membership
121
122

Switch   Switch

Figure 4.8 Two simple protocol-based (IP subnets) VLANs

moves, adds, and changes[1]) and the vendor can prove to you a dramatic performance increase (and be willing to help you set up and diagnose problems), then, I would say, you should give VLANs a shot. Otherwise, wait for 802.1q, frame tagging, to become a standard. My recommendation: Wait.

4.9 Summary

Switches and routers are two very important networking devices used within switched LAN implementations. Switches are multiport bridges that forward frames at high speeds. Routers route packets across your network. Switches do not contain broadcast traffic; routers do. Some switches (designated as layer-3 switches) also perform routing functions. Switches and routers provide solutions that complement each other within a switched LAN.

With the benefits of switching come new management challenges and considerations. By definition, switching greatly augments the use of bridging, making it important to consider standard bridge features such as spanning tree, source routing, and filtering. Likewise the introduction of lots of bridging can result in an increase in bridge-related problems: loops, storms, table overflowing, and excessive broadcasts.

---

1. Unless your are doing a VLAN based on protocol grouping, have your network vendor prove to you by demonstration that VLANs actually simplify management of moves, adds, and changes. I'm not convinced yet.

VLANs are a first attempt at solving some of these problems—namely broadcast containment and the subsequent reduction of storm impact. Nonetheless, the proprietary nature of VLANs makes them far from a perfect solution. Rather, VLANs are an early indication of what's to come, further improving networking at layer 2.

Switching has a bright future. It has clearly refueled the power of bridging and is moving up the stack to layer 3 with developments in routing. Over the next few years we will see more and more networking solutions based on switching technology.

CHAPTER 5

Managing Common Routing Protocols

5.1 Introduction

It is always interesting to put a packet analyzer near the backbone of your switched LAN and get a view of the type, frequency, and pattern of packets that are transmitted. Often it may surprise you to know that your network, not atypical in the least, is servicing many varieties of networking traffic simultaneously—traffic generated by many different networking services and higher-layer protocols working concurrently. The four most common LAN networking protocols are Network Basic Input/Output System (NetBIOS) with its many flavors and add-ons, NetWare, TCP/IP, and AppleTalk.

All of these networking protocols

- have strengths and weaknesses in the LAN.
- leverage some common and some unique techniques and concepts.
- require some common and some unique forms of network management.

This chapter explores these protocols with a focus on the routing aspects of each and enumerates many of the management "hot spots." You will find the key to managing the protocols across your network is managing the protocols *across* your network, that is to think of your network devices as a *composite* configuration, rather than as a collection of separate device configurations. It is the synchronization of configuration across many network devices that, at this layer, is critical to result in a well-behaved network. In short, layer-3 configuration consistency is paramount to keeping your network working smoothly.

At this point you are probably saying What does routing have to do with switching? Technically, nothing. As we discussed earlier, routing is complementary to switching because it provides security, segmentation, and broadcast containment. Subsequently many powerful switches have built-in routing capabilities (earlier we called these switches layer-3 switches). Over time, expect more "switches" to pack routing into their feature set. So when you get right down to it, it is pretty common to have routers and switches in your switched LAN. It is therefore important that we spend time understanding the management issues associated with routing.

One quick note: The information presented in this chapter applies to both *switched and shared LANs*. So if you currently manage a traditional LAN, are in the process of "switching" over, just evaluating switched LANs, or support both switched and traditional LANs, you can leverage the information equally in both environments.

5.2 Revisiting a "Simple" Network

Before we get into routing, we need to finish what we started earlier in the book by completing our simple network. As indicated in Chapter 1, you need a network operating system (NOS), a set of defined services and protocol(s), to provide network access to your applications. This networking software completes the simple network. NOSs come in various flavors from simple to complex. NetBIOS, an IBM standard, is a very early NOS that provides simple networking. We will start with NetBIOS.

When you come right down to what networking provides, there are really two fundamental things: shared media (various types like regular files, multimedia files, graphics, mail, and so on), and shared devices (like printers, scanners, fax machines, CD farms, and so on). Yes, we keep adding to the types of media and devices we support in networks, but fundamentally networking is just files and devices.

NetBIOS provides a simple transport and network-layer function in a LAN environment. NetBIOS is a nonroutable protocol; that is, it can exist within a layer-2 switched environment but it cannot traverse a router (unless the router is functioning as a bridge or switch). This is because it does not require addressing necessary for routing, which keeps the protocol simple, and is easy to set up and get going. Some refer to these qualities as "plug-and-play."

Windows/NT uses the NetBIOS Extended User Interface (NetBEUI) frame (NBF) protocol to provide simple communications among a workgroup and/or domain[1] of users. NetBEUI extends NetBIOS, enabling Windows/NT to share a printer queue and file systems, the server's CD drive, and so on. NetBEUI provides the easiest way to complete our simple network to form a Microsoft LAN. We merely indicate that we want to set up a "Client for

---

1. A Windows/NT domain provides the ability to add significant policy to a workgroup. Access lists, user privileges, and so on can all be configured for a Windows/NT domain. If a system is not part of a domain, it is by default part of the local workgroup and does not require configuration.

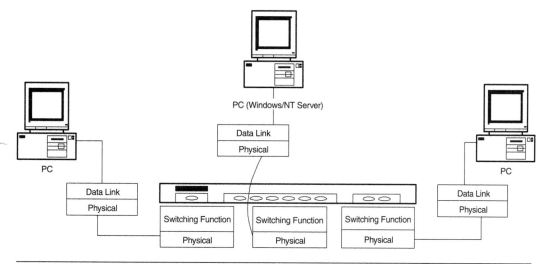

PC (Windows/NT Server)

PC

PC

Figure 5.1 Revisiting a simple network (NetBEUI operate without routing)

Microsoft Networks" from the Network tool within the Control Panel from Windows/95 or Windows/NT V4.0. Voilá! We have completed our simple network. Figure 5.1 illustrates this simple network.

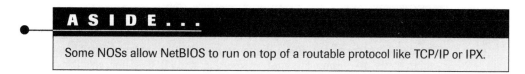

A S I D E . . .

Some NOSs allow NetBIOS to run on top of a routable protocol like TCP/IP or IPX.

5.3 Protocols That Route

AppleTalk, Novell's NetWare, and TCP/IP all provide routing capabilities. Routing is accomplished by switches that perform both layer-2 and layer-3 functionality, routers, or workstations. In the purest sense, switches forward (switch) frames based on MAC addresses between two network devices; routers route packets across a network based on layer-3 addresses. As mentioned previously, vendors keep the terminology concise by referring to these hybrid switches that route as layer-3 switches.

The biggest challenge managing at layer 3 is managing a network configuration in a distributed fashion. Not only do you have the complexities of setting up routing in each switch or router, but you also must ensure that each configuration is synchronized with its switch and/or router buddies. To compound this problem, you often need to manage one or more protocol families simultaneously. Failing to set up routing properly can cause your network to perform poorly, not to work at all, or to work only intermittently (which is the worst problem of all).

The best way to understand the idiosyncrasies of each protocol family is first to understand the similarities. The following chart (Figure 5.2) presents each of the major three families in relation to the OSI seven-layer reference model. This provides us with a quick layer-by-layer road map of each protocol family and its associated services (represented as abbreviations in the chart). In each of the following sections we will "zoom in" on each family's stack and discuss what services each stack offers and how they work together.

Before we dive in, let's briefly itemize the similarities of these three routing protocol families. All of the big three share the following traits:

- **Providing some form of source and destination addressing**: Like conventional mail, when there are several intermediate destinations between the source mailbox and the destination mailbox, a route is required. Flooding and reverse MAC address learning as used by bridges and layer-2 switches just don't work when intermediate destinations (known as hops) are involved. Routers need source and destination addresses so they can determine the "best" multihop path to the desired destination.

A S I D E . . .

The big exception here is Token Ring's Source Routing that *does* specify a route within the layer-2 frame. Ethernet, ATM LANE, and FDDI do not have this capability and therefore require the addressing at the routing (network layer, layer 3) to get across the network. Note that there are some emerging technologies (for example, Fast IP) that minimize the amount of routing done. These will be discussed in detail in Chapter 6.

- **Providing a form of determining link state**: This trait determines whether a node (host) or server is "alive." TCP/IP provides "ping" using ICMP; AppleTalk provides tools called Inter•Poll and AppleTalk Echo Protocol (AEP); NetWare provides an Echo Protocol.

- **Working over the same data link protocols and physical media that were discussed in the previous chapters**: This includes Ethernet, FDDI, Token Ring data link protocols, and UTP/STP and fiber physical media.

- **Providing a datagram, best effort, unreliable service**: Although not exact in functionality (more in concept), TCP/IP provides UDP

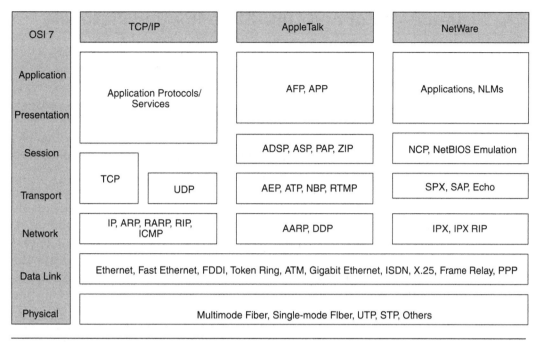

OSI 7	TCP/IP	AppleTalk	NetWare
Application	Application Protocols/ Services	AFP, APP	Applications, NLMs
Presentation			
Session		ADSP, ASP, PAP, ZIP	NCP, NetBIOS Emulation
Transport	TCP UDP	AEP, ATP, NBP, RTMP	SPX, SAP, Echo
Network	IP, ARP, RARP, RIP, ICMP	AARP, DDP	IPX, IPX RIP
Data Link	Ethernet, Fast Ethernet, FDDI, Token Ring, ATM, Gigabit Ethernet, ISDN, X.25, Frame Relay, PPP		
Physical	Multimode Fiber, Single-mode Flber, UTP, STP, Others		

Figure 5.2 Common communication stacks used in LANs

over IP; AppleTalk provides Datagram Delivery Protocol (DDP); and NetWare provides Packet Exchange Protocol (PXP) and, more important, Internetwork Packet Exchange (IPX).

- **Providing a reliable, connection-oriented service**: TCP/IP provides TCP over IP; AppleTalk provides AppleTalk Data Stream Protocol (ADSP); and NetWare provides Sequenced Packet Exchange (SPX).

- **Using a routing protocol to keep routers in synch**: TCP/IP in the LAN uses RIP or Open Shortest Path First (OSPF); AppleTalk uses Routing Table Maintenance Protocol (RTMP); and NetWare uses RIP, which we'll designate as IPX RIP since it is a little different from TCP/IP's RIP. NetWare also uses NetWare Link State Protocol (NLSP).

In addition, both AppleTalk and TCP/IP provide address translation facilities used to translate network addresses into MAC addresses. AppleTalk provides AppleTalk Address Resolution Protocol (AARP), and TCP/IP provides ARP and RARP. NetWare doesn't use an ARP-like service because the MAC address of the client is already part of the network address.

5.4 Distance-Vector and Link-State Routing Protocols

Routing protocols are classified as distance-vector or link-state. Distance-vector protocols are based on the Bellman/Ford algorithm. The protocol uses periodic updates containing neighbor vector of distances (also called hop counts) between each router. Routes (or paths) are computed based exclusively on the fewest number of intermediate routers (or hops) between two network nodes. Apple-Talk's Routing Table Maintenance Protocol (RTMP), IP's Routing Information Protocol (RIP), and IPX's RIP are all based on a distance-vector algorithm.

Distance-vector algorithms are simple to implement, and the algorithm is freely available (developed by the University of California at Berkeley) to implementers; hence distance-vector has become popular. These algorithms do not require extensive computations to maintain the routing table, nor do they converge (stabilize) quickly after a network change such as an adjacent router going up or down. This is largely because distance-vector algorithms do not result in the complete view of the network—rather they result in a "local" view (constructed by the neighbor updates) at each router. Distance-vector algorithms also have the disadvantage of generating lots of router-table update traffic, since routers periodically (as often as every thirty seconds) broadcast routing-table updates.

"Split Horizon" technique, introduced into the distant-vector arena, is designed to minimize the amount of time it takes for the routing tables to converge. Essentially it modifies the update message *not* to include the same routing information it learned from each respective interface it depended on for routes. In short, routes are not advertised on the ports they were learned. Split Horizon can have the side effect of preserving inaccurate information longer in a routing table, since it suppresses some updates.

"Poison Reverse" augments Split Horizon by setting the hop count to destinations learned from adjacent routers to infinity, quickly eliminating potential loops. Poison Reverse greatly increases convergence time to the new route, since it immediately announces the old route with a metric of 16 (that is, infinity), thus avoiding the "counting to infinity" problem.

Link-state routing protocols exchange link states (whether a route is up or down) for each route between routers. These link states are used to construct a complete view or map of the network at each router. IP's Open Shortest Path First (OSPF) is an example of a link-state protocol.

In contrast to distance-vector algorithms, link-state algorithms are complex, require extensive computations to maintain the routing table, and converge very quickly. Since link-state algorithms propagate only changes, they require far less network bandwidth to maintain. This fact explains why link-state protocols such as OSPF are popular across WAN connections.

Now that you understand some of the similarities of distance-vector and link-state, let's go through AppleTalk, NetWare, and TCP/IP and uncover the differences that make each of their routing protocols unique. We base the order of presentation on complexity (not popularity), from AppleTalk to Novell and finally to IP. We spend a bit more time on IP since IP is emerging as the dominant network protocol in today's LANs. The popularity of the Web, the requirement to have TCP/IP for a PPP connection to the Internet, and the availability of applications that run over IP are intensifying IP's penetration in LAN environments.

As always, our coverage will be concise and focused on managing these protocols in a switched LAN environment.

5.5 AppleTalk

AppleTalk was invented in the mid-1980s as a protocol family for connecting many Apple computers to form a client-server-distributed network. Early versions of AppleTalk used LocalTalk over ordinary phone cords; this implementation was called Silver Satin. Subsequent versions (AppleTalk Phases I and II) run over the same conventional link layers (Ethernet, FDDI, and Token Ring) and physical media (UTP and fiber) as other clients.

Like all Apple-based products, AppleTalk was designed to be plug-and-play and as configuration-free to the user as possible. The idea was that networking for the user (access to shared files and printers) should require only a cable connection to make it operational.

And it worked. AppleTalk's Phase I success was followed by that of Phase II, which addressed AppleTalk's popularity by making AppleTalk scale to larger networks. Our discussion will focus on Phase II since most AppleTalk installations today are using Phase II.

5.5.1 Fundamentals and Terminology

Under the simplicity of what AppleTalk provides comes a plethora of terminology that you need to know in order to understand AppleTalk management (see Table 5.1). Figure 5.3 puts AppleTalk terminology into context with the OSI 7-Layer Reference Model:

In AppleTalk jargon:

- a *network* is single cable[2],
- *nodes/devices* are connected to a network,

_____

2. A hub typically has several cables attached to it; all cables, however, are in the same network. See Figure 5.4 for an example of an AppleTalk network.

Table 5.1 AppleTalk Terminology

AARP	AppleTalk Address Resolution Protocol
ADSP	AppleTalk Data Stream Protocol
AEP	AppleTalk Echo Protocol
AFP	AppleTalk Filing Protocol
APP	AppleTalk Print Protocol
ASP	AppleTalk Session Protocol
ATP	AppleTalk Transaction Protocol
DDP	Datagram Delivery Protocol
NBP	Name Binding Protocol
PAP	Printer Access Protocol
RTMP	Routing Table Maintenance Protocol
ZIP	Zone Information Protocol

- *nonextended networks* do not route,
- *extended networks* form an *internet* (or *internetwork*) and do route, and
- *zones* are logical groups of nodes/devices that may span more than one AppleTalk network.

Although AppleTalk does work over the same data link protocols that we discussed in the previous chapters, AppleTalk clients (nodes/devices) use EtherTalk Link Access Protocol (ELAP), TokenTalk Link Access Protocol (TLAP), FDDI Link Access Protocol (FLAP), or LocalTalk Link Access Protocol (LLAP). LocalTalk is a proprietary AppleTalk Protocol. LocalTalk (a rudimentary Ethernet-like technology) is based on a contention access, uses a bus topology, can span 300 meters, and supports up to 32 nodes.

Fundamental to AppleTalk management is zone management. Zones are logical groupings of nodes/devices that enable a network manager to segment services. In a sense, zones are like VLANs as they define the broadcast domain and can span multiple AppleTalk networks. Each AppleTalk node/device is in

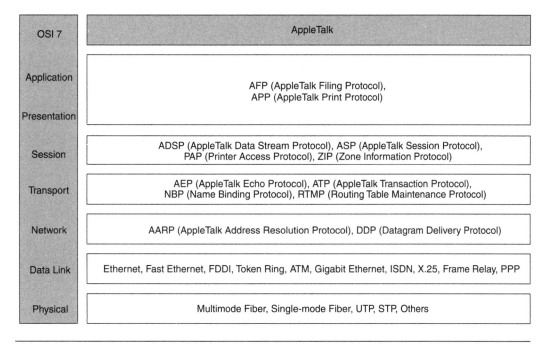

OSI 7	AppleTalk
Application	AFP (AppleTalk Filing Protocol), APP (AppleTalk Print Protocol)
Presentation	
Session	ADSP (AppleTalk Data Stream Protocol), ASP (AppleTalk Session Protocol), PAP (Printer Access Protocol), ZIP (Zone Information Protocol)
Transport	AEP (AppleTalk Echo Protocol), ATP (AppleTalk Transaction Protocol), NBP (Name Binding Protocol), RTMP (Routing Table Maintenance Protocol)
Network	AARP (AppleTalk Address Resolution Protocol), DDP (Datagram Delivery Protocol)
Data Link	Ethernet, Fast Ethernet, FDDI, Token Ring, ATM, Gigabit Ethernet, ISDN, X.25, Frame Relay, PPP
Physical	Multimode Fiber, Single-mode Fiber, UTP, STP, Others

Figure 5.3 AppleTalk

one zone only—chosen at boot time. It is important that you set up your zones optimally for your network. Clearly having a zone that contains lots of local devices across two separate WAN-connected LANs is not optimal (a polite euphemism for bad)—you would end up with a lot of traffic (for example, address resolution for each node when booted) crossing your expensive WAN link. In addition, too many zones can be problematic as you end up with many zones to maintain and manage.

As a rule, grow your zones in increments of 100 nodes/devices, and evaluate the percentage of broadcast traffic as compared to total traffic as you cross each increment of 100 nodes/devices. Try to keep the overhead traffic percentage less than 20 percent. If your network is multiprotocol, the percentage of broadcast traffic will be higher and may warrant inspection at increments of 50 nodes/devices. *This is only a simple rule of thumb, your mileage may vary!*

5.5.2 Addressing

AppleTalk uses a 3-byte addressing scheme to identify each node on the network uniquely; a 2-byte network number coupled with a 1-byte node ID. In addition, AppleTalk forms an Internet socket address by adding an additional 1-byte socket ID to the beginning of the address. Many of AppleTalk's proto-

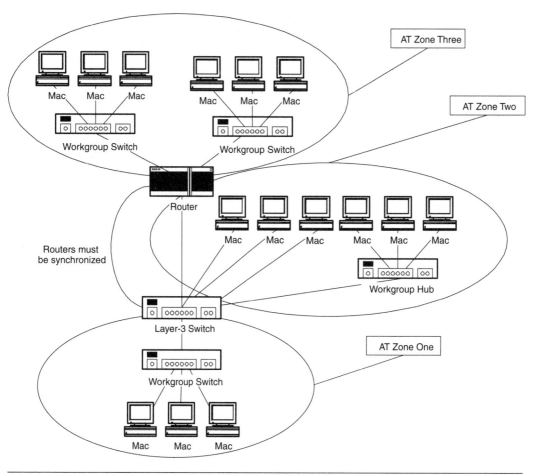

Figure 5.4 AppleTalk network showing zone flexibility

cols (for example, Zone Information Protocol (ZIP)) have preassigned socket numbers, as shown in Table 5.2.

AppleTalk addressing is dynamic; there is no requirement to preconfigure a node's address prior to adding a node to a network. When a node boots into a network for the first time, it constructs a temporary address with a network number ranging from FFF0 to FFFE (a reserved address range for node initialization) and an arbitrary (randomly chosen) node ID from 1 to 254. This temporary address is used to query the *seed router* (a specific router on the network that is configured with the network number range for the network) via the Zone Information Protocol (ZIP) to get a "real" address. If no router is found, the node will use this temporary address, although it will be forced to change addresses when a router comes on board. Once a "real" address is ob-

Table 5.2 Internet Socket Address

1 byte Socket ID	2 byte Network Number	1 byte Node ID

tained, the node will store this address and attempt to use it the next time the node reboots. If during a subsequent reboot the address is already in use, the node will be given a new address.

A S I D E . . .

Since the seed router is responsible for managing dynamic addressing, having more than one seed router on a segment can be dangerous; that is, you may end up handing out duplicate addresses. It is the network manager's responsibility to ensure that, if there are multiple seed routers, the routers are properly synchronized, for example, consistent ranges without overlapping network ranges across the network.

During address resolution at boot, a network node learns the address of a local router and its network-number range. There can be ranges of network addresses associated with any zone name. This allows zones to span beyond 256 (only one byte is used for Node IDs). A network-zone list is maintained by routers; this list is called a Zone Information Table (ZIT).

The AppleTalk Address Resolution Protocol (AARP) is used for mapping AppleTalk addresses to MAC addresses used in Token Ring and Ethernet. The Name Binding Protocol (NBP) is used to convert a network name (identified to AppleTalk users as a network resource) into an internet socket address. Since internet socket addresses are based on dynamic address bindings, the NBP is also done dynamically.

5.5.3 Routing

AppleTalk uses Routing Table Maintenance Protocol (RTMP), a distance-vector protocol, to maintain its routing tables in each router. The routing table maps network number ranges to

- their next hop router (0 in the case where there is no need to route further).
- the number of hops to the router, the port number to route traffic to.
- the state (good to bad or up to down) of the route.

If there are multiple ways to route a packet to zone 2, the "closest" zone in a good state will be chosen. Note also that every time a packet enters a router, its hop count is incremented; packets with a hop count of 16 are considered to have an unreachable destination and are therefore dropped.

The Zone Information Table (ZIT) is where zone names (that is, what the end user sees) are mapped to network numbers. All routers within an AppleTalk internet contain a ZIT; ZIT entries map a network number to a list of zone names. Each AppleTalk II network has a "seed" router (there can be more than one) for certain ZIT mappings; that is, the seed router is preconfigured to "know" a set of ZIT mappings that get distributed to peer routers. Unlike other routers, the seed router does not "listen" to the configuration information it hears. The ZIP protocol is used to map zone names to network numbers, both by routers and by user nodes. As you can gather, judicious management of your ZIT seed entries and orchestrated seed change is critical in keeping your AppleTalk network afloat—network numbers with out-of-date or empty zone information will cause network failure.

AppleTalk Update-based Routing Protocol (AURP) is AppleTalk's answer to the problem of using both distance-vector algorithms across a WAN and a general enhancement that allow AppleTalk networking to scale. AURP provides tunneling of AppleTalk across TCP/IP or Point-to-Point (PPP) links, a way to remap remote network numbers to local numbers to prevent number conflicts, and reduced routing traffic since it advertises just change. Important updates occur when a network is added, when a network is deleted, or when a network route changes.

Like most network-based information, routing information is aged out of tables when periodic refreshes stop. In routing tables a simple state change from good to bad or up to down does the trick and leaves a placeholder for the path as well as bread crumbs for the network manager.

5.5.4 Management Issues

AppleTalk, like all other protocol families, is susceptible to configuration problems. Some of the common problems follow:

- A routing loop is accidentally created. If two AppleTalk internets have more than one connection between them, you have a routing loop. This sounds silly but is easy to do when two LANs are connected via a WAN link. Many recent routers have built-in loop detection.

- Duplicate network numbers are used. Network numbers must be unique throughout AppleTalk network; duplicates cause connectivity and performance problems.

- Timer values are inconsistent within network. Having your network tables out of synchronization causes problems—inconsistent timer values only exacerbate the situation. Remember, the quicker your routing tables converge *consistently* after routing change, the smoother your network will run. Routing tables with incorrect routes results in routing traffic incorrectly and wasted packet processing. Use default timer values as a rule; if you need to customize, change and verify timer values across all routers *at the same time.*

- Policy-based lists (vendor-specific lists defining access) and/or filters are not properly configured. Routers allow you to customize who has access to what; if you choose to implement this level of control, make certain you do it consistently.

- You have too many zones. Design your network to use zones judiciously because having too many zones will increase the multicast traffic and management responsibilities.

- You use invalid zone names in routing tables. It is important that when you make zone name changes that you also orchestrate zone changes in unison, that is, turn off routing across routers for a cooling-off period, make the changes, and then restart.

- You have a ZIP storm; for example, router tables fail to converge, and this occurs when routers propagate a route for which there is currently no corresponding zone name. Again, orchestrate your zone name changes very carefully and judiciously across your network.

- There is invalid AURP tunnel configuration. Make certain that routes can get through AURP tunnels when you initially set up the tunnel.

- When you boot an Apple and it fails to detect its seed router, it will "turn off" AppleTalk and resort to LocalTalk from the printer port. The next time you reboot the machine, it will default to LocalTalk. Reconfigure the machine to AppleTalk and the problem should go away.

5.6 NetWare

NetWare is a pervasive Network Operating System (NOS) introduced in the early 1980s by Novell, Inc. NetWare is built around a client/server model. Examples of servers are database servers, print servers, or file servers; examples of clients are network entities (PCs, workstations, and so on) that use the services provided by the servers. Once NetWare is set up, it provides transparent network access to one or more clients. Fundamental to NetWare's client/server model is the use of remote procedure calls. When a client issues a "call" to the server, the server executes the request and returns the results to the client.

NetWare also provides plug-and-play portability. As long as there is a server (running a compatible version of server software), a client can connect.

Table 5.3 NetWare Terminology

NetWare Abbreviation	
IPX	Internetwork Packet Exchange
SAP	Service Advertising Protocol
SPX	Sequenced Packet Exchange
NCP	NetWare Core Protocol
NLM	NetWare Loadable Module
IPX RIP	NetWare Routing Information Protocol

This means that you can move a client from network connection to network connection without management intervention (that is, client reconfiguration). In fact, in some environments you have portable connectivity even on another LAN within your Intranet with a WAN link in between. Less configuration management is always attractive to a network manager.

NetWare relies on Service Advertising Protocol (SAP) to announce services periodically throughout the network. In a way SAP announcements provide a DNS-like (distributed name service) capability for NetWare; it is used to tell clients what services are available. This is both good and bad—good in that it provides transparent portability and automates "logging" into the network; bad in that there can be lots of SAP traffic (broadcasts that can consume lots of your network bandwidth) on Novell networks. SAP reduction plans, including incremental SAP updates and SAP elimination on certain parts of the network, are common practice for the network manager. Use the amount of SAP traffic and the number of protocols you are routing to tune the size of your IPX networks.

5.6.1 Fundamentals and Terminology

NetWare, too, has its share of terminology. (See Table 5.3.) Figure 5.5 puts the terminology into the familiar context of the OSI 7-Layer Reference Model.

In NetWare jargon:

- routing is done between *networks,*
- each *node/device* belongs to a network,
- NetWare *clients* use services of NetWare *servers,*

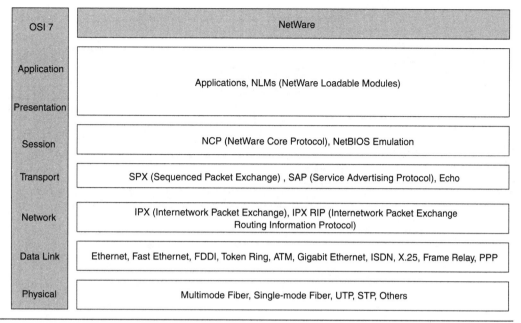

Figure 5.5 NetWare

- *Service Advertising Protocol* (SAP) is used to advertise services available to clients, and
- *IPX RIP* is used as a routing protocol.

Figure 5.6 illustrates a NetWare LAN composed of several NetWare networks.

At the heart of NetWare is IPX. IPX is Novell's IP-like network-layer protocol. Sequenced Packet Exchange (SPX) provides reliable, connection-oriented services—SPX is the most popular NetWare transport protocol. The NetWare Core Protocol (NCP) provides an application programming interface (API) abstraction to services from Novell servers. For example, file access, printer access, and name management are provided via NCP. Novell also provides NetBIOS emulation, allowing Microsoft networking in Windows/95, Windows/NT, or Windows for Workgroups to work in a Novell environment. Network Loadable Modules (NLMs) provide add-on modules (often third party) for alternate communication services (for example, network access to a database). Many core NetWare services are also NLMs.

5.6.2 Addressing

NetWare uses a 10-byte addressing scheme to identify each node on the network uniquely; a 4-byte network number coupled with a 6-byte node ID.

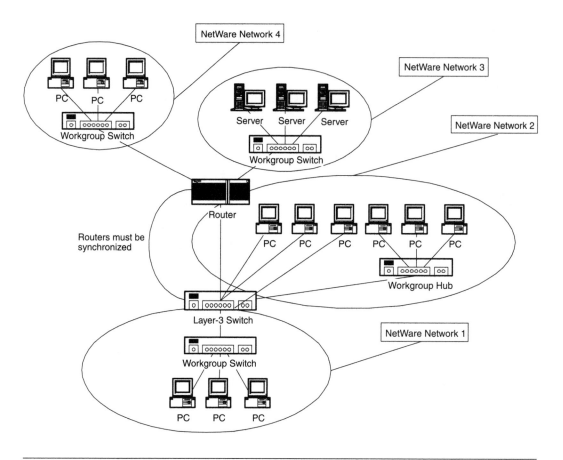

Figure 5.6 NetWare network

Typically a network number is assigned to each "subnet" within your LAN, and the MAC address burned into the NIC is used for the Node Address. As with AppleTalk, socket numbers are used to distinguish client/server processes. A 2-byte socket number is *appended* after the 6-byte node address to form the network address. See Table 5.4.

Each Novell client maintains a local shell (NET.CFG) and a communication process (IPX(ODI).COM) that are used during boot to customize server connection(s) and determine the local network address respectively. The local network address is determined by sending to the router a "Get Local Target Request" that will return a response message containing the source address that may be used to determine the network number. This number, coupled with the local MAC address, forms a valid NetWare address. Once this address is formed, the client sends out a "Get Nearest Server" message. Since this is a

Table 5.4 NetWare Addressing

4-byte Network Number	6-byte Node Address	2-byte Socket Number

broadcast message, all servers respond with their address and the number of hops away they are from the client. Assuming there is a server that is on the same network, the client attaches to the server and the initial client/server "binding" is complete. If, however, none of the servers are on the same network, a subsequent request is made to the local router(s) to get the best route to one of the servers. Once the route is determined, the client connects to the designated server—again, the fewest hops away—completing the initial "binding."

A S I D E . . .

The login process for NetWare Version 3 and NetWare Version 4 is different. NetWare Version 4 does a "Get Nearest Server" request, whereas NetWare Version 3 asks for the route to a specific server.

5.6.3 Routing

IPX uses a RIP-like protocol (one of the routing protocols of the TCP/IP suite) for exchanging routing information. Although this information is often called just RIP, I will call it IPX RIP since it does differ. IPX RIP uses a distance-vector algorithm (the same as TCP/IP RIP and AppleTalk's RTMP) to determine and maintain routes. IPX RIP uses the "split horizon" algorithm to help eliminate "misroutes." Like AppleTalk and RIP (discussed in the next section), IPX RIP has a maximum hop count of 15. Often this maximum count is called the *maximum diameter.* A hop count of 16 means infinity, and destinations within the routing table with a hop count (cost) of 16 are deemed unreachable. If a packet's hop count becomes 16, the packet is dropped, eliminating the problem of "lost" packets clogging the network.

IPX suffers from the same slow convergence and routing-table update problems of TCP/IP's RIP (discussed in detail in the RIP section). These problems are further exacerbated with longer timer update defaults (60 seconds for SAP updates and 4 minutes to age out "stale" SAP entries). One unique feature in IPX is that the update packets contain a tick counter that is associated with each route and can be used by routers as another metric of routing cost—the higher the tick, the greater the routing cost. Unfortunately use of this metric is optional and vendor-specific.

5.6.4 Management Issues

NetWare, like other NOSs, is susceptible to network management problems. Following are some of the common (mostly configuration) problems:

- Frame type mismatch. There are four Ethernet frame types (Ethernet_802.3, Ethernet_802.2, Ethernet_SNAP, and Ethernet_II). There are two Token Ring frame types (Token-Ring_MSB and Token-Ring_SNAP). There are two FDDI frame types (FDDI_802.2 and FDDI_SNAP). Make certain that the version of Novell that you are running supports the frame types configured on both server and client ends. For example, NetWare version 4 supports all common communication-technology frame types, including Ethernet_802.3, Ethernet_ 802.2, Token-Ring_MSB, and FDDI. Note there is one exception where frame-type mismatch is okay: when you have a router between the client and the server. In this case the router converts the frame types appropriately. Make certain your routers and servers have the same frame type.

  Figure 5.7 shows a network where frame types must match, and Figure 5.8 shows a network where frame types are different.

- Network numbers mismatch. All servers attached to the same cable must bind to the same external network number.

- Version mismatch between client(s) and server. Make certain SAPs on servers are properly generated. As an example, a client running version 3 of NetWare can connect to a server running version 4, but not vice versa. Connecting version 4 to version 3 is a "no go" because in version 3 you connect to a server (using Bindery); in version 4 you connect to the network through a server (using ND5). There is no way to emulate connecting to a network by connecting to a version 3 server.

- Inadequate number of user licenses on server. NetWare works on a connection basis; make certain there are enough user licenses to go around.

- Duplicate node numbers on routers. Node numbers on the router must be unique. If you can stick to the MAC addresses that are burned into your NICs and are guaranteed to be unique, then you can blame your NIC vendor if you end up with duplicate addresses.

- Duplicate network numbers. Every network number must be unique throughout an entire NetWare network. This problem is insidious. If you have a duplicate network number across a WAN connection,

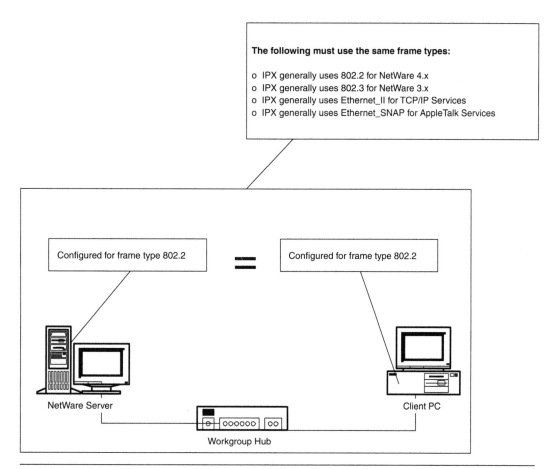

The following must use the same frame types:

o IPX generally uses 802.2 for NetWare 4.x
o IPX generally uses 802.3 for NetWare 3.x
o IPX generally uses Ethernet_II for TCP/IP Services
o IPX generally uses Ethernet_SNAP for AppleTalk Services

Configured for frame type 802.2   Configured for frame type 802.2

NetWare Server   Client PC

Workgroup Hub

Figure 5.7 Picture of network where frame types must match. (On a hub, unlike a switch, all ports share the *same* segment)

through router updates it can propagate from one LAN to another causing serious failure. Network numbers *must* be unique.

- SAP entries missing or misconfigured. If SAP entries are not properly configured on your servers, your clients will not have access to the services.

- Filters or other control lists misconfigured. If you have a lot of services and subsequently lots of SAP traffic, you may want to "turn off" unnecessary SAP traffic. Likewise, your security policy many dictate that you do not offer service XYZ to a network of clients, requiring a correct filter or control list.

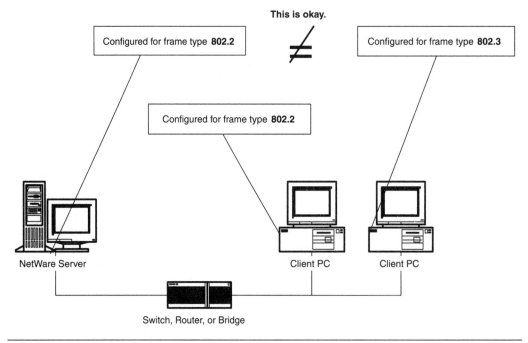

Figure 5.8 Picture of network where different frame types are okay

- NetBIOS over IPX not properly configured. This will cause Windows/95 or Windows/NT networking to fail.
- IPX timer mismatch among routers. The default timers are 60 seconds for table updates and 4 minutes for aging out SAP entries. Mismatched timers result in slower convergence among your routing tables, resulting in misdirected traffic (wasting bandwidth) and lots of resends (possible congestion). Synchronize your timers.
- Misconfigured port filters or misconfigured SAP filters, resulting in no SAP updates. Missing SAP updates in the correct places of your network can preclude services to your clients.
- SAP timer mismatch. Make sure your SAP timers are consistent across your network. Inconsistency results in network unpredictability.
- SAP overrun at server (not being processed as quickly as server generates). Monitor the number and frequency of SAP messages generated.
- Too much SAP traffic. SAP updates use excessive bandwidth; on WANs send SAP updates only when SAP tables changes. Filter out SAP traffic intelligently. Don't advertise services that are not needed or used by a network.

5.7 TCP/IP

The beginnings of Transmission Control Protocol/Internet Protocol (TCP/IP) started in the 1960s by the U.S. Department of Defense as a research project by Advanced Research Project Agency (ARPA). ARPA sponsored research and development of the ARPANET in the late 60s and installation of it began in September 1969. IP and TCP were developed during the last half of the 1970s and deployed in the early 1980s. TCP/IP's openness and its position as the underpinnings of the Internet have made TCP/IP the most widely used protocol suite in the world. In the past few years WWW use has further accelerated TCP/IP's penetration—having a TCP/IP stack is fundamental to having WWW access.

5.7.1 Fundamentals and Terminology

Like AppleTalk and NetWare, TCP/IP works over a common set of datalinks and physical media (see Figure 5.9). In fact, it is not at all uncommon for a PC to be running a Novell stack and a TCP/IP stack at the same time or for an Apple to be running AppleTalk and TCP/IP simultaneously. Table 5.5 provides common TCP/IP terminology.

In TCP/IP jargon:

- networks are divided into *subnets*,

- each *node/device* (commonly known as *host* in TCP/IP lingo) is connected to a subnet,

- a *subnet mask* is a 32-bit value containing ones and zeros and is used to split the network ID and subnet ID from the host ID easily,

- *services* (for example, Telnet, File Transfer Protocol (FTP)) (not *Servers* as in NetWare) are provided,

- *routing* is done between subnets, and

- *RIP* or *OSPF* are the protocols used for LANs (or *Intranets*—LAN to WAN to LAN) routing) while Border Gateway Protocol (BGP) and Exterior Gateway Protocol (EGP) are two protocols used in the *Internet*. See the reference section for a good book describing these non-LAN routing protocols.

Figure 5.10 provides an example of a simple, albeit sparsely populated, TCP/IP LAN.

IP rests at the heart of TCP/IP. IP provides a connectionless, "best effort" datagram service. Simply stated, IP provides a protocol to send chunks of data across many hops within your network; it differs little (except in speed) from a

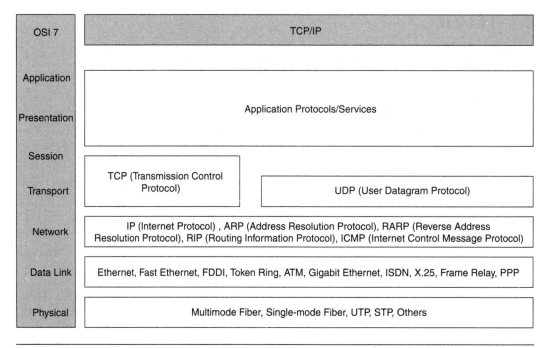

Figure 5.9 TCP/IP

postal service that provides a mechanism for moving letters (datagrams) from one end of the country to the other through many post offices along the way. Two letters sent within hours of one another from destination A to destination B may arrive out of order, travel via different routes, or get lost along the way.

It is the connection-oriented TCP layer that provides the guarantees to deliver; TCP uses sequence numbers and timers to monitor the flow of information from A to B, ensuring that packets arrive correctly ordered and error free. TCP manages retransmission of erroneous packets and provides error messaging when communication fails.

UDP provides a connectionless transport that is layered on top of IP. SNMP is an example of a protocol that uses UDP to perform network management operations.

5.7.2 Addressing

Unlike AppleTalk and NetWare, TCP/IP addressing is complex. In many cases it is the static configuration of TCP/IP addressing that is the root of networking problems. Duplicate IP addresses and incorrect subnet masks will often cause connectivity problems for those nodes or stations involved. It is therefore important for you, the network manager, to have a firm grasp of TCP/IP addressing.

Table 5.5 TCP/IP Terminology

ARP	Address Resolution Protocol
BOOTP	Bootstrap Protocol
DHCP	Dynamic Host Configuration Protocol
IANA	Internet Assigned Numbers Authority
ICMP	Internet Control Message Protocol
IP	Internet Protocol
IPv4	IP Version 4 (version in use on the Internet)
IPv6	IP Version 6
MTU	Maximum Transmission Unit
NFS	Network File System
OSPF	Open Shortest Path First
PING	Packet Internet Groper
RARP	Reverse Address Resolution Protocol
RIP	Routing Information Protocol
TCP	Transmission Control Protocol
TCP/IP	Transmission Control Protocol/Internet Protocol
TELNET	Remote Terminal Protocol
UDP	User Datagram Protocol

Fundamental to TCP/IP's ability to span the world is its hierarchical addressing scheme. Version 4 (IPv4) addresses are 32 bits in length, are represented in dotted decimal notation (x.x.x.x, where x represents each of the 4 bytes, or 8 bits, of the address, for example, 192.168.1.27), and contain a network address and a host address. The first byte within the dotted decimal-formatted address tells you what class the network is—A, B, and C are the most common

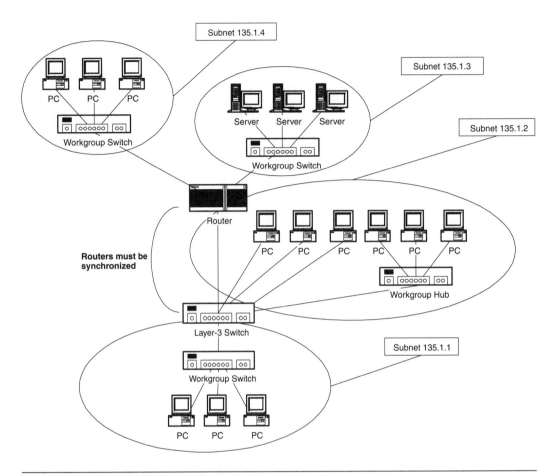

Figure 5.10 TCP/IP network

classes used. There are also class D and class E addresses; class D is used for multicast addressing, and class E addresses are reserved.

Subnets provide a way within TCP/IP to partition your network into logical entities and to contain broadcast traffic. Routing is required between subnets, and broadcast traffic is not typically routed. A subnet mask is a 32-bit number represented by dotted decimal notation that separates the network portion of the address, the subnet, from the host portion when logically "AND'd" to a network address. Routers use the network address to route packets and ignore the node portion of the address. A natural mask is a mask that divides the network and node addresses on byte boundaries, consistent with their class. Note that 255 is equivalent to all 1s or 11111111 in binary.

The following chart, Table 5.6, shows the ranges of addresses for classes A through D, their binary equivalent ranges, and the natural masks for each of

Table 5.6 Address Range

Class	Decimal Range	Binary Equivalent Range	Natural Mask
A	0 to 127	00000000 to 01111111	255.0.0.0
B	128 to 191	10000000 to 10111111	255.255.0.0
C	192 to 223	11000000 to 11011111	255.255.255.0
D	224 to 239	11100000 to 11101111	255.255.255.255

Table 5.7 Binary System

Power of 2	2^7	2^6	2^5	2^4	2^3	2^2	2^1	2^0
Decimal Equivalent	128	64	32	16	8	4	2	1
Example: 25 decimal equals 11001 binary (16+8+1)	0	0	0	1	1	0	0	1
Example: 135 decimal equal 10000111 binary (128 + 4 + 2 + 1)	1	0	0	0	0	1	1	1

the classes. Binary ranges are presented to acclimate you into thinking binary, which is unfortunately necessary to understand how masking is used to separate the network address from the host address.

Table 5.7 illustrates the binary system compared to the decimal system.

A S I D E . . . .

The binary system works by representing all numbers as a combination of 1s and 0s, using powers of 2.

To segment your network beyond your address class, you extend your subnet mask beyond your natural mask. For example, say you have a class B network, 135.1. This means that all connections destined for your network will be 135.1.x.y, where x and y identify the specific destination host address within your network. You can partition this address any way you like. For simplicity though, let's say you use the entire x portion of the address (8 bits) for groups ("subnets" in TCP/IP terminology) and the y portion for members ("hosts" in TCP/IP terminology). This allows you up to 254 subnets, each with 254 hosts. Examples of subnets might include accounting, engineering, MIS, and so on. This network design is accomplished by extending your natural class B mask from 255.255.0.0 to 255.255.255.0.

A S I D E . . .

Why are there 254 subnets and 254 hosts instead of an even power of 2, like 256 subnets and 256 hosts? Traditionally a subnet of all 1s was used for broadcasting, and a subnet address of all 0s was invalid. This simply means that when dividing up the bits between subnets and host addresses you typically subtract 2 from the maximum number. In the purest sense though, a subnet of all 1s and a subnet of all 0s is *valid*. Most routers today know how to deal with such configurations. However, it is true that such a configuration is not recommended for novices. As the IP address space becomes scarce, more efficient use of an IP network number (that is, use of subnet 0 and/or 1) is becoming commonplace.

The notion of masking is best shown by two examples. Table 5.8 and 5.9 illustrate determining a network and host address with a natural mask.

Take an arbitrary class B address, 135.1.43.1, and apply its natural mask to separate the network portion of the address from the host portion (135.1 is the network portion; 43.1 is the host portion of the address). To find the host address, take the inverse mask and apply it to the address.

A S I D E . . .

Applying a mask means to take the logical AND. To do this, first represent the address and mask in binary, then bit by bit. If both bits are 1, then the result is 1 (1 & 1 = 1). If either or both bits are 0, the result is 0 (1 & 0 = 0, 0 & 1 = 0, 0 & 0 = 0).

Using the natural mask for a class B address, we end up with 2^{16} or approximately 65,000 possible addresses. Clearly, that is not manageable as a single entity!

Let's now take the same address but use a nonnatural mask. Nonnatural masks are used to partition further the range of the host addresses possible in any class address. Tables 5.10 and 5.11 illustrate determining a network and host address with a nonnatural mask. For example, say I want to partition my class B network, defined by (135.1) into 62 (2^{6-2}) subnets, each with 1022

Table 5.8 Determining a Network Address with a Natural Mask

	Dotted Decimal	Binary Equivalent
Address	135.1.43.1	10000111.00000001.00101011.00000001
Natural Mask	255.255.0.0	11111111.11111111.00000000.00000000
Network Address	135.1.0.0	10000111.00000001.00000000.00000000

Table 5.9 Determining a Host Address with a Natural Mask

	Dotted Decimal	Binary Equivalent
Address	135.1.43.1	10000111.00000001.00101011.00000001
Inverse Natural Mask	0.0.255.255	00000000.00000000.11111111.11111111
Host Address	0.0.43.1	00000000.00000000.00101011.00000001

Table 5.10 Determining a Network Address with a Non-Natural Mask

	Dotted Decimal	Binary Equivalent
Address	135.1.43.1	10000111.00000001.00101011.00000001
Mask	255.255.252.0	11111111.11111111.11111100.00000000
Network Address	135.1.40.0	10000111.00000001.00101000.00000000

Table 5.11 Determining a Host Address with a Non-Natural Mask

	Dotted Decimal	Binary Equivalent
Address	135.1.43.1	10000111.00000001.00101011.00000001
Inverse Mask	0.0.3.255	00000000.00000000.00000011.11111111
Host Address	0.0.3.1	00000000.00000000.00000011.00000001

Table 5.12 Example <u>A</u>: Determining a <u>Network</u> Address of a Class C Address

	Dotted Decimal	**Binary Equivalent**
Address	192.168.1.1	11000000.10101000.00000001.00000001
Mask	255.255.255.240	11111111.11111111.11111111.11110000
Network Address	192.168.1.0	11000000.10101000.00000001.00000000

Table 5.13 Example <u>A</u>: Determining a <u>Host</u> Address of a Class C Address

	Dotted Decimal	**Binary Equivalent**
Address	192.168.1.1	11000000.10101000.00000001.00000001
Inverse Mask	0.0.0.15	00000000.00000000.00000000.00001111
Host Address	0.0.0.1	00000000.00000000.00000000.00000001

(2^{10-2}) hosts. Note that when you add 6 and 10 you get the 16 bits that you have to play with; the 32-bit mask becomes:

- sixteen 1s for class B (**11111111 11111111**),
- followed by six 1s for subnetting (11111111 11111111 **111111**),
- concluding with ten 0s for host addresses (11111111 11111111 111111**00 00000000**) (16 + 6 + 10 = 32).

Another example, this time a class C address. See Tables 5.12 and 5.13. Suppose we want to take the 8 bits we have to play with in a class C address and devote 4 of them to subnetting and 4 to host addresses. This results in 15 (2^{4-1}) subnets, each with 15 hosts (2^{4-1}). Again 4 + 4 equals the 8 bits we can play with to validate our results. Note that 15 subnets each with 15 hosts may not seem particularly useful to you. A subsequent section discusses a technique on how to extend your switched address space beyond the Class C limitations.

Here's yet another class C address example. See Tables 5.14 and 5.15. Let's devote 2 bits to subnetting and 6 bits to host addresses. This results in 3 (2^{2-1}) subnets (192.168.1.192, 192.168.1.128 and 192.168.1.64), each with 63 (2^{6-1}) hosts.

Table 5.14 Example B: Determining a Network Address of a Class C Address

	Dotted Decimal	**Binary Equivalent**
Address	192.168.1.250	11000000.10101000.00000001.11111010
Mask	255.255.255.192	11111111.11111111.11111111.11000000
Network Address	192.168.1.192	11000000.10101000.00000001.11000000

Table 5.15 Example B: Determining a Host Address of a Class C Address

	Dotted Decimal	**Binary Equivalent**
Address	192.168.1.250	11000000.10101000.00000001.11111010
Inverse Mask	0.0.0.63	00000000.00000000.00000000.00111111
Host Address	0.0.0.58	00000000.00000000.00000000.00111010

You can easily see that in the first example (Table 5.14), you do not need to use a binary calculator to do the masking; in the other examples you might. The point here is to keep your masking as simple (and hence manageable) as possible. When you are looking at routing tables, you may not have your binary calculator, and the last thing you want to do is draw the 0s and 1s necessary to figure out the network and host numbers. A very popular, simple mask for class B networks is 255.255.255.0. This allows for 254 subnets of 254 hosts each. No calculator is required to separate the network number from the host number.

There are four options for setting up your network addresses:

1. You can go directly to the Internet Network Information Center (InterNIC). The InterNIC manages addresses across the Internet, guaranteeing unique addresses.

2. You can get a bunch of class C addresses from your Internet Service Provider (ISP). Beware though, if you change ISPs you will most likely have to give the address back and go through a massive reconfiguration of your addresses across your network.

3. If you don't need access to the Internet (rare, indeed), you can make up your own addresses to be used internally. Again though, once you decide to attach to the Internet you will have to go through an address overhaul. Don't do this.

4. You can make up your own internal addresses and use some kind of proxy address scheme (also known as addressed translation) to get on the Internet. This is a significant management undertaking, but it may be worth the effort to get an internal class B network. Don't do this.

At this point you might be ask, why such a complex addressing scheme—AppleTalk and NetWare have such simple, automatic schemes. It is TCP/IP routing that so greatly leverages the masks, subnets, network addresses, and host addresses defined within TCP/IP addressing; this is discussed in the following sections.

A S I D E . . .

As with AppleTalk zones, use the amount of broadcast traffic as one gauge to help size your subnets.

Another A S I D E . . .

In addition to the IP address, it is worth noting that TCP/IP has predefined, well-known port numbers used to connect to services. For example, normally Telnet is 23, SNMP is 161, SNMP traps come over 162, and WWW http traffic comes in at 80. Often you can trace a problem by mapping the port number back to the service. Note that RFC 1700 is the authority for common association of services and port. Note also that all TCP/IP implementations include a services file. On UNIX this file is /etc/services; on Windows it is \Windows\Services.

5.7.3 Private Addresses

RFC 1597 defined three addresses ranges for use within private Intranets. These are shown in Table 5.16.

These addresses may be used within your LAN without registration. Once you connect to the Internet, however, you must use translation routers to translate to a registered address. When you use private addresses, many believe that you "protect" your PCs and workstations from being seen by the world outside your company's Intranet. In addition, if any of your private routes "leaks" on to the Internet backbone, you do not introduce the problem that you might present with registered addresses. Others believe that private address are bad and eventually result in wholesale address replacement (see RFC 1627).

Table 5.16 Private Intranet Address Ranges

Class A	10.0.0.0 to 10.255.255.255
Class B	172.16.0.0 to 172.31.255.255
Class C	192.168.0.0 to 192.168.255.255

5.7.3.1 Extending Your "Switched" Address Space

As you may have guessed, with the popularity of IP there is an extreme shortage of addresses. Get a class A address—forget it. Get a class B address—good luck. This leaves class C, and one problem with class C addresses is that you have only 254 addresses per network and then you need to route. Once you need to route, you need to add a router to your switched network or move to a layer-3 switch. This can affect performance and result in a network design that is not optimal.

One technique to get around this is to get a series of contiguous class C networks assigned in multiples of 2, 4, 8, 16, and so on, depending on the number of addresses you want to switch together. If you want to switch 500 (roughly 2 * 255) addresses, get addresses that are multiples of 2 (for example, 192.168.**2**.0, 192.168.3.0); 1000 (roughly 4 * 255) addresses get addresses that are multiples of 4 (for example,192.168.**4**.0, 192.168.5.0, 192.168.6.0, 192.168.7.0), and so on. Then set bits in the standard class C subnet mask to 0 to *extend* your networks. Table 5.17 illustrates contiguous class C addresses.

5.7.3.2 Reducing the Size of Your Routing Tables

Another shortcoming with IP addressing is that it is not designed to be hierarchical. This results in large routing tables since they must contain entries for every network or subnet to which they wish to route. Classless interdomain routing (CIDR) is a scheme used to map a group of addresses to a single entry within a routing table. CIDR uses the same technique we defined earlier to map a group of class C addresses with the same subnet mask used to create a large "supernet." The result is that routers need only have one entry in their routing table to define the route to a large region of addresses. This greatly reduces the routing-table space requirements.

5.7.4 Routing

In the LAN there are two major protocols used for TCP/IP routing. Routing Information Protocol (RIP) is widely used because it is so simple; Open

Table 5.17 Contiguous Class C Addresses

Assigned Contiguous Class C addresses	Modified Mask	Modified Mask in Binary
192.168.**2**.0, 192.168.3.0	255.255.254	11111111.11111111.1111111**0**.0
192.168.**4**.0, 192.168.5.0, 192.168.6.0, 192.168.7.0	255.255.252	11111111.11111111.111111**00**.0

Shortest Path First (OSPF), albeit more complex and CPU-intensive, is popular when routing LANs across the WAN since it results in far less traffic. There are other protocols such as Interior Gateway Protocol (IGP), Intermediate System to Intermediate System Protocol (IS-IS), and so on. These protocols are complex and highly specialized.

5.7.4.1 RIP

RIP (RFC 1058) is a widely deployed, simple routing protocol based on the Bellman-Ford distance-vector algorithm. In short, each router maintains a table of routes mapping an IP address to its corresponding IP-gateway network address, telling the router the next hop address to use to forward packets. When a packet comes in, the router uses the subnet mask to AND off the network address from the host address and then searches its routing table for a match. The router selects the gateway/port with the lowest number of hops and routes the packet accordingly. The router ages out each entry in the router table by maintaining a timer for each entry. Periodic refreshes (default is an average of 30 seconds) from neighboring routers keep the routing tables up-to-date.

RIP's biggest shortcoming is that the routing tables tend to converge slowly when routers go down or a route becomes disabled. By "converge" we mean to make adjustments based on changes so that packets are not misrouted. Several factors contribute to this sluggishness:

- Table updates by default happen only every 30 seconds.
- Routes that do not receive updates are held for 180 seconds by default.
- A network can span up to 15 routers (not great for large networks), meaning that in the worse case it may take several 30-second intervals for a change at one end of your routers to propagate to the other end.

When your routing tables are out of sync, you end up with temporary routing loops, extra traffic congestion, and many dropped packets—this obviously has a negative impact on your network. To address convergence, RIP employs split horizon and reverse poison, as discussed previously; RIP also uses triggered updates. Triggered updates are much like SNMP traps where a table update is sent out by a router as soon as it knows about a change rather than waiting for the next scheduled table update. Finally, a technique called "count to infinity" is used to age out dangling paths gradually. This technique is used to remove routes that, due to router disconnect or failure, are no longer available. Count to infinity increments unknown routes by 2 units at each routing table update; this gradually gets these indeterminate routes up to a value of 16 (infinity), disabling the route.

A S I D E . . .

To collect packets that are looping endlessly throughout the network, IP maintains a hop count in the packet header (TTL). When the count is decremented to 0, the destination is deemed to be unreachable, the packet is dropped, and a corresponding ICMP error message packet is fired back.

In addition to the convergence problem, there are some big problems with RIP that, as a network manager, you should be aware of:

- The decision as to which route is best is based exclusively on the hop count (there is no way to account for congestion or other metrics or any way to load balance traffic intelligently across multiple routes).
- There is a significant amount of broadcast traffic generated with periodic, superfluous (no change), routing updates.
- As the network size increases, RIP takes longer and longer to sync up (or converge) its routing tables. Worse yet, sometimes bad paths are left dangling.
- RIP assumes that if subnetting is implemented, it is implemented consistently across the network. This mean that you must use the *same subnet mask* on all your routers across your network.

Nonetheless, its simplicity has made it prevail, except when spanning the WAN. Clearly the last thing you want to do is flood your precious WAN pipe with redundant routing updates. OSPF, an alternative routing protocol, reduces the updates, provides multiple metrics, and converges quickly.

5.7.4.2 OSPF

OSPF is a link-state protocol based on the Dijkstra algorithm. This algorithm supports multiple Type of Service (TOS) values, enabling the network manager to configure routes based on arbitrary metrics such as the largest capacity wire, the most fault-tolerant link, or the speed of transmission. This also provides a mechanism to define several routes to a single destination, differing by the TOS value.

OSPF routing tables are updated via Link State Advertisements (LSAs). In essence, each router maintains a virtual "map" of the network; since each router constructs its map using the same algorithm and data, all routing maps are identical. After initial set up, the maps are maintained only by updates of the changes, not by entire table exchanges as with RIP. These reduce updates, enable OSPF to converge quickly, and eliminate routing loops. OSPF uses multicast packets rather than broadcast packets (RIP); this is beneficial since updates are directed at all routers participating in OSPF rather than at all network devices on your network.

To eliminate redundant updates and hence reduce traffic, OSPF maintains versions of each route in a link-state database. When it's time to refresh, a neighboring router sends its array of links with each link's corresponding version number. The recipient then requests information for only the "interesting" links, the links that have different version numbers.

As the network becomes large, so does the respective link-state database at each router. In addition, the CPU and memory strain on each router participating in the OSPF network increase. To resolve this problem and to reduce traffic across OSPF networks spanning the WAN, OSPF has the concept of areas (see Figure 5.11). These areas enable OSPF to scale to large networks.

Areas are essentially groupings of systems connected to a special backbone area. All areas must be connected to the backbone; areas cannot be connected to another area other than the backbone area, that is, to extend the scope of the OSPF hierarchy. Routers within the area have an area-centric view of the network; only the router connecting to the backbone area has knowledge beyond the area. This router is called the area border router and must maintain both a local and remote link-state database. The area border router serves as the liaison to the rest of the network. Areas are ideal for connections that span the WAN as local router traffic stays local.

5.7.4.3 BOOTP and DHCP

As mentioned previously, one of the big shortcomings of IP is address management. Unlike AppleTalk and NetWare, the TCP/IP's default behavior is *not* to learn a host's address automatically when a host boots. Rather, TCP/IP addresses are by default statically configured at each host in the network. This leaves lots of room for error. Dynamic Host Configuration Protocol (DHCP) and DHCP's predecessor Bootstrap Protocol (BOOTP) provide solutions for automatic IP address assignment.

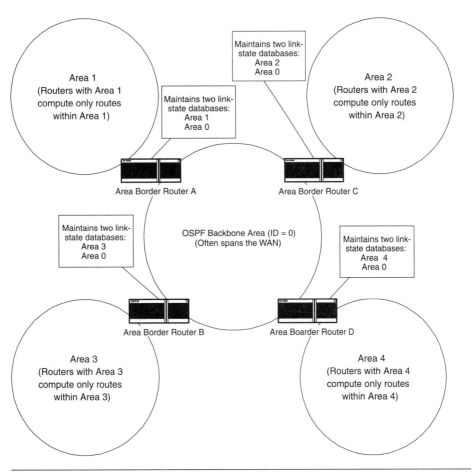

Figure 5.11 Example use of OSPF areas

BOOTP is a protocol that was originally designed for diskless workstations. Essentially, BOOTP uses a single UDP packet to determine its IP address and subnet address. When the diskless workstation boots, it constructs a
link-layer broadcast (it can't construct anything else since it does not have an IP
address or a destination address for the BOOTP server) and broadcasts it out
over the network. Since the server may never respond (for example, if there is
no server), the workstation uses a timer and packet counter to resend the request to some predefined number of retries. A BOOTP server recognizes the
message and maps the MAC address within the link-layer broadcast to a corresponding IP address. A return UDP packet is formed, complete with the IP address, a subnet mask, a default gateway, and a pointer to a boot file. Typically,
the packet is broadcast back and the client uses a series of ARP requests (discussed in Chapter 1) to verify that the address returned is unused. A subse-

quent BOOTP request is now made with the client's correct IP address. After the reply, some more ARPs, and a trivial file transfer protocol (TFTP) exchange to get the boot file, the system boots up to a full TCP/IP stack. TFTP is a boot-strapping file transfer protocol (FTP) that operates over UDP and uses the ".rhosts" or "rhosts.equiv" files for authentication. Network users typically use FTP for their file transfers; this protocol has significantly better authentication.

There are a few problems with BOOTP worth noting. Because BOOTP relies on broadcasts, a BOOTP server must be on the local subnet; BOOTP requests are not typically routed. The solution to this problem is "UDP assist"; a technique common in routers that forwards certain broadcasts "around" the router's normal processing. The BOOTP server must still be manually config-ured with the MAC address to IP address mappings, leaving room for error and inconsistencies among BOOTP servers. BOOTP is still better than RARP because it returns more than just the IP address. DHCP, however, is quickly becoming the popular choice for dynamic address distribution.

DHCP (RFCs 1533, 1541, and 1542) extends BOOTP by providing a general purpose client/server approach to IP address distribution. Like BOOTP, a DHCP server may use the "UDP assist" feature found in router im-plementations to get around the problem of broadcast containment. DHCP uses a similar exchange of packets to get an IP address. The addresses are, however, not stored on the DHCP server as a bunch of static MAC address to IP address mappings; rather the DHCP server maintains a range of addresses that may be distributed and "leased" to any device. Note that the lease period is configurable—from a few minutes to several months. Once a PC obtains a DHCP-served address every time it reboots, it will "refresh" its lease. If the PC fails to refresh its lease within the lease period, the PC may be given a new ad-dress as the server can reclaim addresses of expired leases.

Several DHCP solutions can be distributed across the enterprise as they are able to manage many subnets simultaneously. Many DHCP servers also in-tegrate with DNS services as well as provide central configuration for address management. It is recommended that you install two DHCP servers for redun-dancy; one server remains in standby mode in case the primary server fails. DNS servers follow a similar redundancy model.

Clearly DHCP is an attractive alternative to the static, error-prone con-figuration characteristic of TCP/IP. All it takes is an incorrect subnet mask, in-valid default gateway, or a duplicate IP address to cause a PC not to be networked and to prohibit anyone from communicating to the machines in-volved. If one of the machines involved is a file server upon which multiple users depend, this can cause a serious network problem. With DCHP, the lap-top meeting "goers" can "plug in" across your network campus and have a truly portable network. It is expected that DHCP may be the address acquisition protocol for IPv6 (discussed in the next chapter).

As a network manager evaluating a dynamic IP addressing technology you should ask yourself the following questions:

- Does the technology require the workstation to adapt to the network, or does the network adapt to the workstation?
- Will the technology work over a WAN link?
- Does the technology provide dynamic DNS and gateway information? Does it integrate with a standard DNS service?
- Is the technology available for PCs, MACs, and UNIX boxes?
- Will implementing the technology require visiting every desktop or retrofitting a network?

> **A S I D E . . .**
>
> Many routers that are also communication servers provide DHCP. A caveat here: Implementations, such as Microsoft's DHCP, are often proprietary and cause conflict.

5.7.5 IP Fragmentation and MTU

As David Ginsburg points out in *ATM Solutions for Enterprise Internetworking* (p. 207), care must be taken with setting maximum transmission units (MTUs) across your network. When mixing technologies (using FDDI, ATM, and Ethernet) across your network and using IP, it is important to make your MTU consistent across your network. The MTU determines how big a packet may be before it needs to be broken into several packets. With IP, packets may be broken (or fragmented); the penalty is that if even a 1-byte packet fragment is lost, the entire packet must be retransmitted. This can have performance implications. Likewise fragmentation is done by the router and impacts its performance. The goal is to try and avoid fragmentation by ensuring MTUs are consistent and reflect the lowest common denominator (LCD) across the network.

Suppose you are connecting your primarily Ethernet-based network with an ATM backbone pipe standard 9180 byte IP MTU across your ATM link. The maximum frame size of Ethernet is 1518, of which 1472 bytes may be data. There are two problems here:

- If a packet that is larger than 1472 comes across the ATM link and IP fragmentation is disabled, no connection will be possible to a Ethernet-based host.

■ If the packet comes in and fragmentation is possible, the packet will be fragmented appropriately but possibly with a performance hit by the switch in layer 3 switch.

MTU mismatches often go unnoticed since, assuming IP fragmentation is enabled, the network will be operational, although slow. Traceroute (a tool discussed in Chapter 10) will find the MTU across the network. MIB-2 also has an object for MTU.

5.7.6 Management Issues

TCP/IP, like other NOSs, is susceptible to network management problems. Following are some of the common configuration and performance problems:

■ Network addresses, subnet masks, or gateways are incorrectly configured. Manual configuration of network addresses, masks, and gateways at each end station results in lots of problems. This is why DHCP, which automatically manages this end station configuration, is so attractive. For example,

• A duplicate IP address can cause serious network problems, but only for the users involved.

• An incorrect subnet address will often (depending on how you do subnetting; in certain cases an incorrect address will work) prevent TCP/IP communication.

• An incorrect gateway (default router) will prevent communication beyond the local subnet. It is imperative that configuration be done correctly.

■ Routes are inadvertently disabled or turned off. At the router it is important that routing stays turned on and routes remain properly configured. Verify that the `ipForwarding` (defined in the MIB-2 section following) remains on and that `ifOperStatus` (MIB-2, defined in Chapter 3) for each interface also remains on.

■ Filters are incorrectly defined. It is important that filters and other security lists are configured properly. Refer to Chapter 7 and to the bibliography for more on security. As a rule of thumb, once you attach to the WAN, you must manage security. (There is more information in Chapter 7 on security management.)

■ Subnet masks are set up incorrectly. Make certain that subnet masks on routers (see MIB-2 object, `ipAdEntNetMask`, following) match subnet masks on hosts. If there is a mismatch, packets will be routed to the wrong subnet/host or be dropped altogether. Ensure that your subnet mask is correct:

- Validate that when converted to binary, the subnet mask results in an address with all 1s to the left, resulting in "clean" separation of your network/subnet address from your host addresses. For example, a mask of 255.255.15.0 in binary is 11111111.11111111.00001111 and is most likely not what you intended.

- Validate that when your subnet mask is applied, you do not end up with a host address of zero. In most cases this is probably not what you want.

■ Static routes are set up incorrectly. If you set up static routes, make certain they are retained through device reboot. Validate that your static routes are connected to an operational interface. Check `ipRouteProto` (see MIB-2 object in Table 5.18). Static routes are set to "local" or "netmgmt." Verify the existence of the next hop address and that the address is up. Verify that the next hop of the interface is either local or directly connected.

■ Default routes (sometimes called gateways) are not working in both directions. TCP/IP relies on the default gateway being set correctly in both directions for communication that must be routed to work properly. If A wants to communicate with C through B as default gateway, the default gateway of C must also be set up correctly for A to communicate with C. Routing must be set up properly in both directions for communication to work. It is therefore imperative that, if you have connectivity problems from A to C, you test connectivity in both directions. Monitor ICMP redirects (`icmpOutRedirects`, see MIB-2 object in Table 5.18) received at routers for a sense of validity of client configurations. ICMP redirects are indicative of misconfigured clients, particularly default routes on PC configurations.

■ Parallel routes fail to work. Again, with slow-routing table convergence, a parallel path may fail to work when one path goes down until the routing tables update. Sometimes, though the cause is much simpler, the parallel paths are set up, but they never really worked. They are noticed only when the working one goes down. Always test your configurations immediately after you set them up.

■ Inadvertent configuration of two router interfaces on a router with the same IP address. Make certain that all router interfaces are configured with unique IP addresses (see MIB-2 object, `ipAdEntAddr`, in Table 5.18).

- Sluggish routing table convergence. Validate that your RIP update timers are consistent for all routers in your network. Having timers out of sync will only exacerbate routing table convergence.

- OSPF networks fail to be advertised properly. This is generally an OSPF mask problem—correct the mask.

- OSPF networks are not receiving updates properly. This is often the result of a timer mismatch. Verify that your timers `ospfIfRtrDeadInterval` and `ospfIfHelloInterval` are synchronized across your network. It is important that your routing configurations are synchronized.

- More than one OSPF area is inadvertently assigned to a routing interface. All addresses on an interface must be in the same OSPF area.

- An OSPF interface is inadvertently disabled, or OSPF is inadvertently disabled. Verify that the OSPF interface state (OSPF MIB (RFC 1850) object, `ospfIfAdminStat`) is enabled and that `ospfAdminStat` is enabled.

- Excessive traffic prevents routing updates. Unfortunately, routing updates use the same network as the rest of your traffic, and your traffic can get delayed. This can cause routes to get aged out and constantly (though falsely) "changed." When traffic is excessive (high utilization), monitor the frequency of routing table changes. The MIB-2 variables, that is, `ipRoutingDiscards` and `ipOutNoRoutes` (see MIB-2 object in Table 5.18), are two parameters to monitor as well as any device-specific MIB variables that indicate that the table memory may be low.

- MTU mismatches. Verify that the MIB-2 value `ifMTU` is consistent across your network interfaces. Use traceroute to test MTU across the network or to Internet sites.

5.7.7 Important MIB-2 and OSPF Objects for TCP/IP Management

MIB-2 has a plethora of data associated with managing TCP/IP. The OSPF MIB has useful objects for managing OSPF. The `ip`, `icmp` (covered in a previous section), `tcp`, and `udp` groups are obviously tailored to the TCP/IP protocol suite. Take the time to peruse MIB-2 and learn what counters you can retrieve to help manage your routers and switches. Many of the objects were put into context in the earlier section on management issues. There are, however, many objects that are indicative of performance problems or network faults.

As you know, performance and fault management are critical to your success as a network manager. Therefore it is important that you monitor key MIB-2 `ip` group objects across backbone routers (or other routes that your phone/beeper/e-mail will be ringing/vibrating/flooded if they go down) in your network over time. MIB-2's `ip` group contains many important counters that, can be indicative of performance problems when looked at over time as a percent of total packet flow. MIB-2's `icmp` group contains many error counts that may be cause for alarm when compared against the number of packets transmitted or received. You should monitor these counters as a percentage compared to the total number of packets transmitted across each router.

For example, your network may not be running optimally if your key routers across your network are experiencing a high percentage of

- discarded packets being transmitted or received (`ipInDiscards`, `ipOutDiscards`).

- discarded packets due to no route or unknown protocol (`ipOutNo Routes`, `ipInUnknownProto`).

- packets with errors (`ipInaddrErrors`, `ipInHdrErrors`, `ipReasmFails`, `ipFragFails`).

Also, you are most likely taking a performance hit in your network if you have a high percentage of packets (compared to all packets transmitted) of

- unreachable destinations (`icmpInDestUnreach`).

- received or transmitted time exceeded messages (`icmpInTime Excds` or `icmpOutTimeExcds`).

- received or transmitted source quench messages (`icmpInSrc Quenchs`, `icmpOutSrcQuenchs`) or ICMP messages that were not sent due to problems (`icmpOutErrors`).

You need to monitor these objects over time and designate valid-rate baselines (a snapshot of rates when your network is working well) for your network. Since the network operation of each network is unique, the baselines must be calibrated for your network. It is useful to set a threshold that, when exceeded, makes you aware of the problem. Look for vendor-supplied router management tools to help you with this problem. Table 5.18 provides important MIB objects for managing routing within your network.

5.8 Broadcasting in a Switched Network

When you plan your switched LAN, it is important to remember the impact of broadcast traffic. Because each NIC in each client PC or workstation must pay

Table 5.18 MIB-2 or OSPF MIB Descriptions

Object	Description from MIB-2 or OSPF MIB (prefixed by ospf)
`icmpInDestUnreachs`	The number of ICMP Destination Unreachable messages received.
`icmpInErrors`	The number of ICMP messages the entity received but determined had ICMP-specific errors (bad ICMP checksums, bad length, and so on).
`icmpInMsgs`	The total number of ICMP messages the entity received. Note that this counter includes all those messages counted by icmpInErrors.
`icmpInParmProbs`	The number of ICMP Parameter Problem messages received.
`icmpInSrcQuenchs`	The number of ICMP Source Quench messages received.
`icmpInRedirects`	The number of ICMP Redirect messages received.
`icmpInTimeExcds`	The number of ICMP Time Exceeded messages received.
`icmpOutDestUnreachs`	The number of ICMP Destination Unreachable messages sent.
`icmpOutErrors`	The number of ICMP messages this entity did not send due to problems, such as a lack of buffers, discovered within ICMP. This value should not include errors that are discovered outside the ICMP, such as the inability of IP to route the resultant datagram. In some implementations there may be no types of errors that contribute to this counter's value.
`icmpOutParmProbs`	The number of ICMP Parameter Problems sent.

Continued

Table 5.18 MIB-2 or OSPF MIB Descriptions (*Continued*)

Object	Description from MIB-2 or OSPF MIB (prefixed by ospf)
icmpOutRedirects	The number of ICMP Redirect messages sent. For a host this object will always be zero since hosts do not send redirects.
icmpOutSrcQuenchs	The number of ICMP Source Quench messages sent.
icmpOutTimeExcds	The number of ICMP Time Exceeded messages sent.
ifMtu	The size of the largest datagram that can be sent or received on the interface, specified in octets. For interfaces that are used for transmitting network datagrams, this is the size of the largest network datagram that can be sent on the interface.
ipOutRequests	The total number of IP datagrams that local IP user-protocols (including ICMP) supplied to IP in requests for transmission. Note that this counter does not include any datagrams counted in ipForwDatagrams.
ipReasmFails	The number of failures detected by the IP reassembly algorithm (for whatever reason, including timedout, errors, and so on). Note that this is not necessarily a count of discarded IP fragments since some algorithms (notably the algorithm in RFC 815) can lose track of the number of fragments by combining them as they are received.
ipReasmReqds	The number of IP received fragments that need to be reassembled at this entity.

Continued

Table 5.18 MIB-2 or OSPF MIB Descriptions (*Continued*)

Object	Description from MIB-2 or OSPF MIB (prefixed by ospf)
`ipRouteProto`	`ipRouteProto` is routing protocol for route entry. other(1): none of the following; nonprotocol information, for example, manually configured; local(2): entries set via a network; netmgmt(3): management protocol obtained via ICMP; icmp(4): for example, Redirect; the remaining values are all gateway routing protocols; egp(5) ggp(6) hello(7) rip(8) is-is(9) es-is(10) ciscoIgrp(11) bbnSpfIgp(12) ospf(13) bgp(14)
`ipRoutingDiscards`	The number of routing entries that are chosen to be discarded even though they are valid. One possible reason for discarding such an entry could be to free up buffer space for other routing entries.
`ospfAdminState`	The administrative status of OSPF in the router. The value "enabled" denotes that the OSPF Process is active on at least one interface; "disabled" disables it on all interfaces.
`ospfIfAdminStat`	The OSPF interface's administrative status. The value formed on the interface and the interface will be advertised as an internal route to some area. The value "disabled" denotes that the interface is external to OSPF.

Continued

Table 5.18 MIB-2 or OSPF MIB Descriptions (*Continued*)

Object	Description from MIB-2 or OSPF MIB (prefixed by ospf)
ospfIfHelloInterval	The length of time, in seconds, between the Hello packets that the router sends on the interface. This value must be the same for all routers attached to a common network.
ospfIfRtrDeadInterval	The number of seconds that a router's Hello packets have not been seen before its neighbors declare the router down. This should be some multiple of the Hello interval. This value must be the same for all routers attached to a common network.
tcpAttemptFails	The number of times TCP connections have direct transition to the CLOSED state from either the SYN-SENT state or the SYN-RCVD state, plus the number of times TCP connections have made a direct transition to the LISTEN state from the SYN-RCVD state.
tcpInErrs	The total number of segments received in error (for example, bad TCP checksums).
udpNoPorts	The total number of received UDP datagrams for which there was no application at the destination port.
udpInErrors	The number of received UDP datagrams that could not be delivered for reasons other than the lack of an application at the destination port.
udpOutDatagrams	The total number of UDP datagrams sent from this entity.

attention to broadcast traffic (that is, interrupt the CPU), too much broadcast traffic (a broadcast storm or broadcast-intensive protocols) can literally bring down the network. Minimally excessive broadcasting degrades performance. You can use RMON2 to meter broadcast traffic.

It may be desirable to reduce the size of your IP subnets, AppleTalk zones, and IPX networks and route between each segment as broadcast traffic is not routed. Attempt to follow the 80/20 rule by keeping 80 percent of your traffic local and routing only 20 percent of your traffic to mitigate the performance hit of routing. Another alternative to broadcast containment is the establishment of VLANs as discussed in the previous chapter. Some vendors also provide advanced filtering capabilities at the switch level (filtering is typically done at the routing level); some vendors provide proxy-type functions to contain broadcast traffic.

It is useful to understand how each of the protocols contributes to the broadcast quota for a network. The following gives you an idea as to what is normal in order to baseline your network.

- IP uses ARP, which broadcasts to resolve IP addresses on the network. IP also uses broadcasts for RIP updates. RARP, BOOTP, and DHCP generate broadcast traffic as well.

- AppleTalk uses broadcasting to resolve or request services and to resolve addresses. AppleTalk uses broadcasting to obtain zone information and to keep routing tables up-to-date via the Router Discovery Protocol.

- IPX uses broadcasting to advertise servers, services, and routes. NetWare clients use broadcasting to find servers.

5.9 Summary

AppleTalk, IPX, and IP are common routing protocols used within LANs. It is important that you understand how the routing protocols used within your LAN operate and how to configure them properly.

Routing adds a lot to the challenge of managing a LAN. In addition to maintaining a consistent configuration, managing multiple protocols simultaneously, and managing the overall design of your network as it shrinks and grows, you need to be ready to deal with storms where routing tables do not converge.

With routing, it is imperative that you think of your network as a system (see Chapter 12) and understand all the processes that occur on a regular basis to keep your network intact. Even though you often work on one device at a time, you must remember that routing changes made on one router can have significant impact on your entire network. You must manage routing with the big network picture in mind and validate your designs and changes from multiple points within your network.

You must be able to peel away the complexity introduced with routing, abstract away the debris, and make smart network system decisions. After all, it is routing that ties everything together, making your LANs interconnect, scale, and span to the WAN.

CHAPTER 6

Emerging Technologies Important to Switching

6.1 Introduction

There is no doubt that switching has taken the LAN by storm. It has provided a "drop in" solution to getting more bandwidth across the backbone and to the desktop. Switching clearly has a bright future; there are literally hundreds of vendors who sell switched equipment. So you say, what's next for switching?

- Switching has fatter pipes, for one thing. It wasn't long ago that Fast Ethernet was introduced into the LAN—a technology that moves frames at a rate 10 times that of conventional Ethernet. Now Gigabit Ethernet is on the horizon—100 times faster than conventional Ethernet.

- Switching is moving up the stack—into layer 3. If you can bridge frames at millions of frames per second (FPS), why must you be satisfied with 50,000 packets per second (PPS) typical of routed traffic? All sorts of creative solutions designed to apply the power of switching to the problem of routing are emerging.

- Switching will provide end-to-end service guarantees and traffic prioritization. Multimedia traffic results in large flows of data that can cause network congestion. With multimedia traffic, a small amount of latency becomes an issue. Sure your switches can drop a few frames when faced with congestion, but delays in real-time video are unacceptable. Likewise, voice-over a LAN with delay characteristics found within satellite communications is a real turnoff. The network must be able to do better than "best effort" and provide a means for giving certain traffic first class treatment.

This chapter explores the key technologies that are shaping switching in the future. To lighten things up a bit, I try to use some real-world comparisons dealing with our people transportation system. Network traffic, like rush-hour or

Friday afternoon traffic, exhibits many of the same characteristics. And, our transportation department has come up with some similar solutions.

6.2 Gigabit Ethernet

Our journey begins with data roads—from 10-lane (traditional Ethernet) to 100-lane (Fast Ethernet) to 1000-lane highways (Gigabit Ethernet). No doubt Gigabit Ethernet provides giant data roads for your LAN, roads capable of moving approximately 1.48 million frames per second! (See Table 6.1 for a concise synopsis of important high-bit Ethernet characteristics, and see Figure 6.1 for an example of deploying Gigabit Ethernet.) But guess what? It is still Ethernet!

At the time of this writing, Gigabit Ethernet is an emerging standard (802.3z, expected to be a standard in 1998) that will retain much of the simplicity of traditional Ethernet. It is expected to use CSMA/CD, provide full and possibly half-duplex communications at 1000 Mbps, and retain the frame format/size. It is designed to "drop in" to an existing Ethernet set up without much pain at all, enabling you to scale beyond Fast Ethernet. And, since it is still Ethernet, troubleshooting and network management should be similar, although the pure speed of this technology will challenge current "probing" technologies.

Gigabit Ethernet will place greater restrictions on wire spans—the Gigabit Ethernet committee is shooting for spans of 500 meters of single-mode/multimode fiber, 25 meters for copper coaxial cable, and 100 meters for

Table 6.1 Gigabit Ethernet Information

Standard	802.3z
Important MIB(s)	Ethernet MIB, MIB-2, RMON
Speed	1000 Mbps
Medium	Multimode or single-mode fiber (first planned medium, may support other media after initial standard is ratified)
Segment Length	500 m
Frame Size	64 to 1518 8-bit bytes
Topology	Star

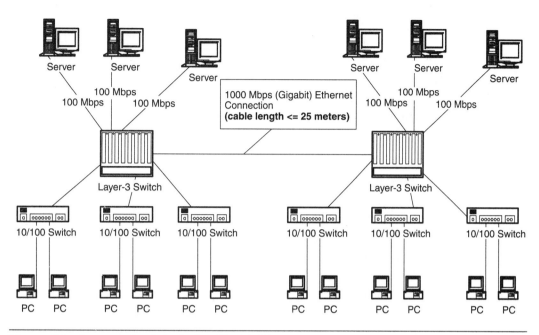

Figure 6.1 An example of deploying Gigabit Ethernet

UTP category 5. These shorter spans are to accommodate the CSMA/CD aspect of Ethernet. As with traditional Ethernet, use of a full-duplex repeater will allow you to increase the span. Gigabit Ethernet will leverage the Fibre Channel interconnection technology for the physical connection, increasing the 800 Mbps signal rate to 1.24 Gbps for a throughput of 1 Gbps.

A S I D E . . .

When you run full-duplex Ethernet, CSMA/CD is disabled. This enables traffic to travel in both directions simultaneously.

Gigabit Ethernet will add carrier extension and packet bursting. Carrier extension increases the number of bits that travel simultaneously through a connection without increasing the minimum frame length. Packet bursting allows end stations to send many frames at once, increasing bandwidth efficiency. Note that packet bursting is a problem, specifically because of the carrier extension requirement.

Five product categories are expected to emerge with Gigabit Ethernet. In the order of our equipment hierarchy defined in Chapter 1, they are:

1. Gigabit Ethernet NICs

2. Gigabit Ethernet Repeaters (There are two types—CSMA/CD or half-duplex repeaters and full-duplex repeaters.)

3. Switches that aggregate Fast Ethernet between Gigabit segments

4. Switches that aggregate Gigabit segments

5. Gigabit Routers

From a network management perspective, it is important to keep a few things in mind when upgrading to or initially deploying Gigabit Ethernet:

- Ensure that any Gigabit NIC you purchase is intelligent so that your server CPU can keep up with the network. The worst thing that can happen is to have your server spend all of its time servicing the network with no time to service the applications it is running.

- Use a hierarchical Ethernet approach. Use Gigabit Ethernet at the core or to a server, Fast Ethernet to connect key servers, and subnets and Ethernet or Fast Ethernet to the desktop. Guard against oversubscription and inadequate links in backbone connections. Carefully consider sharing an Ethernet port instead of providing a dedicated Ethernet port.

- Pay attention to distance. Twenty-five meters (around 80 feet) is pretty short; don't compromise your signal by extending your connections beyond the standards.

- Stay tuned with respect to RMON at gigabit speeds. Polling switch ports that support gigabit Ethernet is also troublesome. Polling is in essence sampling; it is unclear how accurate sampling will be at these speeds. Look for more embedded management, more trap-directed polling, and less reliance on SNMP-based polling of raw data.

6.3 Gigabit Ethernet and ATM

Gigabit Ethernet is often compared head-to-head with ATM because it is the first technology that rivals both 155 Mbps and 622 Mbps connections.

Ethernet is more popular than ATM in the LAN because it has been around a lot longer. Its popularity may persist, though, because it is a lot simpler. It is estimated that about 80 percent of all desktops and servers within LANs use Ethernet.

ATM's biggest strength is that it has built-in Quality of Service (QoS). This enables ATM to offer performance guarantees when communication is established (remember, unlike other LAN technologies, ATM is connection-oriented and uses signaling to negotiate a connection with certain bandwidth requirements), making it very attractive for real time data like multimedia. ATM's QoS can be difficult and expensive to implement, and ATM is enormously complex. Just understanding ATM well enough to deploy is an undertaking.

Ethernet has no guaranteed QoS; it must rely on the layers above to provide any kind of traffic management. Ethernet allows variable-length frames (unlike fixed 53-byte ATM frames); this makes it difficult to regulate real-time flows that may get caught in the middle of a file transfer of consecutive 1500+ byte frames. Many of the topics discussed in this chapter—for example, Resource Reservation Protocol (RSVP), Class of Service (CoS), and 802.1Q and p—provide mechanisms to aid QoS across Ethernet. None of these techniques, however, permits Ethernet to provide ironclad service guarantees since it provides only a connectionless service.

Proponents of Ethernet in many ways leverage the overengineering approach to reduce possible congestion and provide comfort with respect to good response times. Remember Gigabit Ethernet is a fat pipe. It will take considerable traffic to saturate a Gigabit Ethernet link and subsequently, in most cases, overengineering will provide the low latency connections necessary to support multimedia applications over Ethernet.

Finally, Gigabit Ethernet is expected to be less expensive, by about 50 percent, than 622 Mbps ATM. This coupled with the fact that Ethernet is well understood and simple makes Gigabit Ethernet very attractive as an alternative to ATM in the LAN.

A S I D E . . .

Overengineering in this context refers to applying more technology to an anticipated problem without completely analyzing the problem space. In many cases this provides a great safety net, although you run the risk of adding technology that is not really necessary in certain areas of your network. The cost is the initial cost of the technology and maintaining the "extra" technology. Proponents of overengineering in high growth networks often believe that the gains clearly outweigh any cost.

6.4 Load Balancing

Take three double-lane highways and combine them as one, equally distributing traffic among the three highways. What do you have? *Load balancing!*

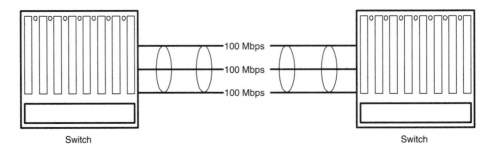

Figure 6.2 Three 100 Mbps connections treated as one 300 Mbps connection

Load balancing (or port grouping, load sharing) is treating two or more parallel network links as a single entity. Figure 6.2 shows a simple example of load balancing between two switches. Logically the combined links appear as one to such software entities as Spanning Tree Protocol (STP) or SNMP; this is especially important with STP, which by definition disables redundant ports.

Of fundamental importance to load balancing is the hashing algorithm used. The most popular technique is to distribute traffic based on Source Address, Destination Address, or both Source and Destination addresses. This preserves packet ordering and provides reasonable, though not necessarily equal, distribution of traffic. This technique is very easy to implement, although it provides no guarantees as to its "balancing" effectiveness, since it is really anything but a random-distribution algorithm.

In terms of management you should consider what happens if one or more of the links goes down, whether the load balancing must be set up statically (that is, the box must reboot to activate it), or whether a fatter pipe might be a simpler and easier-to-manage solution. For example, if you require around a 600 Mbps link, it may be a lot less painful to go with a 1000 Mbps Gigabit Ethernet connection than combining 6 Fast Ethernet connections into a group. Naturally if you need a 2000 Mbps pipe, load balancing is your solution.

A S I D E . . .

Pay careful attention to protocols like STP when using load balancing. Even though your vendor's implementation should be transparent to STP, take the time to ensure that major network trunks are not being inadvertently disabled!

6.5 Layer-2 Tagging

We're all familiar with the UPC-based destination strips airlines use to route our luggage from one city to the next. By applying a destination tag at the source airport, the luggage can automatically be sorted at luggage collection points and directed through the appropriate series of planes necessary to reach the desired destination without actually looking at the true destination address—the city to which you are headed. This happens quickly without much user intervention, without baggage "routers." In much the same way, layer-2 tagging and filtering provides a way to switch frames and quickly sort them by priority.

The current 802.1d bridge specification, which is the foundation for switching, defines a rather simple forwarding process. Recall that the bridge (switch) "learns" where destination MACs are by associating the source MAC address found within the frame header with a port on the bridge. These table entries are automatically "aged out" or deleted from the table after a certain period of time passes with no traffic from a source address seen. Likewise these table entries are refreshed (resetting the aging timer) as new traffic is seen. Static entries may also be configured and may be exempt from the aging process. 802.1Q and 802.1p build upon the 802.1d bridging foundation.

The 802.1Q and 802.1p are emerging IEEE standards, adding significant intelligence to the current 802.1d-based bridge frame forwarding process. Note that it is impossible to talk about one of the specifications without the other, so we will start with the tag header that is fundamental to both and then zoom in on the specifics of each in its own sections.

The Tag Header that is added to the frame directly after the Destination and Source MAC addresses (and routing, if present) is the fundamental component used to filter traffic. The Tag Header contains a Tag Protocol Identifier (TPID), indicating that it is a tagged frame, and Tag Control Information (TCI). Within the TCI there are the following:

- A *user priority* (a number from 0 to 8, represented in 3 bits) that designates the priority of the frame.

- A single bit *Token Ring encapsulation flag* used to designate whether the frame is in IEEE 802.5 Token Ring native format. (This flag is important in the frame translation process.)

- A *VLAN identifier* (a VLAN ID represented in 12 bits) that associates the frame with VLAN membership.

This information enables a bridge to restrict frame forwarding to ports associated with the particular VLAN ID and to prioritize traffic forwarding based on the priority value. More important, this tag is preserved between switches.

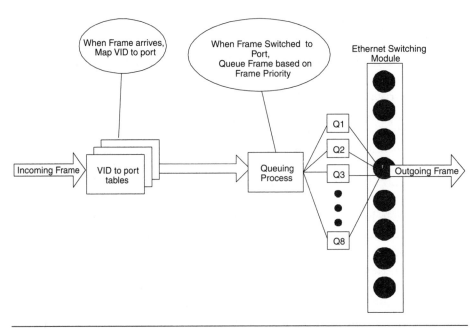

Figure 6.3 Conceptual use of 802.1Q and 802.1p VLAN and priority tagging

Even though bridging is still point-to-point, the tag adds information used to help "route" frames through the network without routing. 802.1p and 802.1Q (see Figure 6.3) are fundamental to Fast IP described in the next section.

A S I D E . . .

The 12-bit VLAN ID may be set to two special values. If it is set to 0, it implies that the Tag Header does not contain VLAN identifier information. If it is set to 1, the frame is associated with the default VLAN; the default VLAN is inclusive of all nodes.

The 802.1Q draft specification provides some nomenclature that is useful to know when talking about tagging:

- **Tagged Frame:** frames with tagging information
- **Untagged Frame:** frames without tagging information
- **VLAN-tagged frame:** frames that contain VLAN information in the tag header
- **Priority-tagged frame:** frames that contain priority information in the tag header

- **Tag-aware regions:** portions of your LAN that utilize tagging for bridging frames
- **Tag-aware bridges:** bridges that recognize and utilize tagging

It is important to realize that when you introduce new technologies into your LAN you should be prepared to deal with mixing the old with the new. Both untagged and tagged frames will be in your network, and there will be areas that leverage tagging (tag-aware regions) and new bridges (or switches) that recognize and utilize tagging. In certain cases the old and the new will coexist well; in other cases, the hybrid will cause problems such as network congestion. Be aware that often when a new technology such as this one is introduced, you have interoperability problems among various vendors' implementations. This is especially the case for tagging since there are already quite a few instances of vendors who overload the frame field for VLAN support, few (if any) of which are capable of coexisting with one another.

6.5.1 802.1Q

The focus of 802.1Q is the formalization of VLANs. Essentially, by using the VLAN, packets may be filtered to go to a particular group of destination addresses (VLAN) rather than flooded to go to the world. Group Address Resolution Protocol (GARP), defined in the 802.1p emerging standard, is used to manage group membership and to distribute group membership among the bridges (or switches) in the LAN.

The initial version of 802.1Q works over a single spanning tree even though it is conceivable that it could have a spanning tree defined per VLAN. The committee felt having a spanning tree per VLAN was overly complex and would have too much overhead associated with it. You can only imagine all the traffic generated by bridges to keep the spanning trees up-to-date! Nothing in the standard, however, precludes having multiple spanning trees in the future.

Bridges supporting 802.1Q are designated as VLAN-aware bridges. These bridges can coexist with non-VLAN-aware bridges for backwards compatibility. According to the specification, control frames addressed to higher layer entities in bridge, like Spanning Tree Bridge Protocol Data Units (BPDUs), GARP PDUs (802.1p) and other management PDUs do not go through the same filtering process. This leaves the existing management frame assumptions unchanged.

Associated with each bridge port may be a set of ingress rules (used to define which frames will be filtered when a frame enters a port) and a set of egress rules (used to define which frames will be filtered when a frame exits a port). These lists are maintained to designate VLAN membership and may be autoconfigured by using the VLAN membership resolution protocol (VMRP).

VMRP is modeled after the GARP protocol defined in 802.1p and is used by both end stations and bridges to communicate VLAN membership among neighboring bridges. A 12-bit VID (VLAN ID) is used to designate each VLAN.

A S I D E . . .

Tagging a full-length packet is one concern with 802.1Q tagging. Since tagging re-lies on adding bytes to the packet, tagging can exceed the total size of the packet. If you exceed the MTU throughout the network, packets may be dropped. Common protocols like FTP use full-length packets by default.

6.5.2 802.1p

802.1p standardizes prioritization of traffic across a LAN, which serves the need for time-critical traffic, a characteristic of multimedia. 802.1p employs frame filtering to achieve a level of QoS regarding latency, overall frame priority, and throughput. Filtering adds intelligence to the existing bridge-forwarding process by limiting frame distribution to portions of the network where there is a high probability of finding the destination rather than just flooding the frame throughout all ports.

802.1p uses GARP to communicate groupings of MACs that are associ-ated with a certain traffic priority. GARP PDUs are identified by having a unique MAC address; when a bridge receives a frame with this MAC address as the source, it knows that this is a GARP packet providing information about group membership. 802.1p also defines port modes that are associated with each bridge port. GARP is used to communicate port modes; a port may be set to one of three modes:

- **mode 1:** forward all addresses (ignore filtering database).
- **mode 2:** forward all unregistered addresses, but use group-registration entries to filter out frames to only those in the group.
- **mode 3:** filter all unregistered frames—require explicit filter to get to port.

Like entries in the bridge, forwarding table filters may be dynamically or statically configured. GARP provides automatic learning of dynamic filtering information via GARP protocol exchanges. Removal of dynamic filter informa-tion is also accomplished via GARP exchanges.

Each group has priority characteristics. Based on this priority, the frame is queued at the exit port. A bridge may have up to eight queues associated with eight traffic classes to prioritize traffic. Priorities may be as granular as on a port basis—each port may have x traffic classes numbered from 0 to N-1. It is not a requirement that all ports in a bridge have the same number of traffic classes and queues.

You can think of each switched port as having eight separate queues. As an example, high-priority traffic waits in queues 7 and 8; medium priority is in queues 5 and 6, and low-priority in the remaining queues. Traffic may be serviced by using the port in a round-robin fashion, by favoring the high-priority queues, by taking more frames from them, or by using some other algorithm. Regardless of the algorithm, higher-priority traffic on the average waits less time in the queue. By sorting traffic by priority, the switch can better service time-sensitive traffic.

There are several good examples of situations where you may want to adjust the priority of certain traffic. For example, you may want give broadcast traffic or IP multicast traffic a lower priority than IP point-to-point (unicast) traffic. Or you may decide to reduce the priority of IPX broadcast traffic or AppleTalk traffic. Traffic prioritization gives you a way to "tune" your network traffic around your corporate policies. If your corporate policy is to limit web use during the workday, you can provide some control by merely giving external IP unicast traffic a lower priority than other traffic from 9 A.M. to 5 P.M.

6.6 Layer-3 Switching

With the success of switching at the data link layer (layer 2) and routers becoming the network bottlenecks, it is no surprise that all vendors want to employ switching technology at the routing layer (layer 3). There are several creative, proprietary solutions proposed for layer-3 switching. We will focus on three solutions, two of which (IP Switching and Fast IP) are positioned for the LAN.

In essence, layer-3 switching is all about putting traffic in the fast or express lane by determining the route only on the first trip and then reusing the route over and over. Sometimes your first trip requires you to go through the city first, traffic lights (routers) slowing you down until you find a more optimal path—perhaps the subway. Sometimes the path stays intact. The essence is to leverage the speed and power of switching, not just between two streets but rather from one building in the city completely across town to another building—end-to-end.

6.6.1 IP Switching

IP Switching (a solution provided by Ipsilon Corporation) provides an alternative to routing all multihop packets. This technique converts IP packets into cells and then sends them over an ATM virtual channel that is already defined.

At the end of the channel the cells are converted back to packets and are locally switched to their final destination. This eliminates the intermediate routing decisions necessary at each hop along the way. The drawbacks of this approach are that initial setup of the virtual channel can be slow and the solution is proprietary and requires ATM in the LAN, which may not be currently employed. It is expected that this technique may lose out over the emerging standard, multiprotocol over ATM (MPOA). The advantages of this approach are that the routing decision is made once and a router table lookup is not necessary for every subsequent packet, resulting in line-speed switching of IP data.

> ## A S I D E . . .
>
> A Virtual Channel does not always have to be set up in this scheme. It is usually set up only if a "flow" has been determined to be "long lived."

6.6.2 Fast IP

Fast IP (a solution provided by 3Com) is a technique used to provide high-speed switched connections across many hops without the need to route data. Fast IP puts "routing" in the hands of end nodes or Fast IP-capable switches—"routing" is not done in the traditional sense, rather Fast IP leverages three standards: 802.1Q, 802.1p, and Next Hop Resolution Protocol (NHRP). Fast IP is best illustrated by the following example:

Let's say User A wants to accelerate data sent to User B located two hops away. An NHRP request containing the source, destination MAC (intermediate bridge as final destination is unknown), IP source and destination addresses, and frame type is sent. The NHRP data includes the source end station's MAC address (important, since the header's source address will change along the way to the destination to reflect the required point-to-point hops) and the VLAN ID. The NHRP is forwarded to the destination end system through the routers. Note that this packet obeys all the normal routing policy, for example, filtering in place between A and B. The destination returns an NHRP response using the source MAC address and VLAN ID found in the data portion of the packet and sending its MAC address so that data from the original source can use the same technique going in the other direction. Switches in between then *bridge* (switch) the data back using the MAC address if it is in the bridging table (that is, it is directly connected) or the VLAN ID if the MAC address is not found (that is, it must be switched to the next switch). Once the packet returns, subsequent data can be "switched" through multiple hops resulting in a very high-speed pipe as it does not require layer-3 routing

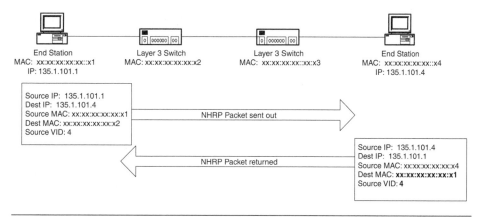

Figure 6.4 Fast IP Next Hop Resolution Protocol (NHRP)

table lookup—rather it utilizes the new features that extend traditional bridging as employed by switching with tagging. Figure 6.4 shows an example of two end stations using Fast IP.

Fast IP does not have to be used for every bit of communication; it can be triggered based on the amount of data flowing from A to B or on some other frequency measurement. Fast IP is fault tolerant in that, if a response NHRP packet is not received upon sending an NHRP request packet, communication will continue as normal. Fast IP is vunerable to GARP-based VLAN ID management working properly and VLAN ID change. If a Fast IP "connection" times out after establishment, the NHRP will have to be done again, possibly to locate another path. While this happens, nothing precludes communication to continue with the normal routed mechanisms. It would be interesting to have a count of the number of NHRP requests made over time, the frequency of "like" NHRP requests, and the number of NHRP "retries" from an end node perspective as well as an intermediate switch perspective.

6.6.3 Tag Switching

Tag switching (a solution provided by Cisco) uses tags assigned at the network edges to route packets across a WAN network. When a packet arrives at a switch, the tag is used to index into a Tag Information Base (TIB), a database of tags that is constructed and maintained by using routing protocols like OSPF. Each entry in the TIB contains an outgoing tag, an outgoing interface, and link status. If there is an exact match and the link status for the outgoing interface is okay, the packet tag is changed to the outgoing tag and pushed out the outgoing interface. This process continues through one or more switches until it comes out at the other edge. One big advantage of tag switching is protocol and media independence—it is not just an IP solution.

6.7 Traffic Management

We all know how wonderful it would be if we could schedule a space on our highway system, guaranteeing our arrival at our destination at a certain time. Sometimes leaving only 10 minutes later results in a delay of 50 minutes—clearly traffic congestion is not linear with respect to time. Commuter lanes (assuming you can find a buddy) offer some relief, but they are not a guarantee. During peak traffic hours there are often delays everywhere.

Networks, too, have peak traffic periods. There are daily peaks, weekly peaks, monthly peaks, quarterly peaks, and so on. And, with the advent of multi-media, which is not so good about "backing off" when things are congested, traffic management is becoming an even bigger problem for which we need strong networking solutions. Having your stock trade waiting on the information highway can be costly.

Traffic management is all about providing quality of service (QoS) and class of service (CoS). QoS is a term that comes from ATM (perhaps the biggest advantage of ATM); it means being able to negotiate a certain, guaranteed service quality prior to communicating. Remember, ATM is a connection-oriented protocol, so during initial setup of the connection, there is a perfect opportunity to specify exactly what kind of service is required and expected. CoS refers to sending data without guarantee but with some specification of service. We are all familiar with first, second, third, and fourth class postage rates—simply stated, CoS works the same way. First class is "better" (first class is more likely to get there sooner than second class). The big distinction is that there are no guarantees—CoS is still a best-effort service, unlike QoS, which provides a guarantee.

This isn't to say that sending something top priority CoS doesn't make a difference, however—because it will. The priority bits specified in the 802.1p specification will be used to queue traffic according to priority and to give higher-priority traffic special treatment in times of normal flow and in times of congestion. Naturally though, heterogeneous environments with a mixture of tag-aware and tag-ignorant bridges will reduce the overall service—the more homogenous the environment is with tag-aware switches, the better the service.

So, you say ATM sounds attractive with its QoS, but what's available in my Ethernet-centric best effort environment that will help guarantee my bandwidth to time critical applications? Resource Reservation Protocol (RSVP) is the emerging protocol that will mitigate delay in an "ATM-less" TCP/IP environment.

6.7.1 RSVP

RSVP is a protocol that is aimed at providing a level resource reservation across a desired communication path. It is positioned as a QoS solution for native TCP/IP LAN environments, but it cannot provide any QoS absolute guarantees because it is built upon connectionless technologies like Ethernet. RSVP requires built-in support from the following network devices across the communication path in order to work:

- **End Stations:** must use an RSVP-enabled protocol stack, for example, WinSock 2.0 described later.
- **Applications:** must employ RTP, a real-time end-to-end protocol that operates at end stations.
- **Routers or layer-3 Switches:** must support RSVP. Reservations are negotiated at each link, not end-to-end like ATM.

A big headache here for the network administrator is getting the RSVP solution installed across the LAN and managing mixed environments (non-RSVP-enabled network devices coupled with RSVP-enabled network devices). Mixed environments are inevitable whenever every device in a network path is involved in a solution. Before tackling these problems, though, it is important first to understand fundamentally how the technology works.

RSVP uses two message formats to set up and maintain a flow between two devices wishing to communicate. It is best explained by the example shown in Figure 6.5.

Device A wants to communicate with Device B. The data flow is critical and time sensitive so the application on Device A decides to use RSVP. The interface to RSVP for Device A is found in extensions to WinSock 2.0, the application's interface to the network. Using WinSock, the application on Device A sends out a "Path" message to Device B. This protocol message goes through each router (for simplicity we will assume that all routers along the way support RSVP, though tunneling through non-RSVP routers is possible). At each router, the state of the RSVP "flow" is saved in a special table. Once the RSVP Path message reaches Device B (assuming that Device B is willing to accept the flow), it sends back a "Resv" to the application on Device A. The "Resv" message goes back through the network using the same path that the "Path" message set up. Along the way each router activates the reservation, possibly debiting some resource counter for RSVP bandwidth. Once the "Resv" makes it back to the sending application, the setup is complete. Note though that the application must periodically pulse (refresh) the reservation using the "Path"/"Resv" protocol. Without these refreshes, the reservation will time out and disappear.

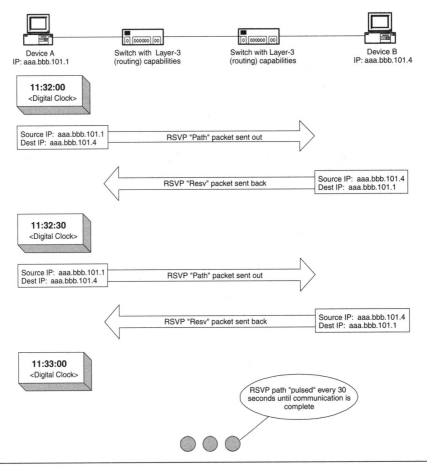

Figure 6.5 RSVP setup and subsequent flow "pulsing"

A S I D E . . .

At the date of this printing, WinSock 2.0 is a fairly new standard that really has not had a chance to "take off." Time will tell how popular the use of this new WinSock functionality, coupled with RSVP, becomes.

Following are some of the key points about RSVP from the IETF RSVP draft specification:

■ RSVP allows for resource reservations for both unicast and multicast applications. RSVP leverages subsequent reservation refresh pulsing to make adjustments for changing group membership and changing routes dynamically.

■ RSVP is receiver-oriented not sender-oriented. The receiver of a data flow initiates and maintains the resource reservation used for that flow.

■ RSVP depends upon present and future routing protocols. RSVP is not a routing protocol; it uses local routing databases to obtain routes.

■ RSVP supports transparent operation through routers that do not support it. Note though that hops through routers that do not support RSVP severely discount the reservation. A Non-RSVP flag bit is used to signal that the reservation is passing through one or more routers that do not support RSVP.

■ RSVP provides QoS for layer 3 (routing) only. It has nothing to do with tagging or prioritization at layer 2 (bridging/switching).

■ RSVP supports merging of flow specifications. Thus an application can attach to an existing flow (that is already set up). This allows RSVP to scale for very large multicast groups. Refresh messages may also be consolidated, although there is no penalty (albeit extra router processing time) for sending out too many refresh messages for a flow.

■ ResrErr and PathErr are messages used to propagate errors; RSVP "teardown" messages are used to remove path and reservation information immediately.

For RSVP management it is useful to be able to diagnose RSVP set-up failure, to know the amount of RSVP use, and to gain some yardstick of the effectiveness of RSVP. There is some interest in tracking flows for accounting purposes, that is, providing a means for charging based on bandwidth reservation services. It would be interesting to compare response times for applications that use RSVP with those that don't, especially in times of network congestion. It will take considerable experimentation to determine how effective this protocol is, where to deploy it, and how to manage it effectively.

RSVP is expected to be used in conjunction with Real-time Transport Protocol (RTP) instead of TCP. RTP (RFC 1889)

■ allows for multicast traffic (not point-to-point, as with TCP).

■ provides a way to limit the delay variation of packets.

■ includes timing information (unlike TCP and UDP) in each packet.

- provides a way to mix streams from multiple sources into a single packet stream.
- runs over UDP.

RTP has a separate control protocol, Real-Time Transport Control Protocol (RTCP). RFC 1889 indicates that RTCP will provide feedback on congestion and performance reports containing errors rates (for example, jitter, lost packets) for both senders and receivers. This will provide network managers a window into how well the RSVP system is working.

6.8 IPv6

Anyone traveling on today's United States highways knows the traffic has increased compared with a decade ago. And guess what? There's not only more traffic, but many more cars, each with its own unique vehicle identification number (VIN)—that cryptic string of 17 letters and numbers that you need to fill in on a loan application when you purchase a car or on a form when you register a car.

Network traffic, especially Internet traffic, has also realized explosive growth within the last decade. The massive movement to the WWW (which rests on the IP-based Internet) has placed great demands on the IP protocol suite. It used to be that the Internet was used only by technology companies to send mail or FTP files across the country. Not any more. Now surfing the WWW is done by many—placing scaling problems on the IP protocol suite. The IPv6 specifications (also called IPng for IP, next generation—see RFC 1726, for starters) is a response to this popularity.

IPv6 resolves many IPv4 (the current IP version) problems. Extending IPv4 addressing is the most important problem that IPv6 tackles. The IPv6 address structure also considers support for other protocol addressing, like IPX and OSI's Network Service Access Point (NSAP). The current 32-bit IP address (x.x.x.x, where x's represent decimal byte values, such as 192.168.1.43) with its hierarchical class scheme simply does not provide enough addresses to service IP's popularity. IPv6 extends the addressing to a full 128-bit representation, represented as eight 16-bit hexadecimal values consisting of four 4-bit "nibbles," each separated by colons (0:0:0:0:0:0:0:0). This provides IPv6 with $10^{**}12$ end systems and $9^{**}10$ network—very, very large numbers indeed. Just imagine 1564 addresses per every square meter on the planet earth—that's a lot of addresses! The address 0:0:0:0:0:0:0:0 is unspecified; 0:0:0:0:0:0:0:1 is a loopback address directed back to the device itself, the same as 127.0.0.1 in IPv4.

A S I D E . . .

You can use the loopback address to verify that your local IP stack is operational. Simply issue the following command:

PING 127.0.0.1

or in the case of IPv6,

PING 0:0:0:0:0:0:0:1

to verify that your stack is operational. This is one of the first tests used to diagnose a connectivity problem.

One of IPv6's biggest requirements is coexisting with existing IPv4 addresses. IPv6 accomplishes this by padding the first six hexadecimal digits as zeros, followed by the four dotted decimal digits used to represent the IP addresses, 0:0:0:0:0:0:x.x.x.x.

IPv6 supports unicast, multicast, and anycast addressing. Unicast and multicast are the same as in IPv4, packets directed to one address, or packets directed to many addresses, respectively; anycast packets go to the closest (the least number of hops) group of devices or to the closest anycast group.

It is expected that IPv6 will enable address autoconfiguration, perhaps based on the 48-bit *unique* MAC address. This is very attractive to network management, since one big problem is duplicate IP addresses, which are tough to find and create serious network havoc for the workstations and/or PCs involved.

Within the IPv6 header is a 24-bit flow label field and a 4-bit priority field. These fields are expected to be used to help optimize the internetworking of packets across multiple hops. The idea is simple—switches can route and forward packets by reading only the flow label, greatly reducing the time to make routing decisions. Likewise, the 4-bit priority field can be used to influence the queuing priority of packets; an example of use might be to give time-sensitive audio a higher priority. Use of the flow field comes with the typical problems of maintaining state information across several devices in the network: aging out stale flow labels from a table, storing many labels, not having a flow label in the table, using some protocol to refresh labels periodically, and interoperating with empty labels. The priority field is considerably simpler as it does not require state storage. It is sufficient to maintain a simple agreement that the bigger the value, the higher the packet priority. This field is expected to help prioritize packets in the state of congestion, where values of 0 to 7 indicate that the packet is resilient to congestion (can be dropped), and values of 8 to 15 would indicate that it is not (for example, multimedia data or a bank debit from your checking account). These issues are expected to be resolved prior to making IPv6 a standard.

IPv6 also includes new security features: optional headers allowing for extensibility and tunneling used to interconnect IPv4 and IPv6 devices. IPv6 also extends ICMP by incorporating many more informational messages. For example, IPv6 is specified to have group membership messages (type 130, 131, 132) to query, report, and terminate group membership; this functionality will replace similar services currently available using the Internet Group Management Protocol (IGMP) in IPv4. Also, ICMPv6 type 135 will replace the ARP protocol used within IPv4 to find out the mapping between an IP address and a MAC address.

6.9 IP Multicast

IP multicast is a methodology used to route a single IP packet to multiple destinations. It makes more efficient use of LAN bandwidth by routing a packet through the network and then, at the final destination, creating a copy of the packet for each packet subscriber. IP multicast is good for multimedia applications, such as video or audio broadcasting, as well as for transferring a single file to many locations at once. Loosely speaking you can think of this as taking a single copy of a report on a plane and, when you get to your destination, running to the photocopier to make 100 copies to distribute to 100 different people. Bringing 100 copies on the plane would be a heavy load for you (and for a network); replicating at the end of your journey is the most efficient, least-effort approach.

IP multicast distribution is based on multicast groups. Hosts subscribe to a particular application's transmissions via IGMP. An IGMP subscription indicates that the host is interested in receiving an application's transmissions. Routers keep track of these groups in the form of source/group pairs and dynamically build distribution "trees" to chart paths from each sender to all receivers. Note also that IP multicast facilitates dynamically, attaching to a data stream in progress; there is no need to synchronize subscription based on the start or stop of a data stream.

There are three IP multicast protocols designated for the LAN: Distance-Vector Multicast Routing Protocol (DVMRP), Multicast Open Shortest Path First (MOSPF), and Protocol-Independent Multicast (PIM). All three protocols are used to build the Multicast Backbone (MBONE), an experimental multicast backbone of multicast router islands that are interconnected by tunneling on top of sections of the Internet. IP multicast relies on tunneling to get through regions of a network that do not support IP multicast traffic. Essentially, a tunnel encapsulates an IP multicast packet into a unicast packet and then unencapsulates it at the other end of the tunnel. The MBONE is designed to test multicast applications before the widespread deployment of multicast routers.

DVMRP (RFC 1075) is a distance-vector protocol that uses reverse path forwarding to define the scope of its multicasting. Essentially reverse path forwarding *floods* the first datagram containing source/group pair to all leaf routers in the network. If the routers do not have any subscriptions, they return *prune* messages that reduce the scope of the multicasting required. After a designated period of time, the pruned branches grow back, giving routers the chance to add subscribers. This prune/grow back practice continues as long as the multicast flow continues. In addition to the grow back mechanism, a graft message may be sent by a leaf router if a leaf host indicates interest in an application's multicast flow. In order to maintain state, DVMRP implements its own routing table, similar to a RIP table. One management problem with DVMRP is that it does not scale well due to excessive use of flooding.

IGMP Snooping is a technique used within switched environments to mitigate the effect of multicast flooding. Essentially IGMP snooping "turns off" the flooding of switch ports (at layer 2), based on promiscuously monitoring different ports for IGMP messages. On the ports where IGMP traffic is found, IP multicast traffic is fowarded; on the ports without IGMP messages, IP multicast traffic is filtered. This greatly reduces the impact of flooding at layer 2 and hence the potential for congestion that leads to frame dropping. See Figure 6.6 for a simple example of IP multicast.

MOSPF (RFC 1584) builds off the base of the link-state protocol, OSPF, and uses the same algorithm as OSPF to determine the shortest reverse path, with the addition of the source/group pair necessary for multicast traffic. MOSPF requires lots of processing power like OSPF and is well suited for environments in which only a few source/group pairs are active. This protocol is particularly poor in environments with unstable links.

MOSPF maintains a local group database of group memberships based on IGMP monitoring. One MOSPF router on each subnet becomes the designed router; this router is solely responsible for listening for IGMP subscriptions and sending host membership reports to all other MOSPF routers. A backup designated router is also configured in the event the designated router goes down. Unlike DVMRP, MOSPF does not support tunneling.

PIM is a scaleable, multienterprise protocol that enables networks running unicast routing protocols to support IP multicast. PIM integrates with Interior Gateway Routing (IGP), Intermediate System to Intermediate System (IS-IS), OSPF, and RIP. PIM has two modes: dense mode and sparse mode. Dense mode is used for LANs where multicast groups are in proximity, and sparse mode is used for WANs where groups are widely distributed. (Since this book is about LANs, we will restrict our discussion to dense mode.) Dense

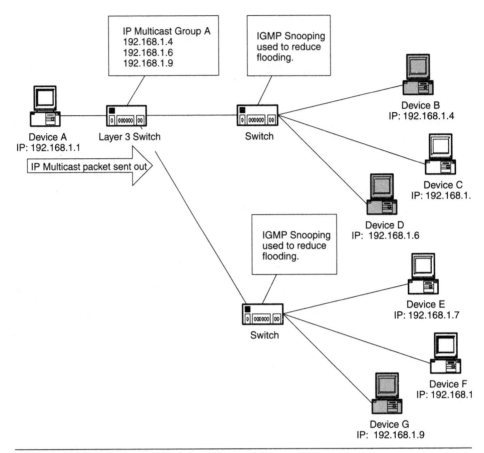

Figure 6.6 Simple example of IP multicast: "Grayed" network devices receive flow based in IGMP subscription; others do not.

mode PIM (DM-PIM) uses reverse path forward routing as used by DVMRP. DM-PIM depends on a running unicast routing protocol (OSPF or RIP in the LAN) for changes in the topology. DM-PIM relies on pruning messages to trim back its transmissions; like DVMRP, DM-PIM supports graft messages.

IP multicast will be a challenge to manage in a switched LAN. This is because it requires so many network devices to interoperate and that it (like routing) has distributed "state" information throughout the LAN. From a management standpoint it might be interesting to

- track bandwidth utilization for multicast, proving that multicast deployment is actually saving bandwidth;
- diagnose situations when users are unable to subscribe to a service, to verify the advertisement of a service, or to monitor IGMP;

- track group-creation membership adds and deletes;
- track top "N" receivers of multicast;
- perhaps limit multicast traffic, restrict multicast traffic, or charge based on subscription to multicast groups; and
- show a physical topology of multicast trees.

6.10 Summary

Our dependency on networking within the LAN and the popularity of line-speed layer-2 switching performance are clearly placing more pressure on extending the scope of switching. More data, more users, time-sensitive data, and data paths requiring routing are motivating the industry to provide fatter pipes (Gigabit Ethernet), better addressing (IPv6), tagging and prioritization protocols (802.1Q and 802.1p), ways to multiplex the same traffic to many clients (IP multicast), accelerated routing (Fast IP), and bandwidth reservation protocols (RSVP). These emerging services will allow LANs to scale to the twenty-first century as networking becomes as fundamental as electricity.

The emerging technologies place many new challenges on network management. The most significant is the need to manage your network as a system, a system that is dependent on itself. More sophisticated services are introducing many new, distributed states and tables across our network, which are dependent on the network for staying accurate. In many networks today, information spanning multiple devices is limited to routing tables and perhaps to Spanning Tree Protocol (STP) state information. We are now introducing RSVP tables, GARP tables, filtering tables, VLAN IDs, and traffic priorities—lots of information is spanning many systems. Network management's biggest challenge is to manage the many emerging technologies that span the network by being able to diagnose, verify consistency, and proactively predict network faults by viewing the network as a system (see Chapter 12), rather than as a set of independent interconnected devices.

CHAPTER 7

Managing WAN Connections

7.1 Introduction

Very few LANs exist today as islands; nearly every LAN is connected to a Wide Area Network (WAN) in some way or another.

This chapter provides the basics on managing and understanding popular WAN connections: dial-in connections, Internet connections, and connections to one or more remote sites. These links allow your network users to work remotely, surf the WWW, and have access to data and resources at remote LANs respectively.

We begin by discussing the basics of LAN-to-WAN connections. The WAN world is an entirely different world, and, after spending the last six chapters in the LAN world, it is important that we do a little bit of WAN acclimation. The discussion then proceeds with solutions for dialing into your LAN, connecting your LAN to another remote site, and providing Internet access. We conclude with a brief discussion of security since security is an important consideration to make when you add WAN exposure to your LAN.

7.2 Fundamentals

Connecting to the WAN world requires you to rely on others for services and to learn about many new technologies like modems, ISDN services, and frame relay. And even if you are not concerned about security within your LAN, the minute you connect to the Internet, you *must* be concerned about security.

With WANs come third parties. Within your LAN you have control over your cabling and interconnections, but within the WAN you have obligatory dependence on telcos (telecommunication companies, the proprietors of WAN connections). Just getting timely service from the telcos can be a challenge in itself!

With WANs come smaller pipes: Their capacity is *significantly* less than the fat pipes we are used to dealing with in switched LANs. Consider the following scenarios:

Take a typical dial-in connection. Employee X is at home and wants to check her e-mail. She connects her laptop to her 28.8 Kbps modem and then to the phone jack. The modem dials out and establishes a connection at 24 Kbps; employee X is happy because usually the line is noisy and falls back to 19.2 Kbps. While at work employee X has a dedicated 10 Mbps Ethernet connection. Her pipe remotely is 24/(10 * 100) Kbps or .024 Mbps—far less than 10 Mbps. Needless to say multimedia over a slow modem connection is not plausible.

Take an outbound connection to the WWW. Employee Y is surfing the net for the latest on Gigabit Ethernet. His place of employment has a single fractional T1 line out to the Internet. This provides employee Y with shared access to a single 64 Kbps pipe. Even if employee Y gets to work at 3:00 A.M. because he is so excited about Gigabit Ethernet developments that he wants the pipe all to himself, his access is still 64/(10*100) Kbps or .064 Mbps.

Undoubtedly you have gotten the picture that WAN connections have far more limited capacity than common switched LAN connections. Just to illustrate how much less capacity, Table 7.1 gives you some popular WAN service levels compared to a single 10 Mpbs switched Ethernet connection.

A S I D E . . .

It is often misleading simply to compare WAN and LAN utilization—that's why we limit our comparison to capacity. On a LAN with light traffic, utilization can hover around 1 percent; a heavily loaded LAN may be near 20 percent, but it rarely exceeds 30–40 percent. It is the bursts of traffic characteristic of networks that test your WAN link and make a low-capacity WAN link appear much slower that a LAN connection.

With WANs come tariffs. Based on the chart, T1, T3, E-1, E-2, and E-3 connections appear to be pretty good options—and they are. The telcos think so, too, especially in regard to fattening their bank accounts. WAN connections are expensive, and the larger the pipe, the bigger the bill. A T1 connection spanning the United States may cost several thousands of dollars monthly. T3 connections are exponentially more expensive.

E-1, E-2, and E-3 service levels will add significantly to your expense budget. Since WAN resources are expensive, they must be treated as a very precious resource to your LAN.

Table 7.1 WAN Service Levels

WAN Service Level	Speed (Mbps)	%Ethernet (10Mbps)
28.8 Kbps (modem)	.0288	.288
56 Kbps[1] (ISDN B Channel) (Fractional T1 (FT1), single channel DS-0)	.056	.56
64 Kpbs (FT1, single channel)	.064	.64
112 Kpbs (ISDN 2B Channels)	.128	1.28
256 Kpbs (Frame Relay)	.256	2.56
1.54 Mpbs (T1)	1.54	15
44.736 Mbps (T3)	~44.7	447
2.048 Mpbs (E-1, European Signal Level 1)	~2	20
8.448 Mpbs (E-2, European Signal Level 2)	~8.4	84
34.368 Mpbs (E-3, European Signal Level 3)	~34.4	344

With WANs come many different management considerations:

If you are providing *dial-in access* to your network, be aware that certain protocols are not particularly resilient to propagation delays. For example, if you have an employee who is remote in Europe and is attempting to read his e-mail, which uses the IPX protocol, the link may fail if it goes via satellite because of propagation delay with satellite communication. IP-based or AppleTalk-based connections tend to be less sensitive to propagation delays such as those introduced by satellite communications. In short, IPX and WANs do not mix well; TCP/IP presents the fewest obstacles to remote access.

If you are *connecting two sites* across a WAN span, you usually do not want to bridge. Fundamental to layer-2 protocols like NetBIOS or NetBEUI that cannot be routed is the fact that they generate lots of broadcast traffic—this traffic goes across your bridge. In addition Novell's IPX is quite

---

1.Technically ISDN and Fractional T1 can be either 56 or 64 Kbps.

chatty. Since WAN bandwidth is such a precious resource, the last thing you want to pay for is lots of LAN broadcast traffic. Routers (and layer-3 switches) operate at layer 3 and do not typically transmit broadcast traffic. Typically you use routers to connect over the WAN. In the future the broadcasting containment featured in VLANs may provide a WAN bridging solution.

Last, if you are providing *Internet access* into your LAN, you will want to focus on security. Your Internet access must be designed to optimize around security and access with the use of firewalls and filters. The last thing you want is for your LAN to be vulnerable to the attack of an outside hacker who has nothing better to do.

The following sections deal with on-demand connections, multiple-site connections, and Internet access. It is hoped that this information will provide you with a minimal basis for management of your links to the WAN.

7.3 Popular On-demand Connections Options

There are two popular mechanisms to getting into your LAN on an ad hoc basis: use of a basic modem connection and use of an ISDN connection. Terminal emulation and remote control are two other on-demand techniques used, but they are not nearly so popular.

A S I D E . . .

By "ad hoc" we mean "temporarily," like access from an employee's home or a traveling employee's hotel room. These connections are often transient and move around a lot. ISDN connections tend to be more permanent than modem connections; ad hoc connections are in contrast to permanent (or dedicated) connections, such as a dedicated link between two sites.

A n o t h e r   A S I D E . . .

Both serial line interface protocol (SLIP) and point-to-point protocol (PPP) are used to transmit IP packets over dial-up or leased lines. PPP is the protocol of choice as it is about 40 percent more efficient than its predecessor, SLIP. PPP is able to encapsulate many different protocols, such as IP, IPX, and AppleTalk; this feature makes it suitable for environments that run many different network layer protocols. PPP also supports a mechanism to assign an IP address automatically; this feature allows a user to connect easily into your LAN from any point.

7.3.1 Modem Dial-up

Typically modem dial-up is used by employees who are traveling or connecting from home. Another use might be to provide an occasional, relatively slow, point-to-point from a remote site. Modem dial-up provides a flexible, on-demand way to get in and provide an extension to your LAN. Remote users want to be on the LAN, that is, to be able to perform tasks as if they were physically there. The classic example is the user of IP services. He wants to be able to Telnet into other nodes, run an IP-based mail service, and, if this user is a network manager, run some SNMP-based tools remotely over UDP. Dial-in IP is facilitated by the PPP protocol. So let's go through how it all works.

Your remote user X plugs her laptop with her 33.6 Kbps modem into the data link jack at her hotel. Prior to her trip she configured her machine with a special IP address and appropriate subnet mask to be used for remote dial up. To ensure the modem worked correctly, she tested out the configuration and modem while on site and ironed out all the kinks.

The modem dials out to the 800 line provided to your LAN. The 800 phone number is "picked" (redirected) by the phone company to a trunk line that supports many simultaneous calls. At this point, the telco will do one of two things depending on the size of your company:

- If your company is large, you will probably have a PBX. In this case the telco will dial into your PBX with one of your local numbers, and your PBX will provide a hunt group to convert the one number into direct inward dial (DID) or an extension that connects it to a free modem. The term *hunt group,* used as the connection, must sequentially go from modem to modem (each address with a separate DID or extension) until it finds one that is free.

- If your company is small, you will probably not have a PBX, and the local telco will provide the hunt group functionality, trying each of the modems with its DID until it finds one that is free or, if all modems are in use, returns a busy signal to the caller. As another alternative, you might configure a remote access service/server (RAS) on a Windows/NT server and use it directly.

After some "hunting" it is detected that modem four is free. The two modems go through their screeching protocol. Because the lines are noisy and the modem pool is a bunch of 28.8 Kbps modems, the connection falls back to 19.2 Kbps. (It is not uncommon for the line to fall back, especially with the noisy lines characteristic of rural areas.) A connection is established. Your user X is prompted to dial in to the network with her password, and then she is on the LAN.

Transparent to the user is the fact that each of your modems in your modem pool is connected via a serial link to an Ethernet port within a remote access server (RAS). The RAS does the data-link conversions necessary and provides the concentration point for all the Ethernet connections, rolling up all possible connections to a single, say 10 Mbps, Ethernet port that is connected to the LAN. Why such a "small" pipe? Do the math. One Kbps equals .001 Mbps, and 24 connections at a maximum of 28.8 Kbps is .6912 Mbps ((28.8 * .001) * 24), a fraction of the 10 Mbps Ethernet connection.

Figures 7.1 and 7.2 illustrate the dial-in connections for both a large and a small company.

7.3.2 ISDN

ISDN is another increasingly popular way to connect to your LAN from afar. ISDN is not nearly so portable. I don't think I've ever been at a hotel with an ISDN option, but this may be an option in the future. What's the big plus for ISDN? Speed and the ability to send both voice and data traffic at the same time. ISDN is also a good backup for dedicated connections (such as a frame relay link, discussed later in this chapter).

ISDN requires a special network termination (NT1) device that connects both to the ISDN line provided by your telco and to your laptop. If you use a straight network termination device, you will also need an ISDN interface for your computer. Many ISDN devices now include an Ethernet connection, allowing you to use your Ethernet adapter directly.

ISDN in the United States comes in two service options:

- A basic rate interface (BRI) provides two B-64 Kpbs lines and one D-16 Kpbs control line; this is a total of 144 Kpbs, five times the capacity of a 28.8 Kpbs line. (Note that long distance B lines often connect at 56 Kpbs.) This is typically the option used by work-at-home employees or at remote sites requiring only low bandwidth.

- A primary rate interface (PRI) provides twenty-three B-64 Kpbs lines and one D-64 Kpbs control line; this is often how a LAN site may service multiple remote ISDN users coming in at the basic rate. PRI is really "transported" on a T1 or E1 (International) line. When you order the line, you must specify whether you want a PRI-T1 or a PRI-E1 line. (We will talk more about T1 and E1 later.)

In order to set up a BRI with ISDN, you need to be *loop qualified.* Loop qualification is being no more than approximately three cable miles (18,000 feet) from the central ISDN site provided by your local telco. After three cable

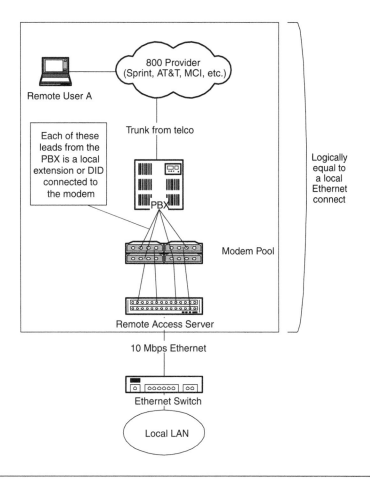

Figure 7.1 Equipment involved in a dial-in connection (large company)

miles, the signal degrades significantly. At the central ISDN site your connection goes into the ISDN network cloud and comes out the other end to connect with your LAN.

At your LAN site, ISDN typically (assuming you have a PRI connection) connects from the telco box—the connection point managed by your telco is called a data service unit (DSU)—to a channel service unit (CSU) to a router. The channel switch unit converts the frames into a signal suitable for the telco and vice versa for the router. The framing and line coding within the CSU and the router must match.

To the user, an ISDN connection looks like a digital pipe remotely pro-

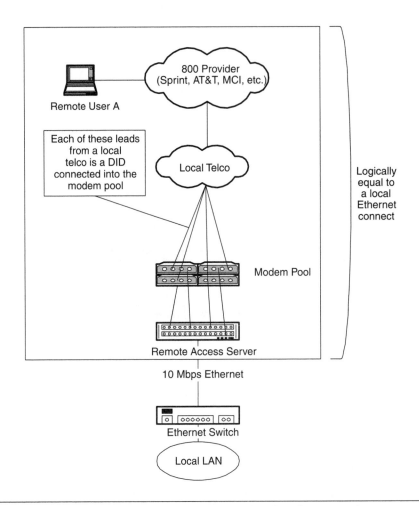

Figure 7.2 Equipment involved in a dial-in connection (small company)

viding full LAN access. Except for picking up printouts from remote LAN printers, ISDN leaves the remote user in pretty good shape. The B channels operate like a full-duplex 64 Kpbs (or 56 Kpbs) line. Connection to the LAN from remote goes through a process similar to that of modem connections, although much faster—only 2 to 3 seconds. This is why ISDN provides an attractive fallback connection for other technologies. Typically a connection starts out at 64 Kpbs (or 56 Kpbs) and then, if needed and available, another B channel is established. This conserves primary interfaces and reduces the overall tariff of the connection.

7.3.3 ISDN and CAPI 2.0

CAPI 2.0 is an API developed by German ISDN board vendors to access ISDN services in a unified way from DOS, OS/2, UNIX, Windows 3.x, Windows/NT, or Windows/95. This standard was approved in 1995 by the European Telecommunications Standards Institute (ETSI). ISDN has become a very popular option in the European market, and CAPI 2.0 is expected further ISDN penetration. ISDN may even displace the current telephone service in Europe.

A S I D E . . .

One small tip with CAPI 2.0: Like other network cards that you plug in, it is a good idea to get drivers that are known to work with the board's manufacturer; drivers are usually shipped with hardware.

A n o t h e r   A S I D E . . .

ISDN in Europe is much different than in the United States. Go to `http://www.acotec.de` or `http://www.stollmann.de` for more information on ISDN and CAPI 2.0.

7.3.4 Terminal Emulation and Remote Control

Terminal emulation and remote control are two other techniques for on-demand WAN communications. Neither of these techniques is very popular as they only provide connectivity in a very limited way.

Terminal emulation enables you to connect to a remote node as if you were local—communication is facilitated by piping screen updates back to you. It wasn't too bad in the old UNIX shell days when all you had to deal with was character-cell graphics. Today, though, the utility of this technique breaks down disproportionally as you start running graphical, bandwidth-intensive applications.

Remote-control access enables you to dial in to a LAN and seize control of a PC. This is useful if you are trying to diagnose a problem remotely, but it is not advantageous if you want to attach to the LAN remotely. With remote control access you tie up both PCs and must use a interface different than your typical Ethernet attachment to the LAN.

7.4 Key On-demand Management Issues

There are three key areas you need to manage with respect to on-demand connections: configuration, faults, security, and configuration. Oops! I put "configuration" there twice because that's where most of the management lies.

7.4.1 On-demand Configuration

Assuming you're using IP, you have to assign and maintain a pool of separate IP PPP addresses. Make certain that your remote users can connect by inspecting their machines—correct IP address, subnet mask, Domain Name System (DNS) server address, and default route and do a test run on site by connecting via an analog line at your site.

If you provide ISDN, make certain that you configure the speed on your Basic Rate Interfaces (BRIs) appropriately. Typically the speed is 56 Kpbs for long distance calls, although 64 Kpbs is an option on many BRIs. A speed mismatch can prevent a call from going through.

With outbound ISDN or modem connections, make certain that you configure your automatic dialer correctly. Each dialer must be configured with the phone number of the remote PRI or the remote modem. Sometimes you must configure each B channel with a phone number.

Make certain that your ISDN framing and line coding match between Channel Service Unit (CSU) and router.

You must correctly configure your network type (given to you by your telco) in your remote ISDN equipment. Optionally your telco may use Service Profile IDs (SPIDs) and Directory Numbers (DNs); these too must be correctly set up in your remote ISDN equipment. Misconfiguration of these parameters is a common source of failure.

7.4.2 On-demand Faults

Periodically check that modem dial-up and your ISDN connections are working at your LAN. Check that all of your modems are working. The following example illustrates a problem that may have been eliminated by some additional preventive maintenance:

We set up dial-in access with pool of 28.8 Kbps modems and did a test of a few connections; everything worked very well. Two weeks later a problem that a user could not get into the facility was reported. We did a test of a few connections—worked great—worst kind of problem—intermittent. It turns out that the problem was that modem number 8 within the modem pool was not operational. So for one to seven users, things worked great. When number 8 tried to dial in, the dead modem was reached, causing the hunt group to assign number 8 to an inoperable modem to which the user could not connect.

If possible, set up faults such as the Ethernet port going down to trigger the pager of a network manager. Nothing is worse than getting a call from an irate employee at 2 A.M. because a user has been trying to get in all evening without luck. If you know *immediately* when the port goes down, you can fix it and perhaps get a good night's sleep. That is where MIB-2 variables like sysLocation, which you may want to include in the automatic page, come in handy.

Finally, if you have set up the rest of your network so that it is operational if the power goes out (that is, installed Uninterruptable Power Supply—UPS—in all your backbone routers), add a UPS to your remote access server. Unfortunately having a UPS in your remote access server, if the rest of the network is down, is not particularly useful. However, making your local power hit transparent to your remote users is a nice thing to do.

7.4.3 On-demand Security

You don't want just anyone dialing into your LAN, so protect it by requiring a dial-in password. Don't use a global password—customize for each user by using a special remote-access password or by reusing an existing one, such as the one used to attach into your Novell network.

7.5 Popular Dedicated Connection Options

Dedicated connections are typically used to link your LAN to another LAN across the WAN or to provide a link to the Internet. To make these connections, you need a router that is capable of Remote Access—note there are many types of routers, and remote access is a special breed. Remote Access Routers come with all of the security and firewall features you need to protect your LAN. When you have private connections to one or more sites across a WAN, you have what is often referred to as an *Intranet*—a private corporate network. There are two options for dedicated WAN connections: use of dedicated point-to-point leased lines or use of cloud technologies.

The advantage of point-to-point leased lines is that they are private and are not shared with other users. The disadvantage is that they offer only point-to-point links. If you have lots of points to connect, you have lots of lines to lease. For short distances (less than 1,000 miles), they are often cheaper than

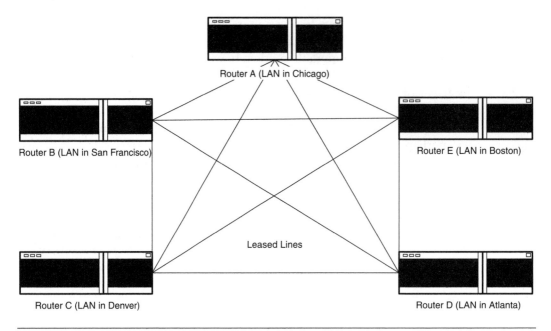

Figure 7.3 Ten leased-line connections necessary to connect five remote sites fully

using cloud technologies. Figure 7.3 illustrates the use of leased lines to connect multiple sites.

Cloud technologies are shared WAN technologies that allow you to connect from multiple points without separate leased lines. For long distances (more than 1,000 miles), cloud technologies are often cheaper than leased lines. Use of cloud technologies is more popular when you have many sites to connect because of the flexibility clouds provide. Figure 7.4 provides a visual example of cloud technologies.

Regardless of whether you use dedicated leased lines or cloud technologies, they both use the same popular connections to connect you to your point at the other end or into the cloud: T1, T3, or fractional T1. A T1 line provides twenty-four 64 Kbps channels or 1.544 Mbps (rounded up to the standard) total bandwidth. A fractional T1 line is a 64 Kbps incremental chunk of a T1 line, anywhere from 64 Kpbs to 1.472 Mpbs (23/24s of a T1). The telco simply divides a T1 among several different customers.

A T3 is twenty-eight T1 lines or 45 Mbps (1.536 Mbps * 28, rounded up to the standard). For a WAN connection this is considered to be a pretty fat pipe and comes with a pretty fat monthly lease of several thousand dollars.

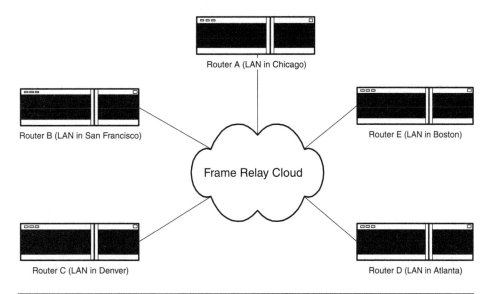

Figure 7.4 Five connections to a frame relay cloud necessary to connect five remote sites fully (Frame relay is explained in the next section.)

There are three cloud services:

- X.25 (the granddaddy)
- Frame Relay (X.25 on steroids)
- ATM (emerging as a data channel)

7.5.1 X.25

Although no longer widely used in the United States, X.25 retains popularity in Europe. X.25 provides a packet-switching data network with data rates up to 64 Kbps. Packet switching is common in WANs—essentially data in packet switched networks are accepted from many sources and divided up into packets. X.25 has lots of error detection and recovery built in. For example, packets are reassembled at each hop, verified for errors, and then passed along.

X.25, like other packet switching, is often represented as a cloud. This is because X.25 provides the specifications at the connection points to the network but not the network itself; what happens in the networking cloud is transparent to the user. As long as the service at the endpoints matches, X.25 or other packet-switching technologies may be used by the telco to provide the service. Table 7.2 shows the advantages and disadvantages of X.25.

Table 7.2 X.25 Advantages and Disadvantages

X.25 Advantages	X.25 Disadvantages
Since it is internationally deployed, in many cases only WAN technology is available. It is popular in Europe.	The maximum rate is a slow 56 Kbps, making it unsuitable for voice or video; data rates are better served by frame relay.
Built-in error correction, flow control, retransmission of lost packets, make it highly reliable, and good for connections that span large distances over noisy lines.	There is high latency. Because packets are reassembled at each node along the way, packet throughput is low, and packet delay is high.

7.5.2 Frame Relay

Frame relay service (FRS) is a widely deployed data-only service that scales with the granularity of a T1 line—from 56 Kbps to 1.544 Mbps. When you set up your frame relay connection with your telco you define a committed information rate (CIR), a committed burst rate (CBR), and sometimes an excess burst size (EBS). The CIR is the guaranteed average data rate that you need, and CBR is the maximum number of bits that can be transmitted over a time interval. So if you select a CIR of 256 Kbps and a CBS of 1024 Kbps, you are guaranteed to be able to transmit 1024 Kbps of data over a 4-second period. (T= CBS/CIR => 4 = 1024/256). This guarantee is a worst case scenario when the network is congested. If the network is not congested, the EBS comes into play. Given an EBS of 512, you would be able to transmit 1536 (1024 + 512) Kbps more during the same time period. You should add a little fluff when specifying both the CIR and CBS for your frame relay connection. A good rule of thumb is to round up by about 10 percent.

The tariff for frame relay is directly related to the distance the link must go and the bandwidth. Generally speaking the bigger the pipe and the longer the distance, the larger the cost. Telcos vary as to how they charge for your frame relay connection. Some carriers base the entire charge on usage; others offer a CIR at a fixed monthly fee. Table 7.3 shows the advantages and disadvantages of frame relay.

Table 7.3 Frame Relay Advantages and Disadvantages

Frame Relay Disadvantages	**Frame Relay Disadvantages**
Frame relay is very fast, taking advantage of the cleaner signals in today's wide area connections by reducing error checking. Latency at intermediate nodes is far less than X.25.	There is an optional bit that may be set within a packet indicating that a packet may be dropped when the frame relay cloud is congested. Unfortunately it is rarely used. Subsequently frame relay is susceptible to congestion problems.
Variable-size frames work with any LAN packet, for example, TCP/IP, Ethernet, Token Ring MAC, or even an X.25 packet. Frame relay thus provides transparency to the user.	There are no special provisions for time-sensitive real-time traffic such as voice or video.
Frame relay provides bandwidth on demand, allowing you to exceed bandwidth to accommodate bursts.	Reduced error checking results in retransmissions when lines are noisy.

7.5.3 ATM

Although privately deployed by the telcos, ATM-based Cell Relay Service (CRS) is not yet publicly available. When available, CRS will utilize T1, T3, and fiber-based lines. An interesting thing about ATM is that it can provide end-to-end communications from LAN to WAN to LAN with ATM attributes like multimedia and quality of service (QoS). ATM is expected to provide much larger pipes, pipes that far exceed the T1 limit of Frame Relay.

7.6 Key Dedicated-Connection Management Issues

Since dedicated connections across the WAN are often mission critical, it is important that they are carefully managed. Figure 7.5 depicts two management stations that are managing a connection across the United States. It is critical to this WAN connection, or your own connection over lines that you do not own, that you work well with your telcos.

The initial setup and maintenance of your leased lines and services lie

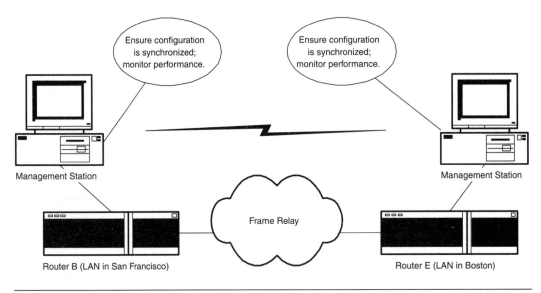

Figure 7.5 Two management stations managing each side of a WAN connection

within the hands of telcos. In fact, once the signal leaves your site at one LAN, your entire management scheme is in the hands of the telco until the signal reaches the other side. And the longer the haul you go with your connection, the more individual telcos you may have to deal with. The following advice is recommended:

- **Diversify:** Select more than one telco to provide service. If one relationship or service goes bad you have a backup.

- **Create redundant links:** For example, if your frame relay link goes down, have an automatic fall over to an ISDN line as a back up. Plan for temporary outages.

- **Plan Ahead:** It can take considerable time to get a connection operational. Plan accordingly.

- **Monitor your pipe:** Monitor each end of the pipe from opposite ends. Ensure that you have reachability from A to B by pinging B from A; and from B to A by pinging A from B. A simple "cron" job (a UNIX job scheduled to execute at periodic intervals) that automatically does a ping to the opposite end will do the trick. Monitor latency as well as connectivity. Generally speaking for PPP expect a latency of 10 milliseconds for each 1,000 miles for a T1 line. Benchmark your connection, and track the latency over time. If the link is slow or down, automatically dispatch an alert to a pager or to mail.

- **Monitor routing changes:** You will probably be using the open shortest path first (OSPF) routing protocol on the WAN to minimize the traffic on the WAN; Routing Information Protocol (RIP) is much chattier. Regardless, ping key backbone nodes beyond the end point from the opposite end—this will help ensure that routes are maintained properly.

- **Set up a WAN administration protocol:** Since changes across the WAN network need to be synchronized at both ends, set up some formal change-order process for orchestrating changes. Included should be the synchronized time of change, a detailed description of the change, and some sign-off mechanism from all parties regarding the change.

- **Synchronize your speeds:** Having a T3 at one end to send data to a T1 at the other is going to result in lots of dropped packets. It sounds trivial, but make certain that you understand and keep track of the pipe sizes at both ends.

- **Monitor your pipe utilization:** Monitor your pipe utilization at both ends. Plan accordingly for capacity expansion or reduction.

- **Consider traffic prioritization schemes:** If you have high utilization, you may consider a prioritization scheme for different types of traffic. For example, the recent introduction of WWW browsers has generated a lot of TCP/IP traffic; you may want to limit TCP/IP to only a certain percentage of your pipe so that SNMP management or IPX gets some bandwidth. Or perhaps you have too much FTP traffic. Many routers allow you to prioritize your traffic based on traffic type.

- **Consider using a RMON probe to monitor traffic flows:** Since your WAN tariff is based on usage, use RMON2 to ensure that WAN usage is appropriate. The RMON historical tables will help you track statistics over time. It is expected that as network use continues to increase, particularly with respect to expensive WAN use, a key network management need will be around network accounting. An application to track network use and provide each network user with a "network bill" based on locality of use, WAN (long distance), LAN (local), or extended LAN use, RMON2 has all the data for this type application.

7.7 Security

Once you open the door to the Internet you *must* concern yourself with network security. Security management is *not* a one-shot deal; you must continuously be concerned about security and devote time and energy to refining and plugging security holes. The last thing you can afford is to have the integrity of your network compromised by some network hacker or by a competitor. The following are examples of ways that hackers will attempt to penetrate your network:

- **IP tunneling:** IP tunneling refers to encrypting IP packets within IP packets. The outer IP packet makes it through your security. Once inside, the router strips off the outer header and passes along the unsecured IP packet within. You may want to explicitly disallow packets that use IP tunneling.

- **IP spoofing:** IP spoofing refers to passing along an IP packet from the external network with a source network address found within your LAN. Because this address is local, it is hoped that it will pass through your packet inspection process. You need to keep track of the direction in which packets are flowing. IP spoofing is really only a concern via an interface like the Internet since dial-up users are validated via passwording and are really just an extension to your internal network.

- **IP fragmentation:** One IP feature is that it allows packets to be fragmented. With fragmentation of large packets the source/destination information is only in the first packet. If you allow these types of packets through, you need to maintain context with these packets until they complete transmission. With contrived fragmentation resulting in very small packets, the IP header may span multiple packets. It is recommended that these packets are simply dropped.

- **IP source routing:** IP has a feature allowing packets that contain their routing information. This information is used to route the packets, rather than making routing decisions at the router. If a packet can define its own flow, it can go around your security. It is recommended that IP source-routed packets be explicitly dropped.

- **Illegitimate UDP packets:** UDP packets (remember SNMP uses UDP) can be problematic. The problem is not the packets that are sent out, but the packets that come back. Since UDP by design does not retain context, there is no way to detect whether the packets coming in are legitimate or not. A "source" UDP packet will not retain the same port number as the "destination" UDP response; this subjects you to port forgery and bad packets destined to your network.

Although it may seem ultraconservative, many LAN administrators choose to turn off UDP traffic on their connection to the Internet. Some LAN administrators may disable UDP for dial-in users. Beware though, since UDP is the underpinnings of many other protocols, turning off UDP comes with a lot of consequences, for example, NFS-mounted file systems will not work and you will not receive all DNS updates. If you choose to disable UDP for dial-in users, make certain your remote users are aware of their dial-in limitations. One policy is to be more restrictive for connections coming directly in from the Internet than for those that are direct-dial and password-protected—especially since you may want to dial in and run a SNMP-based application yourself!

The first thing to note is that security for each of the three common ways you connect to the WAN (modem/ISDN dial-up access, Internet access, and remote site access) needs to be handled differently. Generally speaking traffic to and from your remote site requires more relaxed security than traffic out to the Internet. Figure 7.6 shows an unprotected local LAN. Don't let your LAN be or become unprotected!

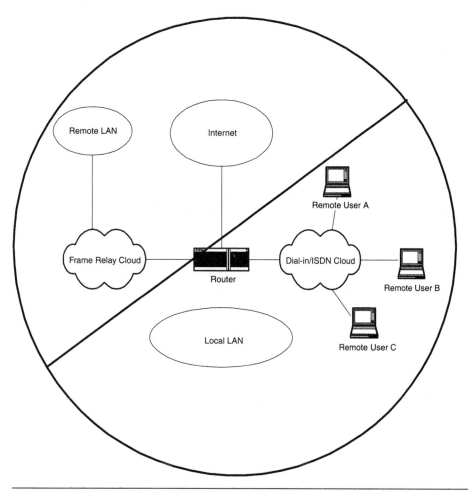

Figure 7.6 Basic WAN connections into a LAN *without* local LAN security

ASIDE . . .

Hacks into your network are often insiders or ex-employees. Shut down all access to your network when an employee leaves.

7.7.1 Dial-In/ISDN Traffic Considerations

It is important that all access into your LAN go through a managed point in your network and is user ID/password protected. Use of modems within your LAN should be restricted to your modem pool; a modem in an employee's office that doesn't use your firewall comprises your security. One easy way to restrict modem use is to use a PBX within your building and make analog lines very sparsely distributed.

7.7.2 Internet Traffic Considerations

Data flowing to and from the Internet require the tightest security. Unlike dial-up that can be password restricted, Internet traffic can travel without validation. The following are some considerations you should make with respect to Internet traffic:

- All Internet traffic must pass through a filter so that it can be inspected. Traffic that does not pass inspection must be dropped.

- Most Internet firewalls do *not* protect against viruses found within files that come from the Internet; viruses are at the application level, not at the transport level at which firewalls work. It is important for your network users to recognize this fact and be cautious of any foreign files.

- SNMP, traceroute, whois, ping, finger, and telnet should not pass your firewall into your LAN from the Internet. All these tools provide access to proprietary network information that can be used to learn and attack your network.

7.7.3 LAN to External LAN Considerations

It would seem that LAN-to-LAN connections, which privately connect different parts of your own organization (that is, provides your Intranet), probably requires the most relaxed security—not so! As a general rule, anything in your LAN that connects with a foreign source (something you do not personally manage) is suspect to break in. You must protect all connections going into your LAN in order to maintain your LAN's integrity. Always keep in mind the three As of security: authentication, authorization, and accounting.

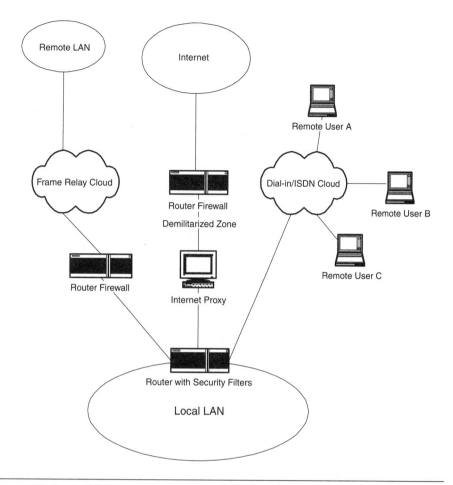

Figure 7.7 Basic WAN connections into a LAN *with* WAN security

7.7.4 One Approach to Security

Figure 7.7 illustrates a solution to the three common WAN connections. Use or adapt it to fit your needs.

The first line of defense is the packet-filtering router to the Internet. Each packet that flows to and from the Internet passes through a series of filters. There are two strategies to filtering: deny certain packets or define explicitly which packets pass through filtering.

The first strategy leaves you vulnerable to the unorthodox use of protocols. Remember TCP indicates that the common use of Telnet is via the well-known port, 23—it does not require this. This strategy also requires that you explicitly know up front what to filter out—you may not, until security is compromised.

The second strategy is defensive and recommended; packets that are not explicitly recognized are dropped. You open up your network as needed and as required. Such a strategy prevents surprises but, depending on the size of your filter, may slow down your traffic. It is felt that security wins out over speed in this case. Note that the order of filtering matters from a performance point of view; you should filter based on most likely to least likely. That way many packets will be filtered out early on without the need to pass through all the filter tests, which take time to process.

Traffic that passes the first line of defense is in the Demilitarized Zone. This traffic can use certain well-known servers like FTP, but it must pass through a proxy server to get to your LAN. The proxy server is used to screen all traffic bidirectionally. For example, if an employee on your LAN wishes to Telnet to a node on the Internet, the proxy server actually establishes the Telnet session and monitors data to and from the employee's workstation.

If you are a bit skittish about setting up your own firewall to the Internet, consider letting your Internet Service Provider (ISP) do the firewalling for you. Most ISPs have many options, including firewalling, and are very willing to create a customized solution for you. Note that there are many fine books on security; consult the bibliography for more information.

Note also the firewall between your LANs—this protects against foreign objects coming in from the cables you do not own. This is often overlooked, but it is a very important part of your security scheme. To save money, you may want to go through the same router as your Internet connection—this scheme provides more flexibility.

7.8 Summary

Connecting to the WAN opens up the door to a whole new set of challenges for the network manager. New services (dial-in, remote access), new technologies (Frame Relay, ISDN), and new requirements (for example, increased security, WAN bandwidth allocation) all have to be understood, deployed, and managed.

Ideally your network users want their distributed Intranet to be transparent. Regardless whether a server exists locally or at a remote site, the user wants 7 * 24 (all day, every day), fast access. Access to the WWW and the Internet is becoming a critical part of the way business is being done. Being able to dial up from anywhere and the establishment of higher-speed ISDN lines are now expected.

Perhaps, though, the most challenging part of WAN management is dealing with the third parties, the telcos of the world. Because telcos manage the connectivity between ends of your WAN pipe, you are heavily dependent on them. This requires lots of advanced planning, vendor diversification, and establishment of fallback and redundant links.

PART THREE

Building a Switched LAN Management System

CHAPTER 8

Troubleshooting Problems in Your Switched LAN

8.1 Introduction

Thus far we have

- built a firm grasp of what network management is and what the key standards are,
- developed a solid understanding of what the components of a switched LAN are,
- constructed a good base of the layer-2 and layer-3 technologies, and
- identified many of the problems associated with switched LANs.

It is now time to *apply* what we have learned to real network management troubleshooting.

This is the first of two chapters that use the knowledge base we have developed to solve real network-management problems. We start by clearly defining "reactive" and "proactive" management, since these are important methodologies that you will use to keep your network healthy. We then define the techniques that are useful for problem solving and talk a bit about layer-1 problems that may be the cause of many of the problems you will encounter. We conclude by building the problem inventory that we will apply in the next chapter to solve some classic problems. This inventory should serve as a base for your own *custom* problem inventory.

Before we begin, there are a few caveats:

- First, I have been careful not to repeat the problems and tips identified in Chapters 1–7. Rather, this chapter attempts to put the knowledge base into context, keeping the book light by avoiding repetition.
- Second, the approach tries to take advantage of the same techniques used to solve engineering problems. We tend to look at problems from many views: from the bottom up and from the top down. We even put

things on a pedestal that can be whirled around to give us a look at the sides. My approach is clearly different than what I've seen presented in the field of network management: Bear with me; I think you will find it effective.

Sound good? Then let's get started . . .

8.2 Proactive versus Reactive Management

Reactive management is really an euphemism for fire fighting. The network is down, a user cannot get to a server, the president of the company cannot read his or her e-mail. You get the idea. There's no time for coffee; you and your team need to jump on the problem immediately.

Proactive management refers to monitoring your network to anticipate and resolve problems *before* they turn into a fire. This is ideally where you want to spend the majority of your time. Proactive management prepares you well for the fires, enables you to plan your network, and gives you a little time for a cup of coffee now and then. Proactive management involves

- monitoring the state of your network by collecting MIB objects and using your vendor-provided network management tools;

- keeping statistics over time and generating reports that give you an idea as to how your network is doing and when it is time to upgrade network devices on your LAN; and

- maintaining configuration records and scripts that make it easy to recover when problems arise, enabling rollback to a known state, or setting up a replacement switch quickly and accurately.

Note that some fire fighting is inevitable; the goal, however, is to minimize the flames and thus keep you sane and better able to provide consistent quality for your network subscribers.

A S I D E   .   .   .

It is often good to keep some spare equipment (for example, a backup switch, an assortment of cables, or an extra concentrator) in the event of failure. Naturally how much you keep depends both on your network size and on your budget. A good rule of thumb is to keep one spare of every individual component you use to build your switched LAN.

8.3 Troubleshooting Techniques

Before we get going on understanding how to resolve the "classic" problems in the next chapter, we need to learn the tricks of the trade of network management—the techniques that will help you identify and resolve networking problems quickly.

8.3.1 Physical and Logical Visualization

Let's face it, LANs tend to become big and rely on many components and software entities to function properly. It is absolutely imperative that you are able to visualize your network and construct a simple diagram containing each of the physical and logical components that make up your network. In fact, the first thing you need to do to solve a connectivity problem is to create a simple diagram (either mentally or on paper) that represents each of the key physical and logical components of your problem space. If you are lucky, your problem space will be only a small subset of your network; if you are not, as with some network brownouts, your entire LAN (or a significant portion thereof) will need to be considered or examined in the diagnosis.

Software can help quite a bit, but it doesn't always provide enough granularity. All the network-management platforms provide autodiscovery of your network, and many vendors provide ways to inventory your network-device configurations. Obviously, automatic and software-driven map generators are better—they save you time (networks change frequently) and reduce human error (but they sometimes introduce software errors).

You must keep your image of your LAN up-to-date as much as possible. Networks are spread out and change frequently—often it is a single change or a combination of changes that is the root of a problem. Users add network devices on their own without your knowledge and change configurations without your consent. The more accurate and detailed your picture is, the faster you will zoom in on solutions and be able to reduce your problem queue. Sometimes you will have to fill in details that have changed from your previous network snapshot. This updating obviously will slow you down and make you vulnerable to the chicken-and-the-egg syndrome. If the network is broken and you are relying on the network to get your information, you are in trouble.

What should you care about? How much detail do you need? Unfortunately you need to know a lot. Often it is the one detail that you don't know that is the root of the problem.

From a *physical* side you need to care about the following:

- **All internal devices:** switches, layer-3 switches, routers, bridges, hubs/concentrators, repeaters, NICs, workstations/PCs/Apples, file servers, and printers

- **All cabling:** multimode fiber, single-mode fiber, UTP/STP, and legacy coaxial cable

- **All device connectors:** all intermediate cable splicing/connectors

- **All physical proximities and conditions:** cable locations, cable lengths, device locations, power sources, and environmental conditions (temperature/humidity)

From a *logical* side you should care about the following:

- **All software versions, network address(es), vendor/model/versions of boards running on all devices**

- **All device configurations:** switch, hub, and router configurations

A S I D E . . .

Maintaining up-to-date network device configurations for a large network can be difficult. Prioritize accuracy of backbone network devices.

- **All underlying protocols:** Ethernet, Fast Ethernet, FDDI, Token Ring, ATM LANE, Gigabit Ethernet across each link in your physical picture

- **Use of Bridging/Switching and Bridging protocols (STP)**

- **Use of Routing and Routing protocols:** RIP/OSPF, IPX RIP, ATRP, DVMRP, PIM, MOSPF

- **Use of DHCP or BOOTP**

- **Use of local IP addressing, local MAC addressing**

- **Use of NOSs and versions:** AppleTalk, NetWare, TCP/IP, NetBIOS

- **Use of VLANs:** composition and membership

- **Use of File Servers:** location and protocols in use

- **Use of Printers:** location and queue implementations

- **Use of network application software:** mail, client/server applications, databases, NFS, and so on.

Figure 8.1 shows an example of a LAN calling out some key management details.

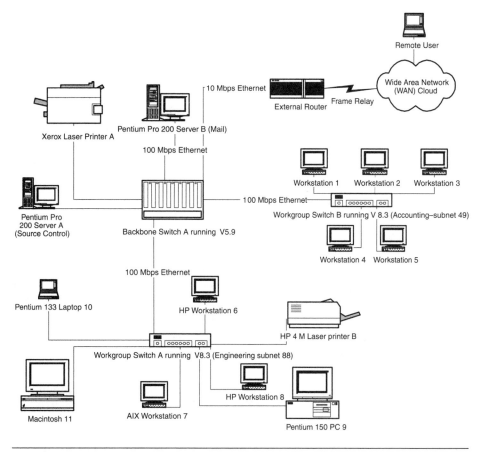

Figure 8.1 Example of switched LAN picture with some detail

8.3.1.1 Background Network Processes

Now that we have a picture of our LAN and a corresponding inventory, we need to think about the background network processes that are going on, with or without network user activity. I define *background network processes* as the set of events that happens on a normal basis that keeps internal network-device tables up-to-date and the set of exception events that happens when something goes awry. Often these processes are network dependent. For example, in order to keep the routing tables synchronized, periodic routing updates across the network are made. These processes include the things that happen behind the scenes, automatically, that keep your network in an operational state.

Events (traps) that notify you when there may be trouble brewing are also included.

8.3.1.2 Network Control Processes

Network control processes are the processes that use your network and device caches to keep the devices in your network synchronized and hence keep your network operating smoothly. Obviously the normal network control processes that happen on your network depend on the physical outlay of your network (now would be a good time to take out your masterpiece picture) and the configuration that you have imposed. Note that one of the most effective ways to validate and identify many of your normal processes is to put a protocol analyzer or probe on your network at various points and then notice the frames and patterns of frames going by. It is best to do this exercise when traffic is minimal so you are not sifting through user traffic to observe your network-control traffic. Another way is to use a MIB browser and dump out your routing and bridging tables.

Let's apply what we learned in the first part of the book and go through some examples of what network control processes to expect. Suppose you have:

- Multiple Layer-3 Switch/Routers in the network.
  - Expect some periodic routing updates to happen—separate updates for each protocol that is routed (IPX, AT, IP). Intervals may be set; default intervals are 30 or 60 seconds.
  - Normally expect static configuration that you set up in your routers and switches to be intact at network device reboot. Sometimes though, even a simple power outage may corrupt flash RAM contents, so don't always assume that static configuration will be preserved. Have your backup ready.
  - Expect router tables to converge quickly, like a router or a route going down or a router coming up as network conditions happen.
  - Expect routes to age out of the routing table(s); expect routing tables to be sufficiently large to store routes without constantly needing to overwrite entries due to lack of space.
- Multiple Switches (Layer 2) in network.
  - If Spanning Tree Protocol (STP) is configured (must be on all switches and bridges that participate in the spanning tree separately; usually means all your switches and bridges), expect periodic BPDUs to be broadcast to prevent bridge loops and dynamically to "open up" redundant paths as needed.

- Single or Multiple Switches (Layer 2) in network.
  - Expect bridges to maintain a forwarding table, to age things out appropriately, to reverse learn new MACs when communication happens, and to have sufficiently large tables so that entries are not constantly "aged out" prematurely.
- Network Servers.
  - Expect periodic SAP traffic from Novell File Servers, printers, and NetWare processes.
  - Expect periodic NetBEUI traffic from Windows/NT File Server(s) and Windows Clients.
- PCs, workstations, Apples boot up for the day or reboot during the day.
  - Ensure that these end stations can secure their network addresses and populate their local routing caches.

The point is that there are many normal traffic flows that you should expect on your network, even without any users! Your network uses the network *itself* to stay consistent. This is why it is so critical that the physical links stay intact and that updates happen quickly and efficiently without the backlash of a storm. A broadcast storm, ZIP storm, or excessive RIP or IPX RIP updates can prevent updates and subsequently cause network failure. Figure 8.2 shows a sample collection of notes for a LAN.

8.3.1.3 Exception Events

Exception events are events that do not happen on the same periodic intervals. These are events that signal network failure. Examples include the following:

- Links go down.
  - Trigger SNMP traps to management station(s); management signifies segments of network as unreachable.
  - Routing table updates.
  - Switches "age out" devices from forwarding tables.
  - With STP switches/bridges, BPDUs open up standby connections.
- Links come up.
  - Trigger SNMP traps to management station(s); management signifies segments of network as reachable.
  - Routing table updates.
  - Switches learn new devices in forwarding tables as they communicate.
  - New service traffic SAPs; NetBEUI commences if servers come online with link establishment.

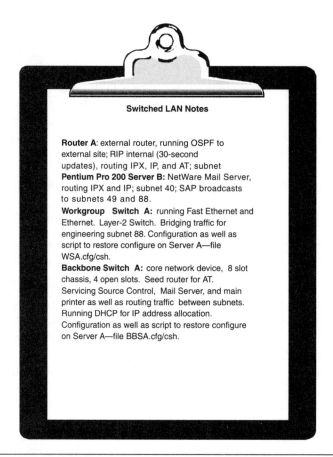

Switched LAN Notes

Router A: external router, running OSPF to external site; RIP internal (30-second updates), routing IPX, IP, and AT; subnet
Pentium Pro 200 Server B: NetWare Mail Server, routing IPX and IP; subnet 40; SAP broadcasts to subnets 49 and 88.
Workgroup Switch A: running Fast Ethernet and Ethernet. Layer-2 Switch. Bridging traffic for engineering subnet 88. Configuration as well as script to restore configure on Server A—file WSA.cfg/csh.
Backbone Switch A: core network device, 8 slot chassis, 4 open slots. Seed router for AT. Servicing Source Control, Mail Server, and main printer as well as routing traffic between subnets. Running DHCP for IP address allocation. Configuration as well as script to restore configure on Server A—file BBSA.cfg/csh.

Figure 8.2 Sample detailed notes about the switched LAN shown in Figure 8.1 (Choose a spreadsheet format if you have a large network.)

- Power outages; power comes back on.
  - Multiple link ups/down as defined previously; remaining network attempts to stabilize.
- Technology-specific events.
  - FDDI/Token Ring beaconing, technology traps indicative of failure.
  - Backbone device traps from switches and routers.
  - Various network logs are populated with exception events (also normal events).
- Proliferation of routing updates, broadcast traffic.
  - One or more devices are flooding your network with useless traffic.

If you are fortunate, you will receive an exception event that gives you immediate notice of network failure, helping you "get on" the problem(s) immediately. There are many unimportant events that trigger traps; it is important that you tune your notification to the correct set of events so that you are not spending lots of time filtering out what is unimportant. Unfortunately, you will often need to sift through events since it is the composite of multiple events across your network that is indicative of the real problem.

8.3.2 Divide-and-Conquer

The next technique to master is problem isolation. You have the big picture; now you need to reduce the size of the picture and test various assumptions along the way. Be prepared to reduce and reduce again based on your probing. Often a test will indicate that other network components besides the one you are focused on should be considered in order to resolve a problem.

Divide-and-conquer is the most powerful technique you will use to solve networking problems. With this technique you methodically reduce the problem space by making various assumptions and tests that disprove certain possibilities. *It is just as important to determine what the problem isn't—this is key and fundamental to converging on what the problem is.* Often by simply going through a process of elimination of what the problem isn't, you will discover what the problem is, even if you have never encountered the problem before. Figure 8.3 illustrates the process of eliminating possible problems.

Once you solve a problem, take the time to document the problem and its solution in your problem-tracking database (see the following section). That way someone else may benefit from your solution if the same or a similar problem occurs. Frequently occurring problems should be looked at carefully to see if there is a more permanent solution. For example, say you discover that a static route is missing from your IP routing table. You add the route, and everything is fine—until the next day. You again add the route and then look further. You discover that every night there is a process that loads a stale router configuration down to the router without the recently defined static route. You save the configuration and update the stale router configuration used by the process so the problem does not recur.

Let's take a connectivity problem from A to B. The first things we need to do are to find out the exact path through which A connects to B and to rid our big picture of extraneous devices and paths—that is, to reduce the scope of the problem. Then we need to validate the path (each hop) along the way from both ends. If it is difficult to get to each end, we might start in the middle and along the way look at the various routing and bridging tables in our switches and routers. Often use of substitution is useful. For example, can device C connect to B? If I use an alternate cable, does the connection work?

Figure 8.3 Network manager eliminating problem possibilities

By reducing the scope of the problem, we are able to narrow down the root of the problem.

8.3.3 Baselining

There is no substitute for knowing what is "normal." This is especially important when diagnosing perceived "performance" problems, such as when a user reports that the network is slow. Often maintaining simple ping-based response times for various connections gives you an indication that a link is not normal.

In addition to baselining performance, it is important that you keep accurate baselines of your network-device configurations, especially for your backbone switches and routers. You need to be able to roll back to a previous "working" configuration and/or software level in the event that problems are caused by a new configuration. In addition, you need to be able to compare and contrast two configurations in order to identify changes that cause problems.

Baselining is also useful for trending and forecasting when you have "outgrown" your network. By keeping accurate samplings of each switch port's utilization, you can determine when you need to reconfigure or add or replace equipment.

Like other records, the more automated you can keep your baselining, the better. Ideally you would like management software to help you significantly with baselining and even to predict pending failures, required network changes, or performance problems.

8.3.4 Plan of Action

Keeping an accurate plan of action is essential in keeping your network operational. Defining one (and maintaining it) keeps you keen on:

- what can go wrong,
- what your action will be,
- who will perform the action, and
- what preventive maintenance is necessary.

It is important that you be defensive with respect to your network devices. You should assume that

- every network device will fail at some point.
- each port on a network device may fail at some point.
- you will lose the configuration of each network device at some point and need to rebuild it.

A good way to keep your network downtime to a minimum is to construct a comprehensive plan of action with a game of "What if?" What if network device xyz turns into a boat anchor (a dramatic way to say "useless piece of iron")? What if cable 123 breaks? What if utilization at this point in the network exceeded a certain threshold? You need to be prepared for the worst and know precisely what you or your team's action will be in the inevitable event of failure. You can also use your "what if?" matrix to track when you must change your network design to accommodate growth. Ideally you can set thresholds across your network to help trigger immediate problems (failure) and growth opportunities that send you to your "what if?" matrix.

Take the time to construct a "what if?" matrix for critical network components as shown in Table 8.1

Your "what if?" matrix will reduce your overall response time to problems. There is nothing worse than having to scramble because you are not prepared for an emergency. And when you do have to scramble on certain unanticipated problems, take the time to add these to your "what if?" matrix for the next time they occur.

8.3.5 Problem-Tracking Database

It is imperative that you establish and maintain a problem-tracking database. Problems have a way of recurring, and often a simple search in a well-maintained problem-tracking database may give you the clues and information necessary to solve a new problem that is reported. In addition, if certain problems occur frequently, you many want to take some preventive measures or in-

Table 8.1 "What If? Matrix

What if?	Action
Device xyz fails?	Substitute spare device xyz2.
Cable 123 fails to work?	Substitute alternate cable 124; diagnose which cable fails. If not repairable, mark as bad and add to list of down cables to be replaced when cabling is done.

vestigate employing a new technology that will reduce future problems. Converting from static IP address assignment to DHCP is an example of a technology upgrade that may save you many headaches caused by duplicate IP addresses, incorrect subset masks, and default routers.

Your database should include an entry for each problem and a way to search. A web solution is ideal for logging problems as it is so accessible from many locations. There are many good search engines on the web that can give you ideas as to what kind of search solution you need for your own problem database. Ideally you will find a help-desk solution that enables you to create and maintain your problem-tracking database and allows you to tie the database in with the rest of your management solution.

Figure 8.4 is a sample entry containing some of the information that will be useful to help you troubleshoot future problems.

8.4 Layer-1 Basics

In earlier chapters we covered in great detail the data-link and network layers, layers 2 and 3. These are fundamental to switching and routing and hence paramount to effective management. Although not specific to switching or routing, layer 1 (physical connectivity) is also critical to keeping your network operational; without operational cabling you do not have a working network.

A S I D E . . .

To lighten things up a bit, I offer a garden-hose analogy for cabling. I think you will find it effective in helping to remember the rules of cabling.

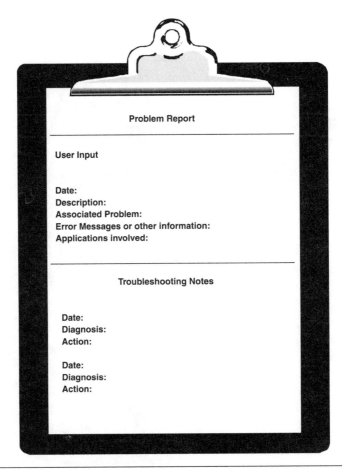

Figure 8.4 Sample contents of each entry in problem database

I have devised ten basic rules for cabling. These rules apply to new cabling that you might do or existing cabling that you already depend on.

Figure 8.5 illustrates a pile of garden hoses that are out-of-control. Don't let your cabling get out-of-control.

Ten Basic Rules to Cabling

1. Use high-quality connectors and cable. Don't skimp on cable! Don't use cable that has not been certified. Plan for expansion—overcable.

   Remember that $2.99 garden hose you bought at a discount store? Remember how it leaked on both ends and froze stiffly in colder months? *Likewise inexpensive networking cable is not the place to save money.*

Figure 8.5 Garden hoses out-of-control

2. If you can avoid it, don't mix cable types—multimode to single-mode fiber, Cat 5 to Cat 3 UTP, and so on. In many cases it will work, in some it will not, and in others it will be the source of an intermittent failure.

Remember when you connected two different brands of garden hose together to reach the garden and the connector leaked incessantly? *Consistency is good.*

3. Mark cables at each end. Use color coding judiciously as there are only so many distinguishable colors. Consider UPC-based marking.

Remember when you set up for the last drought with your "network" of water hoses? Remember when you tried to instruct your neighbor on what was attached to what—and you got pretty wet? *Know what cable connects to what by marking each ahead of time.*

4. Keep track of distance. Distance matters! Pay attention to the standards that were discussed in Chapter 3.

   Remember when you strung together four 100-foot hoses to water your neighbor's shrub? Remember how bad the water pressure was? Protocols like Ethernet are particularly sensitive to distance. *Don't risk intermittent failure by trying to stretch the limits of the standards.*

5. Be neat! Create sensible fiber bends that conform to standards, and guard your cables—avoid dangerous installation places like across the floor.

   We all know how embarrassing it is to have company trip over your garden hose. Likewise getting wet because of a tangled web of hosing isn't always fun. *Don't leave your network vulnerable to sloppy installations.*

6. Avoid excessive intermediate connections between cable end points. Remember there are limits to the number of repeaters that you may daisy chain together and still run Ethernet successfully.

   How many times can you splice a hose and still keep the sprinklers going? You hypothesize as you discover leaks at every connector and cable splice. *Daisy chaining makes your life difficult as a network manager. Avoid it.*

7. Avoid excessive connectors and the overuse of patch panels. Not only are these difficult to trace in the event of problems, but each connector introduces potential network problems: total disconnect, intermittent connector failure, or network noise.

   It is no fun tracing a hose 100 feet through a convoluted web to determine that you're just 10 feet from your starting location. *Don't turn your cabling into an adventure games. Your colleagues will become very angry with you.*

8. Use connectors only in places you can get to. A connector that fails under 12 feet of concrete will put the cables it connects out of service. Typically building codes disallow connectors that are inaccessible.

   Recall the huge spigot in an out-of-reach place—like on the house behind the mound of garden equipment and a very prickly shrub? *Don't make network cable maintenance an adventure game.*

9. If possible, locate cables in areas that are somewhat accessible. If you can choose a drop ceiling over a concrete floor, pick the concrete floor—just kidding!

   Recall the neighbor who buried her garden hoses for aesthetics only to find our they leaked excessively the next spring after the water inside froze during the winter. *Hiding cables can be a bad idea!*

10. Test cables when they are easy to get to.

It is much easier to verify a 100-foot hose close to the house spigot than 100 feet away. *Verify that your cables work prior to installation.*

8.4.1 Media Types

There are basically three media types used in switched LANs:

1. *Coaxial Cable:* Both 10b2 (10 Mpbs base 2) and 10b5 (10 Mbps base 5) for Ethernet.
2. *UTP/STP:* Unshield/Shielded Twisted Pair, 10bT (10 Mbps base T), and 100bT (100 Mbps base T).
3. *Multimode and Single-mode fiber:* 10bFL (10 Mbps base FL), 100bFL (100 Mbps base FL), FDDI, and ATM.

UTP/STP and multimode fiber dominate switched LANs and new installations; this is due largely to cost and ease of installation. Although very popular in the 1980s, coaxial cable is still quite expensive and not nearly as easy to maintain (early installations often lack the nice modular plugs provided by UTP/STP and multimode fiber). Use of single-mode fiber is more difficult to work with than multimode, is significantly more expensive, and is really intended for longer distances than characteristic of most LAN installations. For completeness we will discuss common problems associated with each type of medium.

8.4.1.1 Layer 1 (Connection) Problems

Before we get into media specifics, let's identify the generic media problems and possible causes. See Table 8.2.

8.4.1.2 Coaxial Cable

In terms of problems, coaxial cable's biggest weakness is connecting to the cable. Historically, connecting to coaxial cable required cutting the cable and installing connections and a tap to the device you were connecting. There was a lot of room for error in this manual process. Then modular terminators and other connection options as well as the vampire plug became available. Vampire plugs allow you to attach to a cable by drilling into the cable to a certain depth and attaching the plug without breaking the cable.

Table 8.2 Generic Media Problems

Symptom	Possible Cause	Action
• Sudden connection failure	Loose connector, connector goes bad.	Identify bad connector and replace.
• No link status • Unreachable devices	Bad connector, loose connector, kink or break in cable.	Identify bad connector and/or cable and replace.
• Signal attenuation • Late collisions with Ethernet • Irregular error patterns • Lots of errors (for example, excessive collisions with Ethernet) • Intermittent failure	Exceeding distance restrictions, loose connector.	• Reduce distance or insert a device (e.g. repeater, concentrator) in cable length to make two lengths within distance restrictions. • Verify all connectors are attached firmly.

Aside from the modular connectors, the other manual connection options are prone to error. Drilling too deeply or too shallowly into the cable can cause your vampire-connected device, as well as the rest of the network devices on the cable, to fail. Loose connectors are also problematic. The worst part about coaxial cable connections is intermittent failures or failures introduced when an inadvertent tug on the cable is made.

A S I D E . . .

There is an inexpensive plastic device that will prevent vampire connections that are too shallow or too deep. Buy the device if you use vampire connections to connect into your coaxial cable.

If you are stuck with coaxial cable, minimize the manual connection points and maximize the modular connectors. Be on the lookout for generic symptoms with respect to connections. Do new installations with fiber and STP/UTP (save your extra coaxial cable for your cable-TV connection), and migrate to fiber and STP/UTP as possible.

8.4.1.3 STP/UTP

No doubt STP and UTP are less problematic than coaxial cable and a lot less expensive to install. Nonetheless, be on the lookout for the basic problems, including the following unique problem:

- Cross talk by pin misassignment. Wires 1 and 2 should go with pins 1 and 2; wires 3 and 4 should go with 3 and 4. Inadvertent assignment of wires 1 and 2 with pins 1 and 3 and wires 3 and 4 with pins 2 and 4 will result in cross talk. Be aware of this if you install your own jacks.

As new higher-speed technologies such as Gigabit Ethernet emerge and more installations require Fast Ethernet, existing STP/UTP installations may be challenged. We all know that attempting to run Fast Ethernet over anything less than two pairs of Category 5 or four pairs of Category 3 or 4 will cause problems. Now there is another alternative called *enhanced Category 5,* which is supposedly better suited for higher speeds. Category 6 is also emerging as an international standard. The point is to take new installations very seriously since cabling is expensive and often difficult to redo. Overcable and install the best quality you can to ensure you have a strong upgrade path as new higher-speed technologies emerge.

8.4.1.4 Fiber

Multimode fiber is pretty easy to use and now is nearly as pliable as STP/UTP. Single-mode is much more sensitive to bending and poor splicing. Even with multimode though, if you can get by without doing your own splicing, do. There are problems that are unique to fiber.

- If you are running FDDI and are leveraging the fault tolerance of both paths, you must remember to connect A to B and B to A with FDDI to prevent a ring wrap.
- As said previously, with splicing come problems; avoid splicing.
- Although fiber has become much more pliable over the years, it is more sensitive to bends than copper. Remember light travels through the cable, not through electric signals.
- Multimode fiber is much more sensitive to distance restrictions than single-mode fiber.

8.4.2 Cascading Ethernet

Generally speaking it is not great practice to *cascade* Ethernet in a switched environment. By cascading we mean having several layers of repeaters or hubs between your end stations and your switched port (see Figure 8.6). I recom-

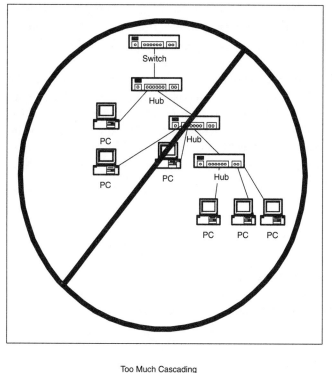

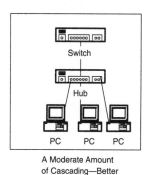

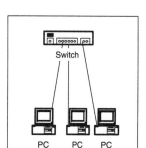

Figure 8.6 Three scenarios showing too much cascading, a moderate amount of cascading, no cascading

mend keeping things very flat; never use more than one hub or repeater per switched segment. This means to "fan out" a segment in only one place (or not at all if you can afford a dedicated connection for each end station). This will save you management headaches associated with disconnected cables, loose connections, and signal problems.

8.5 Problem Inventory

When diagnosing problems, it is useful to have a previously built inventory of potential problems. Your problem inventory complements your problem-tracking database. Your problem-tracking database provides records of actual problems your network has encountered; your problem inventory contains potential or possible problems you *might* encounter. Often it turns problem determination into multiple choice rather than fill-in-the-blank, and we all know that multiple choice is easier.

Tables 8.3 to 8.10 present a problem inventory organized by layer. This can be used as a "starter" for your own "customized" inventory. Since each switched network is customized for its installation, you will probably want to take the time to organize your problem inventory to suit your LAN. Typically you will not be alerted of security problems. You must, however, proactively manage security as negligence can compromise your network. For emphasis only, I include Table 8.11.

Table 8.3 General Link-Layer Protocol Problems

Symptom	Possible Layer-2 Cause (generic problems)	Action
• Sudden connection failure	• Duplicate MAC comes online. • Loose connector.	• Identify device with duplicate MAC and disable. • Use protocol analyzer to find, or use other tool that monitors bridge-table changes over time. • Verify connector integrity at all connection points.
• No link status • Unreachable devices	• Intermediate device (for example, switch, concentrator) goes down. • Intermediate device rebooted with changed (invalid) configuration.	• Locate device and reboot, or or simply plug in. • Restore configuration.

Table 8.4 Ethernet Problems

Symptom	Possible Layer-2 Cause (Ethernet problems)	Action
• Poor or denigrated performance	• Lots of noise. • High rate of collisions. • High rate of bad packets (runts). • High rate of FCS errors. • High utilization.	• Locate cable and switched port and user(s) or server with problem. If many users are attached or utilization is high, consider moving them to another port. • Verify cable integrity.

Table 8.5 FDDI Problems

Symptom	Possible Layer-2 Cause (FDDI problems)	Action
• Poor or denigrated performance	• High rate of link errors • High utilization.	• Locate cable and switched port and user(s), server, or other network device with problem. If many users or other network devices are attached or utilization is high, consider moving some users or network devices to another port.
• Excessive beaconing	• Any of FDDI errors defined in Chapter 3	• Locate cable and switched port and user(s) or server with problem. • Beacon should give you the upstream neighbor, which should help you narrow down to the culprit. Replace cable or NIC, or switch connector to another port.
• Poor performance • High error rates	• Distance between stations exceeds 500 meters (multimedia fiber). • Loose connector. • Poor signal.	• Validate cable lengths, connector integrity.

Table 8.6 Token Ring Problems

Symptom	Possible Layer-2 Cause (Token Ring problems)	Action
• Burst error • Line errors	• Hardware problem (bad cable, NIC, or MAU).	• Isolate faulty component(s) and replace.
• Failure to log into ring	• Duplicate MAC.	• Reassign MAC, or use vendor defaults that are unique.
• Poor or denigrated performance	• Excessive token errors, beaconing, or other soft errors.	• Recall all recent changes, monitor utilization, reduce number of stations on ring, and monitor percentage of NetBIOS and IPX SAP packets.
• Ring failure • Excessive beaconing	• Mismatch of ring speed among stations, switches, bridges, or routers.	• Verify ring speed matches on each ring. (Note it is okay to have different speeds on different rings defined by different bridge ports. You cannot, however, mix speeds on the same ring.)

Table 8.7 ATM LANE Problems

Symptom	Possible Layer-2 Cause (ATM LANE problems)	Action
• Sudden connection failure	• Misconfigured VLAN • Inability for device to access BUS.	• Isolate and fix configuration problem. • Dump out VLAN tables or use management application to determine VLAN membership.
• Poor or denigrated performance	• High error rates.	• Monitor error rates and replace any faulty hardware. • Compare performance to baseline and adjacent systems.

Table 8.8 Layer-2 Switching Problems

Symptom	Possible Switching (Layer-2) Cause	Action
• No connection	• Invalid filter installed at port. For example, filtering out UDP traffic will prevent a large majority of IP traffic. • Invalid or misconfigured layer-2 VLAN. • Bridge or switch is down. • Port disabled.	• Verify filters at all ports affecting station. • Dump out VLAN tables, or use management application to determine VLAN membership. • Reboot bridge or switch if down. • Enable port.
• Sudden loss of connection	• Learning mode in switch turned off. • Loose or bad connector at switch. • Port inadvertently disabled.	• Verify learning mode is on. • Verify link status at switched port and at all intermediate connections in between.
• Intermittent connection problems • Network performance problems	• Lots of switch or bridge cascading resulting in lots of timeouts. • Broadcast storm. • Bridge loop. • Lots of dropped packets. • Address table always full. • Excessive broadcast/ multicast traffic.	• Monitor timeouts. Draw accurate picture of configuration, and eliminate one or more intermediate switches if possible. • Monitor network for broadcast storm. • Isolate and detect bridge loop, consider spanning tree, or ensure spanning tree is turned on across all switches. • Verify that switch is not dropping excessive number of packets. • Verify that switch is not aging out entries prematurely due to consistently full bridge table. • Monitor amount of broadcast/multicast traffic, set thresholds for alarming or cutting off traffic to alert of potential storm.

Table 8.9 Layer-3 Routing Problems

Symptom	Possible Layer 3 Cause (Layer-3 switch/routing problems)	Action
• Connection for one or more systems suddenly fails	• Invalid router configuration caused by recent reboot. • Invalid end-node configuration.	• Verify router configuration and restore previous configuration if necessary • If using TCP/IP and not DHCP, validate network mask, default route, name server, and unique IP address at all network devices involved in failure.
• Poor or denigrated performance	• Excessive router table updating. • Misconfigured routers. • Excessive rerouting.	• Monitor routing updates; verify tables are of adequate size and timers for updates are consistent and long enough; verify routes are set up efficiently based on physical topology. • Monitor routing error rates.
• No Connection	• Router inactive. • Invalid filters. • Routes get aged out of table or are inadvertently removed.	• Verify router is up and operational. • Verify all filters through which connection passes. • Verify protocol required is active. • Ensure that your configuration of static routes is intact and consistent across your network.

Table 8.10 Miscellaneous Problems

Symptom	Possible Layer-3 Cause (Layer-3 switch/routing problems)	Action
• Failure of printer to work	• Out of paper. • Not plugged in. • Offline. • Toner low. • Jammed. • Queue is plugged. • Inadvertently disconnected from network	• Verify printer is not displaying error messsage; if so, correct problem. • Verify queue is not hanging on error. Often a queued file that has format problems or is requesting different paper sizes will stall the queue for all printing. • Plug into network.
• Failure of network application to work	• Distributed server portion of application has failed or is not running. • Application is misconfigured. • One or more servers (DNS, NetWare, and so on) are no longer operational.	• Verify server portion of application is operational. Restart if necessary. • Verify configuration of application. Pay particular attention around addressing information. • Sometimes rebooting client solves problem. • Verify all servers are operational.

Table 8.11 Security Problems

Symptom	Possible Security Cause	Action
Wrong devices have access to wrong data.	• Invalid firewall. • Invalid filtering. • Misconfigured VLANs.	• Verify all security measures periodically. • Spot check access periodically.

8.6 Summary

Effective LAN troubleshooting, problem-resolution exercises, and key problem-solving skills include the following:

- visualization (both physical and logical)
- baselining and record keeping
- divide-and-conquer

In addition, it is critical that you maintain an understanding and accountability of the network processes that keep your network operational. Routing table updates, spanning tree updates, service advertisements, and VLAN table synchronization are a few of the processes that are dependent on the network. If these processes fail or get out of control (for example, ZIP or broadcast storm), they can disable network service and in extreme cases might even bring your network down.

Over the next few years we will see an increase in the amount of logical content in LANs. We see this already with the introduction of VLANs. Ensuring that you have a physical connection is no longer sufficient to ensuring connectivity. This phenomenon further underscores the importance of being able to visualize your network from a logical as well as a physical standpoint, and the dependency on management tools that help us do this.

Troubleshooting problems in your LAN can be difficult. The trick is to stay *ahead* of many emerging problems by monitoring your network and maintaining good records and reports so that you can extinguish potential problems before they become fires. Proactive management can and will reduce reactive management.

CHAPTER 9

Troubleshooting Common Network Problems

9.1 Introduction

This chapter is about troubleshooting the problems that consume the majority of your troubleshooting time. These problems are general in nature but comprehensive in scope. The step-by-step diagnostics presented are applicable to both switched and traditional LANs. It is hoped that by going through common problem scenarios you will gain an understanding as to how to define and solve other problems that are unique to your own network.

We start by identifying the classic problems that will consume a fair amount of your time as a network manager. We then identify a key set of techniques for resolving problems and conclude by going through each of our classic problems and applying the techniques.

Unlike other chapters in this book, it is important that we begin this chapter with a small caveat: *We do not want to get too prescriptive about problem solving*. Although this chapter walks through typical scenarios and goes through step-by-step diagnostics for solving specific problems, you should not view these techniques as the only ways to arrive at a solution or as a 100 percent guarantee for a solution. Rather, you should look at these scenarios as examples of how to isolate and resolve problems in your own network. Do not underestimate the importance of problem isolation as the key to keeping your network fully operational. Once you effectively isolate a problem, the solution will often follow.

9.2 Your Challenge: Keeping Ahead of the Classic Problems

What's the first thing you expect when you pick up the telephone and put your ear to the receiver? A dial tone—correct? What about when you turn on an electric light? The bulb illuminates—right? You expect this every time, failing only when a serious external storm is brewing. Networks are no different; and since businesses are often built around networks, networks that are down can cost a significant amount of money. Maintaining nearly 100 percent of time and user connectivity is your number one priority as a network manager.

Your number two priority is response time. There is nothing more annoying than picking up your phone, dialing a long-distance number, and being told that all long distance carriers are busy and to please try your call later. Or plugging in a second appliance in your kitchen and tripping a circuit breaker, causing your kitchen lights to go out and toaster to stop browning. Your network needs adequate capacity for network bursts, and users expect decent response time and throughput. After all, this is the fundamental reason you upgraded to switching in the first place.

The bottom line is that users care about two things:

- reliability and
- response time/throughput

Subsequently we will talk about the classic network problems that interfere with those attributes your users measure your effectiveness on. Believe me; the quicker you can turn around the following problems, the closer you will get to hero status within your organization.

- **No Connectivity:** inability to reach any devices.
- **Partial Connectivity:** inability to reach certain devices.
- **Intermittent Connectivity:** inability to reach any or certain devices at certain times.
- **"Poor" Performance:** perceived poor performance.
- **Network Brownout:** the LAN becomes completely inoperable.

9.3 The Classic Problem Scenarios

The following scenarios utilize the troubleshooting techniques presented in the previous chapter:

- Physical and logical visualization
- Divide-and-conquer
- Substitution and elimination
- Baselining

These techniques are fundamental to troubleshooting network problems and can be used in many different combinations and adaptations to discover and resolve network problems.

The steps presented are not necessarily in the order in which you will want to perform them—this order really depends on the situation at hand. Once you solve your problem, you can simply abort the rest of the steps. Generally speaking each step stands on its own. It is expected that you will adapt the order in which you follow these steps and customize it to suit your own needs and your own network to get to the resolution most expeditiously. Often you can jump into a problem without a comprehensive diagnosis up front; sometimes you will need to backtrack to gain resolution.

Some of the first questions you should ask when attacking any problem are:

- Did this ever work?

- If so, when?

- If so, what changed?

- If so, when were the changes made?

You get the idea. By determining whether this is a newly created problem or a problem created as a result of forging new frontiers, you can save yourself considerable time in your diagnosis and problem resolution.

9.3.1 No Connectivity

No connectivity is the classic "can't get there from here" problem. There are many reasons why a network fails to work from two points. The following steps go through the thought process necessary to resolve the typical problem of no connectivity.

1. As discussed in the previous chapter, we start by creating a picture containing point A and point B and all the network devices and components in between. It is important to consider all physical components in this picture: cable, connectors, concentrators, repeaters, hubs, switches, routers, and so on. If you use discovery software to construct the base of your picture, be sure that the discovery is up-to-date.

2. We then need to overlay the logical components onto our physical picture. Ask yourself what logical processes are going on between A and B. Are VLANs employed? If routing is employed, what protocol(s) are used?

3. Now that we have a visual image of the problem space, the first question we should ask is, "Did the connection ever work?" If so, what changed in your network since it last worked? Physical network layout? Switch configurations? Routing configurations? VLAN configurations? Use of a new monitoring tool? Migration to DHCP? Even if you think a change is unrelated, write it down.

4. If an end station (PC, UNIX, or Macintosh) is involved, check the configuration. If IP routing is involved,

- do a "ping" test within the subnet and outside of the subnet.
- verify the end-node address is unique, the default route is valid, the subnet mask is valid, and the name server is valid, especially if not using DHCP.

  If multiple protocols are used simultaneously, see if any of them work. Connection to Windows/NT server? Connection to NetWare server? Connection to AppleTalk end station? Connection to adjacent TCP/IP node?

5. Verify you are plugged into network and reseat all connections. Verify link status (typically green LED on NIC card). If no link status and you have an alternate cable that you can connect to, try the alternate cable. Verify the link status at the next immediate connecting device (typically a repeater, concentrator, hub, or switch). Ensure link status is fine from point A to point B and between all intermediate network devices along the way.

6. Can others see device A? Can you get from B to A? Check that the MAC address for A is in the bridge tables and that the corresponding slot/port mapping in the table match your expectations. (Note that you may have to read up on how the bridge-address table entries map to slot and port; this is vendor-specific.) Do the same for B.

7. If a router or multiple routers are involved, verify their configurations. Verify that the routes are valid and are properly configured. Verify that you can get from each intermediate point along the way between A and B. Substitute known cable and switch ports as available along the way.

8. Verify all devices along the path are plugged in and operational. Are there other connectivity problems? Look at trace logs of devices to see recent faults.

9. Compare all configurations of all devices along the way against their baselines for all devices for which you have baselines. If routers are involved, verify the consistency of parameters between routers. Are routing updates happening? Can you get to other end stations on the same IP subnet, AppleTalk network, Novell network?

10. Use other devices to verify the integrity of each intermediate repeater, hub, switch, router, and concentrator along the way.

9.3.2 Partial Connectivity

Partial connectivity means that you can connect to certain network devices but not to all network devices or that you can see certain network devices with only one protocol. For example, you can see a NetWare device using IPX-based routing but not using IP-based routing.

1. First, verify that there is a connectivity problem. Often poor performance (attributed to an overloaded network) is interpreted as "no connectivity." Increase the length of time for your ping and traceroute traces if you have an IP network.

2. Repeat steps 1–4 in the No Connectivity section.

3. Construct an inventory of network devices to which you can connect and those to which you cannot connect, including network protocols. Include layer-2 transitions, such as Ethernet to switch, FDDI to another switch, Ethernet to network device B, or LANE at the backbone. The more complete this inventory is, the easier it will be to determine if any problem exists.

4. If protocol does not matter, you need to walk through your diagram and prove the viability of all cabling, and hardware along the way.
   - Are all concentrators working correctly? Can you connect to network devices with which you share the segment? Usually a simple ping test will suffice.
   - Are all switches working correctly? Can you see other network devices on all ports on the bridge? What do the forwarding tables look like? What is the port status of your connection and other adjacent ports to which you wish to connect?
   - Are there excessive error rates associated with your port? Reseat the connector if you are at the switch.
   - Are there filters applied to your port? Were the filters recently introduced? Are they correct?
   - Are there any port-based or MAC-based VLANs? Are they set up correctly? Have they changed recently?
   - Is routing required? (Is it a common problem that you can see network devices locally but not when routing is required?) Verify that the routing configuration (filters, routes, tables) is intact, the routing tables look viable, and the end stations, both ends, have correct configurations (for IP without DHCP this includes subnet mask, unique IP address, optionally a name server, and a default route).

Remember, too, that with IP, routing must be set up properly on both ends for it to work from either end.

- If servers are involved, verify their configurations. Ensure that services are properly advertised and that the advertisements are not inadvertently getting filtered out.

5. Check all logs to see if any network devices were recently rebooted.

6. If WAN link involved, verify that that link is up.

7. If necessary, place a network analyzer or probe at different points in your LAN along the path. See what traffic is passing by and verify that the necessary control traffic, such as RIP updates, is being propagated correctly.

9.3.3 Intermittent Connectivity

Intermittent "anything" is the worst problem, especially if the frequency between when it works and when it doesn't work is excessive. Generally speaking, the longer it takes to reproduce the problem, the longer it takes to fix the problem.

Trend analysis, that is, collecting network statistics over time for analyzing trends, can be very helpful in resolving intermittent problems. In fact, you can often anticipate a problem before it is even reported. Classic examples include the following:

- Seeing a high Link Error Rates (LER) is characteristic of having a bad connector on FDDI networks.

- Observing lots of Ethernet errors is characteristic of bad cabling or connectors.

- Reports of many configuration changes to network devices across your network, especially when unauthorized changes are made (security breach), is often the cause of network problems.

1. Repeat steps 1–4 in the No Connectivity section.

2. Validate the integrity of all devices, cables, and connectors on the way. Take a look at any network management reports you have over time. Carefully note configuration changes and their frequency. One invaluable trap that many network devices provide is an indication that some part of the configuration changed. Network management tools that enable you to track this are especially valuable in locating potential "spots."

3. Look for patterns, such as high utilization, lots of layer-2 errors, periodic configuration changes. Track time of day, day of week, span in frequency, and so on. Map patterns to your trending statistics.

4. If available try alternate cables; reseat all connectors along the way.

9.3.4 Poor Performance

How many times have you heard, "The network is slow" or "Something is really not working"? Sound familiar? The first thing that comes to mind should be, "slow"—compared to what? It is essential that you maintain accurate performance data so that you know what is normal. Note that "normal" will change during peak-load periods and even on different days of the week or the month or an event at the end of business quarters.

It also helps to know the composition and distribution of traffic. How much traffic is going over the WAN? How much traffic is contained within each VLAN? How much traffic is routed as opposed to switched? How much AppleTalk, NetWare, or IP overhead traffic is there? What applications consume the network? RMON2 really shines here. With good RMON2 network monitoring tools you can determine your traffic patterns and tune your network. For now, though, let's assume your network is tuned and that a user has filed a complaint about poor performance.

1. First, find out
   - if sluggishness is confined to time of day, week, month, and so on.
   - what the user is doing.
   - how slowness was perceived (compared to what).
2. Repeat steps 1–4 in the No Connectivity section.
3. Using your picture visualization to determine who or what was involved, look for patterns, look at utilization and trending reports, and look at data gathered by RMON and RMON2 applications.
4. Look for signs that
   - there is a broadcast storm (hook a scope at a central place in your network).
   - there is bridge loop.
   - one or more pieces of equipment in your backbone are down or rebooting excessively.
   - there is one or more duplicate IP addresses.
   - a WAN link is down.
   - a WAN link is very slow.
   - routing is not converging quickly in your network.
   - routing tables are overflowing; routes are being repeatedly aged out prematurely.
   - buffers in routers are overflowing.
   - an excessive number of packets is being dropped.

- an excessive number of frames is being dropped.
- error counters are high.
- switch tables are overflowing.
- a server is overloaded or running low on disk space.
- excessive routing is required to reach destination.
- broadcast/multicast traffic is high.
- traffic must pass through several complex filters that will slow traffic down.
- an end station is not itself overloaded.
- any VLAN configuration in place results in excessive routing.
- there is a sudden, expected, excessive generation of traffic, perhaps put on your network by your engineering crew for testing purposes.

5. Examine all recent configuration changes. Examine network growth and draw any correlation between the area of growth and the problem area.

6. Look at error rates.

7. If IP is being used, use ping and traceroute to record response time and paths from various points in network.

9.3.5 Network Brownout

Network brownout refers to the state when nothing works from a network perspective. In a switched environment the most likely causes are

- a power failure (complete, partial, or excessive power spikes),
- WAN network failure,
- a broadcast storm,
- a routing storm (routing tables do not converge),
- bridge loop,
- duplicate IP addresses or duplicate MAC addresses, or
- a central cable is severed or crushed.

Loops and storms can be difficult to find, although many packet analyzers now detect such problems. The trick with a switched network is locating the analyzer at the correct spot; sometimes (especially with larger networks) it will be worth the extra investment to have more than one analyzer so you can converge more quickly on solutions.

Uninterrupted Power Supplies (UPS) can help with power failures and can even help protect your equipment against power spikes. Use UPS on core devices so that in the event of power problems you do not suffer from complete brownout of your network.

Network redundancy is another good preventive measure. Often devices come with two power supplies just in case one burns out; we all know the importance of having alternate spare cables and network components. Backup WAN connections, such as an ISDN line to use if a Frame Relay connection goes down, can be instrumental in times of failure. Backup LAN connections for critical links are also important.

It is often useful to assess the cost of network failure (loss of productivity, loss of important data transfer, and so on) to determine the amount of redundancy and backup systems you need to put in place. Clearly you do not want to waste money; however, your network "brownout plan" must line up with your business' overall cost of network failure.

Network brownout uses the same techniques as discussed in the sections on the other classic problems for troubleshooting; I will not repeat the text here.

9.4 Summary

The more experience you have with troubleshooting network problems, the better you will become at resolving complaints quickly and efficiently. Troubleshooting is all about looking for patterns, visualizing the problem, and disproving a set of assumptions until you "zero in" on the solution.

Keeping an accurate inventory of your network and its associated problems will help you to solve future problems and to know when certain aspects of your network design are problematic. It is important that you keep your problem-tracking database and problem inventory up-to-date with respect to problems and solutions—this will especially help you to train new network managers.

There is not a prescription for solving all problems within a switched LAN. Experience and step-by step problem isolation are fundamental to problem solving. Network troubleshooting is all about reducing the scope of the problem; determining what the problem *isn't* becomes key to determining what the problem *is*.

CHAPTER 10

Selecting Switched LAN Management Tools

10.1 Introduction

At this point you have gained a pretty good appreciation for the number of technologies involved in switched LANs and the problems that you are likely to encounter. Now you probably feel like shouting, "Help!"

Help is precisely what you are looking for when you select your management tools. It is important that you look beyond the flash, fancy charts, and slick graphics and select tools that greatly assist you in managing your network. Tools that solve real management problems are valuable; tools that flood you with esoteric "data" are not.

This chapter is all about tools—that is, selecting tools. We start by building a mindset for the motivation of using tools and the basics of what to look for. We purposely do not go into specific vendor tools (with the exception of mentioning a few network analyzer tools), as this information tends to become dated very quickly and doesn't leave you with the framework for proper tool selection for your custom switched LAN. By knowing exactly what to look for, you can be self-sufficient; this is far more valuable than taking someone's tool kit and clumsily retrofitting it to your own switched LAN.

Switched LANs are different from traditional LANs and intensify the requirements of tools. It is, therefore, important that we focus on the correct attributes. After discussing tool requirements, we go through the tool families and conclude with a quick discussion of some very useful "free" tools for diagnosing problems with IP networks. Tools can make a big difference; they can help put you in control of your switched LAN.

10.2 Motivation for Using Tools

We have established that the network is a valuable resource upon which your company depends. The network must adapt and grow as your business requirements change. When the network is down your company is unproductive; hence one of your goals is to keep your network up at all times. When a new employee starts, you need to have the employee online ASAP, in the same way that he is provided with office space and a workstation.

Your most valuable resource is your staff who enable you to satisfy these business needs. Unfortunately, though, there is a finite pool of talented network managers, and your resources are limited to what your business can afford. It is the right combination of network management tools coupled with your limited staff that enable you to be successful; this is why it is so important that you select the correct tools to help you manage your network. In a sense, your tools are your second line of defense. The correct combination can enable you to solve more problems with fewer staff; the incorrect combination can keep you working 80-hour weeks.

10.3 Day-to-Day Life Cycles and Tools

One way to understand what tools you need to manage your switched LAN is to look at the life cycles that you encounter. There are two life cycles—the network life cycle and the problem life cycle—and a simple set of five or so questions that you should consider when you put together your tool kit.

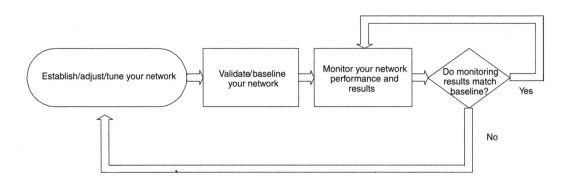

Figure 10.1 Network life cycle

Table 10.1 Network Life Cycle

1.	**Establish/adjust/tune your network:** This is the state when you build your initial LAN, extend your LAN, recover from network failure, or make configuration adjustments to try to optimize your LAN.
2.	**Validate/baseline your network:** This is the state when you validate that your network is working correctly, and you take a snapshot of key configuration and performance statistics. Baselines give you a reference point for a healthy LAN.
3.	**Monitor your network for performance and faults:** This is the state when you (and your tools) watch the network for faults and periodically poll the network to ensure that everything is working properly and as planned. Your tools use your reference baseline for comparison of what is a healthy network; this is steady state.

The first life cycle is the *network life cycle* (See Figure 10.1). This cycle covers the changes that your network goes through as you adapt the network to your business. Table 10.1 shows the three states of the network life cycle.

Steady state, that is, the state when your network is running without intervention, is state three. You and your staff would like to spend most of the time having your tools automatically monitor your network while you and your staff are planning and designing your next generation network. There are several actions that will send you back to state one:

- Adding new users or equipment to your network
- Moving users or equipment on your network
- Upgrading your network equipment
- Responding to network faults and performance needs

In addition you may have more actions that are specific to your network to add to this list. Tools that help you get back to steady state and provide "auto" monitoring capabilities are useful. Some tools even cycle through simple instances of states 1 and 2 and resume "auto monitoring."

The second life cycle is the *problem life cycle*. This cycle refers to the steps that you take to resolve problems when they occur. Ideally you enter the problem life cycle automatically from state 3 of the network life cycle; your monitoring tools anticipate or tell you there is a problem. Realistically you also enter the problem life cycle when a user calls and says, "My network is down."

The problem life cycle, as shown in Table 10.2, can be remembered by referencing a strange mnemonic—**DLAIRDI**.

Table 10.2 Problem Life Cycle

1.	**D**etect that there is a problem.
2.	**L**og the problem in a database.
3.	**A**ssign the problem to someone to spearhead fixing it.
4.	**I**solate the problem.
5.	**R**esolve the problem and make any baseline adjustments you need to make.
6.	**D**ocument the resolution with the problem so that you can quickly solve the same problem the next time.
7.	**I**nstall new network devices and upgrade existing network devices to get them on line and operational quickly.

10.4 How Tools Can Help

So where can tools help you out in the problem life cycle? Tools can help you in all stages in the DLAIRDI problem life cycle as well as in the network life cycle.

Good tools can help you set up your network, establish baselines, track key configurations, monitor performance statistics, and alert you of problems across your switched LAN. These are all important elements of the network life cycle.

A good help desk application can help you manage your problem database by providing a way for you to *log*, *assign*, and *document* problems. Often help desks provide a way for your users to do the problem logging and to alert you or your team of the problem via phone, e-mail, or a beeper.

There are many tools that will help you to *detect* problems, even before they occur, helping you to manage your network proactively. They rely on device traps, polling, and trap-directed polling as discussed in the first chapter of this book. RMON2, coupled with an RMON2 application, can help predict traffic patterns and future congestion problems.

There is also a set of tools that will help to you *isolate* problems, speeding up network recovery, helping you manage your network reactively and *resolve* problems quickly. For example, ping and traceroute are essential in IP networks; and having a network analyzer is fundamental to help isolate problems such as a broadcast storm. Some analyzers can also detect certain problems based on traffic monitoring.

And last, there are tools that enable your to *install* new network devices and get them up and operational with out-of-the-box configuration and configuration cloning (using another network device as the base configuration for a new device). These tools are useful and important to manage your network, especially if your network is large.

10.5 A Tool-Kit Model

You can think of your tool kit as three concentric circles (a bulls' eye), with criticality at the core of the circles, at the inner circle. As your tool kit enlarges, so does the richness of your tool-based management. In the inner circle you have the basic "get the network operational" tools. This is where installation tools and out-of-the-box setups are useful. The inner circle is core and fundamental as proper configuration makes your network operational.

The next circle of tools helps with reactive management. Tools that help identify, troubleshoot, and fix network problems fall here.

In the outer circle are the capacity planning tools, the modeling tools, the tools that do trend analysis based on previously established baselines. Your goal is to spend your time using tools in this outermost circle. The better the tools are within the core, the more time you will be able to spend using the outer circle tools. Figure 10.2 illustrates the conceptual bull's-eye view of a tool kit.

At this point you should have developed an appreciation for the fact that tools can help keep you and your staff planning and designing your next generation network—the state where you want to be spending your time. Now let's explore the key functional requirements of excellent tools and highly maintainable switched hardware.

10.6 Key Tool Requirements

As a tool consumer you need to be particularly picky about which tools you invest in. Remember, investment includes learning, deploying, and monitoring the tools. Following are some key questions you should ask when selecting tools for your tool kit:

- **What network problem (or problems) does the tool solve?** Many tools have great architectures but little built-in utility. Infrastructure and architecture help you scale your tools, but infrastructure and architecture alone do not solve problems. Matching the problems you have to your set of chosen tools is paramount, and based on information in earlier chapters, you know the problems of switched LANs. So be selective and don't get too excited about fancy architectures. Always ask What built-in functionality does the fancy architecture come with?

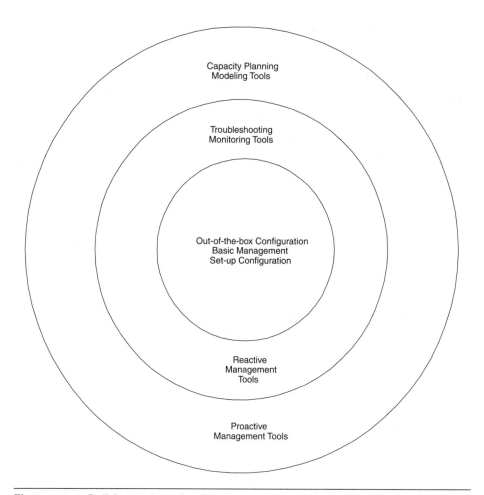

Figure 10.2 Bulls'-eye view of tools

- **How close does the tool get to resolving problems?** Does it rely on you to understand MIB dumps and lots of raw data, or does it zero in on what's important and reduce the complexity for you and your staff? How much of your time does the tool require?

- **What is the "cost" of ownership?** Is the tool easy to install? Does it come with reasonable defaults, or do you need to spend hours configuring the tool? How well is the tool documented? What support is provided? Does the tool require a PhD to learn? Do you need to have someone sit and watch the tool for red/green/yellow/blue color change, or does it alert via other ways like tying into a beeper or your e-mail system? How stable is the tool—a core dumper, a perpetually changing GUI? Does it require a hardware purchase, such as a RMON probe? What are the maintenance costs of the tool? How much time does it take to keep the tool happy?

- **How well does it integrate with the rest of your tools?** Can you get at any data that the tool stores with standard SQL or by reading a flat text file? Can you launch the tool from another tool (such as a network management platform) with context? How well does it integrate with your network management platform? Does it require its own dedicated monitor?

- **Does the tool scale to your network needs?** What is the load placed on the network? Does it leverage trap-directed polling, or does it flood your network with SNMP traffic? Will it be able to maintain an inventory for your 60,000 workstations?

- **How portable is the tool?** Do you need to buy a high-end UNIX workstation to run the tool, or will it run on your inexpensive Windows/NT server? Do you need a 21-inch monitor to use the tool? Does it have a Web client interface from which you can see the data anywhere? Do you have to run back to your central site to use the tool, or does the tool enable you to view data from anywhere on the network?

- **How much resource does the tool consume?** Do you need to add hard disks, memory? How much overall network resource does the tool consume?

- **Does the tool provide useful reports?** Can you customize the reports for your own needs? Do the reports help you with proactive management and network design and planning?

- **Can you customize the tool?** Does the tool provide a way to script repetitive tasks, that is, a way to walk through a menu structure automatically and record a set of key strokes that can later be reapplied?

- **How does the tool perform?** How long will you need to wait when your network is in crisis? How much data are persistently between invocation to speed up the tool?

10.7 Key Switching Tool Requirements

In addition to general-purpose network management tools designed for traditional networks, switched LANs require tools that are tailored to analyzing switches. After sorting out the general applicability of a tool, it is useful to ask yourself some questions around specific applicability to your switched LAN:

- Is the tool designed for switched LANs?
- Does it help you with monitoring many different LANs at once (remember each port on a switch is its own LAN)? Does it help you apply a single change to many different switches/ports at once?
- Do your switches meet the SNMP MIB requirements? That is, do they provide the correct standard MIB support?
- Is the tool generally applicable to switch components coming from other vendors?

At this point you have determined that a tool is a useful management tool and generally applies (or at least is advertised) to managing switched LANs. Now one final pass at weeding out the greats from the not-so-greats. Does the tool

- provide management granularity to the port level?
- provide useful reports about each of your switched ports?
- store data about each of your switched ports over time, allowing you to do trend analysis?
- utilize port-level embedded RMON and RMON-2 data to help you with trending and capacity planning of your switched LAN?
- enable you to configure several devices or ports at once without lots of manual intervention? Does it allow you to define and set and alarm (send out a trap) on key thresholds such as broadcast/multicast across many ports simultaneously?
- provide baselining and consistency checking of key configuration parameters across the many ports within your switched LAN?
- provide device-level baselining and consistency checking across your switches, for example, management of community strings or console passwords?
- provide a way to back up and restore device configurations across your many switches?

10.8 Hardware Tools

We've covered the twenty plus questions, and we now know how to be an intelligent switch tool shopper. So let's see what's available for hardware tools.

10.8.1 Cable Testers

If your network is of any size at all and you don't have the luxury of easily swapping cables, you need a cable tester (possibly several testers, depending on the wire types you have). Cable testers verify the overall integrity of the cable; they detect such problems as cross talk, signal attenuation, miswiring, and excessive noise. There are fiber cable testers and twisted pair testers. Some twisted pair testers work on specific wire categories. In addition to ensuring that the tool will work for your existing environment, ensure that the tester has a migration path to the next wire grade. All cables should be verified at installation; subsequent cable testing should be done when network fault points to a cable problem.

> **A S I D E . . .**
>
> Cable testers tend to be expensive and hard to use. It may make sense to have a contractor install and verify your cables when you need to extend your network.

10.8.2 Protocol Analyzers

Again, if your network is of any size at all, you should invest in a protocol analyzer. These devices are expensive but invaluable in diagnosing and alerting of problems such as broadcast storms, bridge loops, or duplicate IP addresses. Protocol analyzers enable you to see the exact traffic on your network from any point on your network. As we have discussed, switched LANs have the disadvantage of requiring you to monitor your network from several points, since each point typically represents its own segment. However, there are usually central points going through the backbone that serve as good locations for a packet analyzer.

With a protocol analyzer you can see all the IPX, TCP/IP, AppleTalk control packets as well as NetWare SAP traffic, SNMP traffic, and normal network traffic. These tools decode the packets in real time making them more readable to you. Typically an analyzer comes with reports and the ability to set thresholds based on statistical counts of certain packets observed.

Network General's Sniffer, one of today's most popular analyzers, provides an expert system that detects several common network problems by counting packets and observing packet trends. This product also comes as a portable or as a Distributed Sniffer System (DSS). The DSS enables you to place several distributed services out on the network to roll up data to a single console. This mitigates the problem of having many "key" vantage points in switched LANs.

If funds are tight and you have a RMON probe and a RMON application, you can use the probe to get a peek into your network and observe traffic characteristics and patterns. For example, by using the Packet Capture group you can capture packets based on a given filter equation. In fact, since many switches are now coming with many (or all) of the RMON groups built in at the port level, all you really need is a RMON application. One disadvantage of this approach is you lose the notion of automatic detection of key problems; at least I don't know of a RMON application that provides the same problem detection capabilities as a product like the Network General Sniffer.

10.8.3 RMON Probes

RMON probes are hardware devices that can be configured to collect RMON data. RMON probes generally support all RMON groups: Statistics, History, Alarm, Host, HostTopN, Matrix, Filter, Packet Capture, Event, and Token Ring. Embedded RMON (or RMON built in to the switch) monitoring each switched port is generally more limited than what a probe can provide because collecting RMON data is CPU-intensive and memory intensive. As discussed in Chapter 2, this can significantly drain a switch's performance. Since having RMON data at every port is so much better than having to position a probe at the "correct" location, switch vendors will be adding more processing power and hence more RMON at the port level. The other advantage is saving you the cost of purchasing a separate probe; probes are expensive. A RMON probe is useful to zoom in on a port after one or more problems have been detected.

RMON2, providing statistics on layer 3 and above, is also supported by many probes. As discussed in Chapter 2, it adds ten more groups. RMON2 will also be addressed by embedded solutions.

10.8.4 Traffic Generators

So why would you want to generate traffic? Traffic generation is extremely important when you need to validate a network design or a network design change. By flooding the network with traffic, you can observe how the network reacts with regard to congestion levels, behavior when certain thresholds are exceeded, and so on. These tools enable you to test a change before implementing a change to your network design. Many protocol analyzers provide a way to generate network traffic or to record and play it back.

> **A S I D E . . .**
>
> Make certain you use traffic generation correctly and as intended! The last thing you want is to be responsible for bringing down your network by inundating it with test traffic!

10.8.5 Agent Simulators

Agent simulators provide a way to record an agent's capabilities and then simulate the agent with known SNMP MIB values for certain objects. Agent simulators are particularly valuable for tool development as they provide a way to simulate error conditions as well as to validate the accuracy of statistics. In your environment you might use the agent simulator to validate the accuracy of any tools that you purchase.

> **A S I D E . . .**
>
> Agent simulators can be expensive. Using a MIB browser (provided with network management platforms), you can also compare and contrast the values of various MIB objects with your tools for far less cost.

10.9 Software Tools

It's now time to see what's available for software tools aimed at switched LANs. Because there are many network management tools, it is important to recognize that many of them fall short with respect to managing switched LANs. It is important to keep the key tool requirements in mind when you select your software tools.

10.9.1 Software Analyzers

Often complete protocol analysis requires dedicated hardware to keep up with the traffic on your network. The hardware required is a dedicated PC with a special network card and software. Once installed, the PC boots up as an analyzer. There are some analyzers that run as an application. EtherPeek is a product that helps with Ethernet networks; LANdecoder provides Token Ring assistance. These tools generally provide a reduced view of what's going across the wire, since they are unable to keep up with the traffic across a busy link.

With the advent of higher performing PCs, workstations, and switching at the edges of your network, these are worth looking at. Make certain you ask any potential vendor to give you a demonstration on your switched LAN at the location where you intend to use the device, next to a dedicated analyzer. A software analyzer may be perfectly fine for your network, save your considerable money, and enable you to run other tools simultaneously on your management station. You may decide that you need a hardware analyzer for your backbone and one or more software analyzers for the edges of your network.

10.9.2 Network Management Platforms

There are four major platforms that have been available for a long time, as shown in Table 10.3. Platforms are intended to provide a common integration point for all network devices. Unfortunately, "common" often means surface-level management capabilities. Platforms run on both PCs and UNIX boxes (various kinds of UNIX). Until very recently the PC versions of the platforms had less functionality than the UNIX versions, due largely to the overall lack of horsepower of a PC. With the recent advent of PC megaboxes and Windows/NT, platforms are quickly converging to have the same functionality on both Windows/NT and UNIX.

I confess I'm not a platform enthusiast. They tend to be expensive and not granular enough for switched LAN management; they do, however, do a few things very well:

- They provide autodiscovery of your network, from scratch, and incrementally update an existing topology. Although you will most likely want to adjust the topological layout, the basic map of a large LAN kept up-to-date is invaluable for network management. It provides you with a high-level view of all your key core devices and gives you an instant status via color-coded status. If the devices are red, there is a problem; blue unreachable; yellow worth looking at; green okay.

- They provide a common launch point. When you are in a hurry you want to get into a specific tool with the context of where you are coming from. Platforms make it easy for vendors to integrate their tools loosely by launching with context.

- They provide a MIB browser. You can usually load MIBs into a database, and they allow you to walk through and dump out key SNMP objects and tables. Some platforms also allow you to trigger an alarm based on the periodic polling of a specific object. This can be invaluable when you are filling in cracks from your switch vendor's tool offerings.

Table 10.3 Network Management Platforms

Vendor	Major Platforms	More Information
Cabletron	Spectrum	http://www.cabletron.com
Hewlett Packard	HP OpenView	http://www.hp.com
IBM	NetView	http://www.ibm.com
Sun Microsystems	Solstice SunNet Manager	http://www.sun.com

A S I D E . . .

One large problem with platform autodiscovery is that it is usually based on a layer-3 algorithm and often results in not seeing devices at layer 2. For example, cascaded switches at layer 2 are lumped together making it impossible to see the true connectivity between the devices. Algorithms that include Spanning Tree can discern network devices at the layer-2 level, as long as the switches within the LAN are running the Spanning Tree Algorithm.

Platforms fall short especially with respect to switched management. Platforms by their very nature tend to be general purpose, not exploiting, recognizing, or providing management for vendor-specific switch features. Platforms provide a high-level view of your network, depicting devices and device-level reachability. With a switch it is important that you manage at the port level as each port often represents a separate switched LAN; managing at the port level includes monitoring performance as well as configuration consistency checking and application of many configuration changes at once.

You can use a MIB browser to augment some of the management capabilities of the platform, although with lots of switches and their respective ports it is often very painful and time-consuming to manage manually and to get a detailed view of the health of your overall switched LAN.

10.9.3 MIB Browsers

MIB browsers provide a graphical way to walk a MIB. They also enable you to exercise a SNMP command (GET, SET, GET NEXT) easily against one or more devices and see the results. With a browser you can see the results for a single object, a table of objects, or multiple scalar objects at once. Browsers generally come loaded with standard MIBs, including MIB-2 and RMON, and allow you to download into the browser database new MIBs that are specific to your network device(s).

As mentioned, platforms come with a browser. With the advent of the Web, there are now a few Web-based browser solutions independent of a platform. Web-based solutions are useful as they provide built-in O/S portability allowing you to pop up a browser literally anywhere in your network—you don't have to run back to your network control center where your platform is installed.

The main disadvantage of using a browser is that you must be extremely knowledgeable about the MIB. You need to be able to walk the MIB, know what objects are important, and understand the indexing schemes used for tables that you want to view. Although MIB-2 is quite palatable, many vendor-specific MIBs are quite complex. MIBs for switched devices tend to have multiple indexing schemes, further complicating the MIB and increasing the difficulty for you.

10.9.4 Vendor-Specific Tools

One of the key requirements when you purchase any network device is manageability, and switch acquisition is no exception. From our earlier discussions you know what is specifically important for managing your switch tools. Vendor-specific tools tend to fill in the holes of platforms and generic tools. Some useful value-added tools from your switch vendor are tools that

- give you a software view of the state of the device with integrated, comprehensive device configuration.
- scale across your enterprise and integrate with the rest of your management environment.
- help you manage and monitor configuration change of your switches.
- help you monitor your performance and assist with capacity planning and network design.
- help you automate physical and logical topology map generation.
- help you baseline and consistency check your many switched ports and switch devices, tools that provide bulk operations (that is, do a configuration task to many).
- provide port-by-port statistics and alarming, enabling you to manage each of your switched ports.
- provide you with top "N" statistics across all switched ports.

- provide you with utilization on all MAC layer protocols, at all ports.
- help you diagnose, isolate, and fix problems associated with switched LANs.

Table 10.4 gives you some URLs of large networking vendors. Use this chart, the preceding platform chart, your equipment inventory, and your own research to surf the Web for the latest on networking tools. Before buying, remember to ensure that the tools are tailored for *your* switched LAN.

> **A S I D E . . .**
>
> Don't discount management that is built into a network device. Often RMON, RMON-2, threshold setting, autolearning of thresholds, and a robust set of traps alerting you to problems are built into the network device. Remember, too, that management station software is only as good as the MIBs on which it is built; if your network device doesn't support a strong set of standard MIBs and useful proprietary MIBs, management station software for the network device will be lacking. It is especially important that you choose network devices that support standard MIBs so tools that work across vendors (those based on standard MIBs) have a chance of working well on your network devices.

10.10 Free TCP/IP Tools

The TCP/IP protocol stack has a set of very rich and powerful tools that are extremely useful when managing your network. We have already talked briefly about ping and traceroute; this section provides more complete coverage of TCP/IP tools with their many options. For convenience, options of both UNIX and PC (Windows/95 and Windows/NT) tools are discussed. Only the most important options of each tool are discussed; consult your respective "man" pages on UNIX or help on Windows for a comprehensive list of all options.

10.10.1 The Ping Tool

Ping is an invaluable tool to help diagnose connectivity and performance problems. Ping uses ICMP to send an *echo request* packet to a destination; the destination answers by sending an *echo response* packet back to the sender. With ping you can determine if you have end-to-end connectivity and get a measure of the amount of time it takes to send a packet (round-trip) to any destination.

Ping is perhaps the first tool a network administrator will use to diagnose TCP/IP connectivity problems. With just three "pings" you can determine a lot about an end node's connectivity.

Table 10.4 Large Networking Vendors

Vendor	Tool Family	More Information
3Com	Transcend	http://www.3com.com
Bay Networks	Optivity	http://www.baynetworks.com
Cisco	CiscoWorks	http://www.cisco.com
Intel	LANDesk	http://www.intel.com

1. First ping yourself (current workstation, address, 127.0.0.1) to confirm that your TCP/IP stack is operational. Note that some stacks cheat a bit here, and this test does not verify completely that the stack is okay.

2. Then ping a station on the same segment verifying local communication, through a switch or hub.

3. Finally ping stations on other segments or across the WAN verifying remote communication, through a router.

On both Windows and UNIX the basic command line for the tool is

ping <destination>, where destination may
be an IP address or DNS hostname

Unfortunately that's where the similarity between O/Ss ends. The UNIX version has the following:

- wait flag (-i <seconds>)
- size flag (-s <packet size>)
- flood flag (-f) to flood with ping as fast as responses come in

The Windows version has the following:

- continuous flag (-t)
- DNS resolve flag (-a) used to resolve an IP address to a DNS name
- (-l <length>) flag used to specify the length of the ICMP packet
- timeout flag (-w <timeout>) that enables us to specify the time-out interval in milliseconds.

10.10.2 The Traceroute (Tracert) Tool

The traceroute enables you to determine the path taken between two systems. Traceroute provides more detail than just ping; it shows the exact route along the way—including each intermediate router that is used to get you from your local workstation to a remote workstation.

On UNIX the basic command line for the tool is

traceroute <destination>, where destination may
be an IP address or DNS hostname

The UNIX version

- displays gateway addresses numerically (-n);

- uses specific IP addresses for multihomes host (-s);

- operates in verbose mode, displays all ICMP messages (-v); and

- uses a specified maximum number of hops (default is 30) (-m <number>).

On Windows the basic command line for the tool is

tracert <destination>, where destination may
be an IP address or DNS hostname

The Windows version

- does not resolve IP addresses (-d);

- uses host list as "loose" route (-j <host list>); and

- uses a specified maximum number of hops (-h <number>).

10.10.3 The Netstat Tool

The netstat tool provides TCP/IP, and UDP connection statistics. This tool provides information about all active network connections.

On UNIX the basic command line for the tool is

netstat

The UNIX version

- provides a list of all available sockets (-a);

- executes the command continuously (-c);

- resolves networks and hostnames when displaying remote and local addresses (-n);

- provides routing table information (-r);

- lists all packets transmitted by protocol (-s);
- displays only TCP socket information (-t);
- displays only UDP socket information (-u); and
- prints out interface information (-i).

On Windows the basic command line for the tool is:

netstat <interval>

Windows has its own options, including

- providing a list of all current connections and listening ports (-a);
- providing network statistics since computer booting (-e);
- providing statistics by protocols (-p);
- providing statistics for a particular protocol (-p <UPD|TCP|IP| ICMP>).
- providing routing table information (-r); and
- executing continuously over a specified interval (in seconds) (<interval>).

10.10.4 The Arp Tool

The arp tool provides a table of mappings between MAC addresses and IP addresses. You can also use this tool selectively to delete entries within the local arp cache.

On UNIX the basic command line for the tool is

arp

UNIX options include:

- displaying all entries (-a);
- removing a specific entry (-d <hostname>);
- displaying only a specific entry (<hostname>); and
- adding a specific entry (-s <hostname> <MAC address>).

On Windows the basic command line for the tool is

arp

Windows options include:

- displaying all entries (-a);
- displaying only a specific entry (-a <IP address>);

- removing a specific entry (-d <IP address>); and
- adding a specific entry (-s <IP address> <MAC address>).

10.10.5 Other Useful TCP/IP Tools

There are a few other tools that on occasion you will find useful to diagnose problems. Consult the UNIX "man" pages or Windows help to find out all the details on these tools. Here are a few tools that you may find useful:

For UNIX only:

- ripquery: examines any RIP-based routing table.

For Windows only:

- nbtstat: displays status of NetBIOS over TCP/IP.
- ipconfig: shows TCP/IP configuration (available at the time of this writing on Windows/NT only).
- route: manages the local routing table.

For both UNIX and Windows/NT:

- hostname: returns the name of the computer.

10.11 Future Tools

As switched LAN demands and the overall complexity of switched LANs increase, the demand for better, smarter, more comprehensive tools intensifies. Expect some of the following tool advances:

- Better use of RMON/RMON-2 data, especially for accounting/billing, network design, planning, proactive management.
- Tools that validate network device addition/change in the context of the entire network. Tools that ensure that even after additions/deletions and changes the network is still healthy, or even healthier.
- Assistance with providing service-level agreements by leveraging Class of Service (CoS) and Quality of Service (QoS) network attributes. Tools that help with end-to-end management.
- Design tools that help with tuning the network, monitoring the network over time, and suggesting changes that optimize the configuration—tools that provide "what if" capabilities.

- Tools that help provide a logical view of your network as related to the physical view of your network.
- Tools that provide better distribution and leverage Java and Web technologies.

10.11.1 Java and Web Tools

Clearly the accessibility and platform independence offered by Web browsers makes tools that operate within the web framework very attractive. The tools don't need to be installed in multiple locations; they work equally well from Windows and UNIX and leverage a common GUI that is easy and intuitive to use. That nearly every workstation or PC already has a browser installed and can access a server-based network management application without any client installation is a *huge* benefit. These advantages, coupled with the JAVA programming language for more sophisticated tools, makes Web-based tools very attractive for consumers and vendors of network management software.

With web-based tools there are a few challenges that need to be (and currently are being) resolved to make Web solutions ubiquitous and even to displace native UNIX and Windows applications.

- Improve JAVA performance. JAVA currently compiles to an interpretive language and hence it executes slowly. Just-in-time compilation (JIT) is one recent advancement that greatly helps performance. It is expected that there will be compilers that build native JAVA applets that will address overall tool performance. The only caveat is that you will need to use different applets based on platform, but this should not be too difficult for your vendors to pull off.
- Develop better GUI controls. Prebuild components like tree views, progress bars, and so on. Windows provides a very rich GUI environment and has resulted in some very slick GUIs; JAVA is still catching up.
- Assist with security. It will be important for Web-based applications to have access levels, particularly with network configuration tools.

10.12 Summary

Putting together your tool kit is an important part of managing your switched network. You do not have the energy to use hundreds of tools or the screen real estate or the time to monitor many user interfaces concurrently.

Your basic switching tool kit should include the following:

- assistance with initial setup and network device configuration.

- a mechanism to discover automatically and augment incrementally your high-level network picture and to show device-level reachability. Platforms do this pretty well.

- software to enable you to configure each network device easily and to show you device-specific status via a graphical picture of your device. Most vendors provide this software for their network devices.

- a way to monitor all of your switched ports for performance and faults.

- a mechanism to configure many switch ports at once.

- a way to configure and manage key common device-level objects such as SNMP community strings, software versions, and setting-up trap destinations. This tool should inventory all your network device configurations so that you can easily roll back or ahead with respect to network device configurations.

- assistance with baselining your network and restoring/rolling back network device configurations.

- rudimentary reachability tools like ping and traceroute.

Your advanced switching tool kit might include the following:

- a tool to inventory your network devices, showing you configurations, agent versions of software running, and boards installed;

- tools to analyze network data over time and to help with capacity planning; and

- tools that diagnose and automatically fix certain simple network problems.

It is important that your tools fit together, provide adequate coverage, and assist you with initial setup and reactive and proactive management of your network. The proper tool set will keep you out of the fires doing proactive planning and fire prevention.

CHAPTER 11

Switched LAN Design

11.1 Introduction

At this point you

- know what network management is all about;
- understand the key components of switched LANs;
- have a laundry list of the problems associated with switched LANs; and
- have a grasp of some of the tool requirements you will need to fulfill in order to manage a switched LAN.

In short, you've read the instructions, and you are ready to build (or enhance) your switched LAN. You proceed with network management in mind—a key component of evolving your switched LAN into a network management system, our final frontier.

Clearly there are a lot of choices and decisions to make when building your switched LAN. Where do you route? Where do you switch? How do you connect to the WAN? Will you use Ethernet primarily with Gigabit and Fast Ethernet at the core of your network, or will ATM LANE be your backbone solution? What about FDDI? How many protocols do you need to route? Do you expect to support multimedia in the future? Will management be central or distributed? How fault tolerant must your network be? How secure must your network be? How quickly do you expect your network to grow? Will you be connecting to multiple LANs across the WAN; that is, will you be establishing an Intranet?

These are just a few of the myriad questions that you must answer when you design, build, or upgrade an existing network. It is important that you take the time to ask and answer the questions up front and plan your network. Planning up front costs the least in time, effort, and funds. Planning before implementation can add a significant amount of stability in your LAN.

Good network design is difficult. It involves many trade-offs and adjustments as well as customization based on your needs. This chapter provides direction on building a manageable network with specific strategies on designing your network with manageability in mind. It is believed that if you build something that you cannot manage you have created a problem. If you don't believe it, take a look at your neighbor who haphazardly landscaped his yard and is now regretting the amount of management the jungle needs. Don't let your network become a jungle.

11.2 Cardinal Rules of Design

There are a few fundamental rules of design that you should follow. Although these rules are tailored for switched LAN design, the basic gist of each can be applied to other areas equally well.

- **Don't shortchange the amount of time you take to design your LAN.** The time you spend up front understanding how your LAN will work, be managed, and grow will pay dividends by making your life easier. It is easy to justify throwing away a few hours of design and a couple rough sketches; disposing of several hundreds (or thousands) of dollars worth of equipment and accounting for hours of downtime is significantly harder to justify.

- **Always design with manageability in mind.** Select network devices with built-in management. Select network devices that have good network management applications and support common MIBs. Select network devices whose management will integrate into the rest of your management system. This practice will keep you out of your fire-fighting garb and free you up to improve your network design.

- **Don't get too caught up with every technical fad.** Every technical addition has a cost and a purpose. Do you really need VLANs with a 20-user network? Do you really want to have both an ATM LANE backbone and an FDDI backbone? You can do a lot with just a few components. Remember, if you have fewer parts, you have fewer parts that can break.

- **Have a redeployment plan for every network device you purchase.** Technology moves quickly and often needs to be upgraded. It is frugal to consider exactly how you will reuse a piece of equipment, even at the time of initial purchase. In this way you will not be adding to the junkyard every time you upgrade your LAN. Backbone equipment can often be migrated to the edges of your network.

- **Follow the KISS principle—keep it super simple.** Over-engineering your LAN will be problematic for you in many regards. It will be hard to maintain, difficult to train new administrators, and vulnerable to failure. Add complexity only as required.

- **Always know what you have.** There is no substitute for a complete inventory of your network. And if you live in an engineering environment, network devices that were not even installed by you may suddenly appear on your network. Sometimes these network devices can create significant problems. If you keep your inventory up-to-date and leverage incremental discovery of your network via a platform tool, you will be better able to respond to change, fix problems, make accurate network adjustments, and extend your network as needed.

- **Consider modular network equipment that can be upgraded at a later date.** Modular equipment provides a built-in upgrade path.

- **Pay attention to electrical power and cooling requirements when locating your network devices.** Network devices often consume significant power and generate lots of heat; you do not want your network going down because of an insufficient electrical supply or inadequate cooling or heating.

11.3 Hierarchy of Network Design Components

When you design a network, it is essential that you have a good list of available components. The following list comes from the previous chapters and is organized top down by network layers. To get more detail on each component, refer back to the Chapter(s) in parenthesis.

- Management Tools (Chapter 10)
  - Cable testers
  - Protocol analyzers
  - RMON probes
  - Network management platforms
  - MIB browsers
  - Vendor-specific management tools
  - TCP/IP tools

- WAN options (Chapter 7)
    - Modem dial-up
    - ISDN
    - X-25 (mostly in Europe)
    - Frame relay
    - ATM
    - Internet connections
    - PPP
    - Remote access equipment
- Network layer technologies (Chapters 4 and 5)
    - IP
    - IPX
    - AT
    - VLANs
- Data link technologies (Chapters 3, 4, and 6)
    - Ethernet
    - Fast Ethernet
    - Gigabit Ethernet
    - FDDI
    - Token Ring
    - ATM LANE
    - VLANs
- Network devices/components (Chapter 1)
    - Backbone switches
    - Routers
    - Workgroup switches
    - Chassis hubs
    - Stackable hubs
    - Repeaters
    - NICs
- Cabling (Chapters 3 and 8)
    - multimode fiber

- single-mode fiber
- UTP, STP
- coaxial cable

11.4 LAN Design

You have so many decisions and choices to make and components to choose from. Where do you start? This section goes through a brainstorming exercise to get you thinking about building or expanding an existing network. For simplicity the text assumes you are building a network; the techniques, however, work equally well for expanding an existing network with a set of givens. The following steps walk you through network design modeling:

1. First you need to establish your goals in priority order. What is most important about your network? High performance? Zero downtime? Redundancy? Security? Expandability? Is there anything that is unimportant? Cost? Keeping state-of-the-art?

2. Next you need to understand the size of your network today and the expected size over the next few years. How quickly will your needs grow? What are your plans with the WAN? What parts of your network will grow?

3. Then you need to enumerate your constraints. What is the composition of your LAN? Is your LAN contained within a single building? Multiple buildings? Distributed across the WAN? Based on your business, what are your data flow expectations? Are there noteworthy, expected patterns? What applications will be used?

4. You now need to construct various network designs. They should reflect your goals and your anticipated growth. For a network of any size you should come up with at least three designs.

5. Now is the fun part—breaking the designs! You break the designs by applying manageability to them. Ask yourself the following questions about each design:

   - How many technologies are employed? How much training do you need? How current are the technologies? Do you really need ATM LANE, Gigabit Ethernet, Fast Ethernet, Ethernet, and FDDI, or can you standardize on just Ethernet?

- Where will you route; where will you switch? How much traffic is predicted to stay local? Have you oversegmented? How much WAN traffic is expected?

- What are your growth points? What will you do with old equipment as you grow? Can the old equipment be redeployed on the edges?

- Where are you vulnerable with respect to security? Broadcast storms? Loops? Configuration problems? Bottlenecks? What will be the corrective action for these problems?

- Where will you put in redundancy? Where is the design vulnerable to breakage? What will you do if device X breaks? Device Y?

6. Now iterate your designs, making fixes and corrections until you converge on a design that works—one that you can justify.

7. Finally, if you have the luxury, prototype your design, or prototype bits and pieces of the design to validate that the design is correct.

11.5 Physical Design Scenarios

Call them "canned designs," "classic designs," or "design scenarios"—the following are switched LAN designs that have been built in the past and work. Each design has its own set of advantages and disadvantages; each design has its own suitability to network size. The designs are presented from simple to more complex. Complexity is added to build from servicing a small LAN to a larger LAN and finally to a distributed enterprise.

In this section we focus on the physical layout of switched LANs. The section after this follows with management design considerations that can be "applied" to each physical layout.

11.5.1 Simple Hub or Switch

Here we go again; we have the simple network we started out with in Chapter 1. The "starter" network that can support a small workgroup can be built with a simple 10BASET Ethernet hub, a few NICs, and an out-of-the-box NOS like Windows Networking. The result: a low-cost, low-overhead network. As network collisions increase with the number of users and more bandwidth is needed, the network can be easily migrated to a small 10BASET switch or a switch with a combination of 10BASET Ethernet and Fast Ethernet. The hub can still be used to service a small group of users that are switched up to the main switch.

Figure 11.1 illustrates a simple network. Tables 11.1 and 11.2 provide features and management concerns for a simple hub design and small switch design respectively.

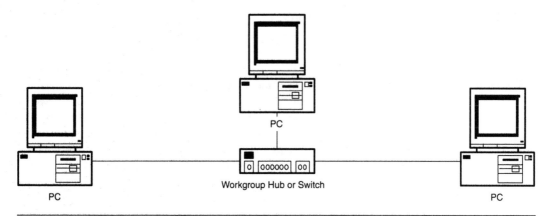

Figure 11.1 Simple network

Table 11.1 Simple Hub Design Information

Simple Hub	
Key Features	■ Inexpensive, entry-level solution. ■ Virtually no configuration to make operational. Supports a few users adequately. Solution has been around for years.
Management Concerns	■ Single Ethernet LAN, single broadcast and collision domain. Solution breaks down as more users come on board. ■ Key to monitor error rates, collisions, and utilization. ■ Often modem(s) is/are used to gain Internet access via an ISP—some concern over security—dialing in to modem without any router filter/firewall features.
Scalability	■ Does not scale well beyond a few moderate users. ■ Easy upgrade path to switch—just swap hub with switch without any end node change.
Equipment Reuse	■ Easy to reuse a hub. Can be moved to the edge of a switch to fan out a single port.

Table 11.2 Small Switch Design Information

Small Switch	
Key Features	■ Moderately priced solution. ■ Transparent upgrade to users from hub solution—yet generally huge performance gains (see Aside)! Very little configuration to make operational. Easy to configure as layer-2 solution. ■ Supports many more users than a simple hub. Number of users is dependent on number and speed of switch ports—10 Mbps ports, 10/100 Mbps ports, 100 Mbps, or a combination. Generally speaking, place only a few users on each port, or ideally give each user his or her own port.
Management Concerns	■ Often modem(s) is/are used to gain Internet access via an ISP—some concern over security—dialing in to modem without any router filter/firewall features.
Scalability	■ Scales well with moderate number of users. Many vendors allow you to stack many small switches together to increase port density. ■ As size of broadcast domain becomes larger, consider VLANs and/or segmentation via a router (see the next section for more information). Remember, even without broadcast storms, the overhead on end nodes of broadcast traffic like SAP and RIP frames may be problematic with respect to your overall performance needs.
Equipment Reuse	■ Easy to reuse a small switch. Can be moved to the edge of a larger switch to fan out a single port.

A S I D E . . .

There is one noteworthy case where the replacement of a hub with a switch can actually result in worse performance. This case is when you move a server and all of its clients from a single hub to a switch, each with its own switched port. Because switching provides unicast containment, the server gets bombarded with requests. With the server and clients on a shared Ethernet segment, each station must wait its turn to make server requests. When you change from a hub to a switch, make certain your server has the capacity for a fat pipe.

11.5.2 Hierarchy of Switches and Hubs

We continue to build our network into a hierarchy of switches and hubs. We purchase some switches, including a routing component, often dubbed as layer-3 switches. This practice provides for future extensibility. We also buy a few switches with modular designs that take different cards (or modules or blades); this gives us a path to other technologies like ATM LANE or FDDI. Hubs are effectively used to fan out switched ports. Our network performs well because of so many dedicated 10BASET and 100BASET connections. Because it is all based on Ethernet, management is simple—except for one big problem: too much broadcast traffic. And what happens when we have a broadcast storm? Our entire flat (layer 2) network is hosed! We suffer from having only a single broadcast domain. There are two lines of attack for broadcast containment: VLANs and routing.

With a VLAN we can still stay flat with layer 2 by constructing port-, MAC-, or protocol-based VLANs. This is a software solution that our switch vendors provide and makes effective use of our existing hardware. The cost of VLANs is increased complexity with respect to management as we now have a "logical" component to our network that must be managed. And, like routing, VLAN tables must be synchronized between switches.

Routing is another line of attack; we need to get into addressing with routing. With routing we can construct AppleTalk zones, IPX networks, and IP subnets. With routing we get

- broadcast containment (protection from broadcast storms and reduced broadcast traffic which all end nodes must process)
- intelligent route selection
- increased security
- protocol filtering
- ease in creating redundant links

The cost of routing over switching is

- performance
- more complex network device configuration
- more complex overall management (the interdependency of network devices on other network devices)
- protocol-specific routing

Both VLANs and routing will work; you can use a combination of VLANs and routing and even have protocol-sensitive VLANs. We will show both solutions in the next two sections.

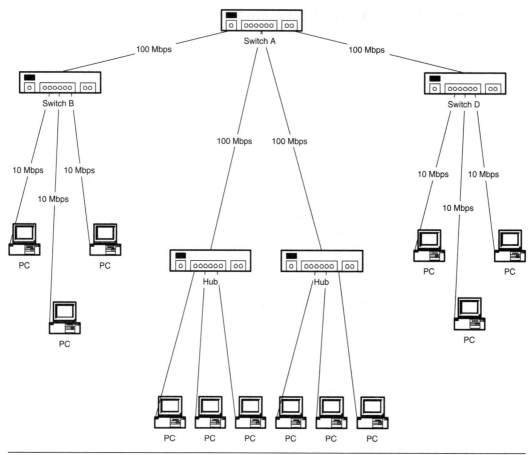

Figure 11.2 Hierarchy of switches and hubs

Figure 11.2 illustrates a hierarchical switch design. Table 11.3 presents the key features and management concerns of a hierarchical switch design.

11.5.3 Hierarchy of Switches and Hubs with VLANs

The success of VLANs is largely dependent on the management software that comes with the network devices. Since VLANs are not yet standard, construction of VLANs usually requires you to stick with one vendor. Figure 11.4 takes our previous hierarchy and introduces port-based VLANs.

Table 11.3 Hierarchical Switch Design Information

Key Features	<ul><li>Cost is virtually on a per-port basis. Can generally add to hierarchy in increments of eight ports. Can stack many switches and fan out ports with hubs.</li><li>Virtually no configuration needed to make operational. Supports many users.</li><li>Good solution to help "flatten" a router-based solution with a solution that will have better performance (see information on routing and switches that follow).</li><li>Consider buying some core switches that have built-in routing.</li></ul>
Management Concerns	<ul><li>Several Ethernet LANs (one per switched port), each with its own collision domain yet the entire hierarchy forms a single broadcast domain. Solution is vulnerable to a broadcast storm that will bring down entire network.</li><li>Key to monitor error rates, collisions, and utilization on a per-port basis.</li><li>Monitor broadcast storms and loops.</li><li>At this network size, remote access should be via an outbound router. Modems are taboo.</li><li>Monitor RMON statistics and utilization at each port. Identify any overloaded ports.</li><li>It is important that you remember to fan out line speed. For example, position 100 Mbps at the core connecting key critical, shared resources like database servers; 10 Mbps out to end nodes or hubs; and shared 10 Mpbs from hubs out to end stations.</li></ul>
Scalability	<ul><li>Major scaling concerns are broadcast traffic with single domain. Consider VLANs or router segmentation.</li></ul>
Equipment Reuse	<ul><li>Easy to reuse a hub or switch. Either can be moved to the edge of another switch to fan out a single port. Be careful of doing too much cascading, though.</li></ul>

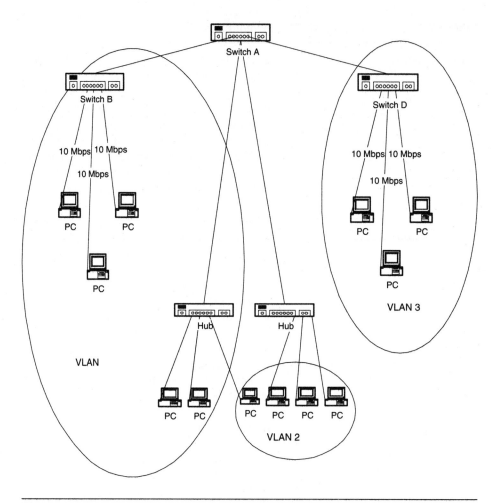

Figure 11.3 Hierarchy of switches and hubs with possible port-based VLANs

Figure 11.3 illustrates a hierarchical switch and hub design with VLANs. Table 11.4 presents the key features and management concerns of a hierarchical switch and hub design with VLANs.

11.5.4 Routed Backbone

As our network grows, we might consider constructing a routed backbone. We can do this with the high end layer-3 switches that have routing built in. We might choose a FDDI ring as the routed backbone between the high end layer-3 switches; FDDI provides fault tolerance and is a mature, proven technology.

Table 11.4 Hierarchical Switch and Hub Design with VLANs Information

Key Features	■ Broadcast containment with VLANs. Limits broadcast traffic and contains storms to single VLAN.
Management Concerns	■ Key to monitor error rates, collisions, and utilization. ■ If routing is used with switches that route, important to attempt to try to segment based on traffic patterns. Try to follow 80/20 rule where 80 percent of the traffic is kept local and not routed. The 80/20 rule applies to VLAN configuration as well. ■ VLANs add a logical abstraction to the network, making it more difficult to resolve and troubleshoot problems. Monitor VLAN administration closely. ■ A good rule of thumb is to keep less than 200 users within a multiprotocol (for example, IPX, AT, and IP) broadcast domain.
Scalability	■ Scales well—can add new users or switches easily.
Equipment Reuse	■ Easy to reuse a hub or switch. Either can be moved to the edge of another switch to fan out a single port. Be careful of doing too much cascading, though.

Always remember *switch* where you can, *route* where you must. Routing requires significantly more processing than switching and can be significantly slower (this is changing and some routers are already quite fast). Switches provide bandwidth; routers provide security, redundancy, control, and broadcast containment.

Figure 11.4 illustrates a routed backbone design. Table 11.5 presents the key features and management concerns of a routed backbone design.

11.5.5 Fault-Tolerant FDDI Routed Backbone

FDDI really shines when it comes to building a fault-tolerant backbone. By dual homing our backbone, the network can survive multiple faults and still be operational. Look at Figure 11.5. If switch B goes down, the PCs directly attached lose their network connection, but the rest of the network stays operational. Likewise if switch A or C goes down, the network stays up. If switch D

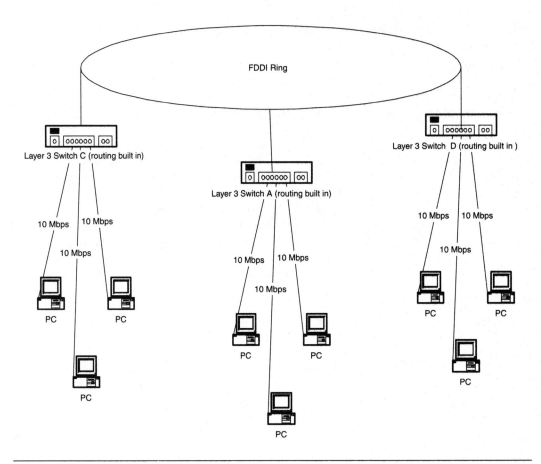

Figure 11.4 Backbone ring or layer-3 switches

goes down, E comes online automatically by moving over to path B, and the network stays operational. This network is resilient to failure. In fact, this design is often employed by large institutions like banks where having the network go down costs serious dollars. You simply do not get the same level of fault tolerance with a simple hierarchical switch design. Table 11.6 also gives information on a fault-tolerant FDDI backbone design.

11.5.6 ATM Switch Backbone

Our last single LAN scenario uses a core ATM switch backbone by segmented groups of LANs into ELANs. VLANs may also be used. Although this design is

Table 11.5 Routed Backbone Design Information

Key Features	■ Broadcast containment and security with routing through backbone.
Management Concerns	■ Key to monitor error rates, collisions, and utilization at each switched port. ■ Attempt to try to segment based on traffic patterns—minimize traffic that routes. Try to follow 80/20 rule where 80 percent of the traffic is kept local and not routed. Use RMON2 probe/application to determine traffic patterns.
	■ Must manage subnets, AppleTalk zones, and/or NetWare networks. Important to set up policies on adding new users and maintain good records of addresses. ■ Many more available technologies to understand and monitor.
Scalability	■ Scales well. More overhead, though, with the addition of new users.
Equipment Reuse	■ Easy to reuse a hub or switch. Either can be moved to the edge of another switch to fan out a single port. Be careful of doing too much cascading, though. ■ Routers can also be repositioned fairly easily.

fairly expensive, it is very high powered. There are many ATM switch backbones emerging for the high bandwidth, scalability, and CoS/QoS support. It is expected that Gigabit Ethernet will be used as an alternative to the ATM LANE backbone.

Figure 11.6 and Table 11.7 detail the ATM switch backbone design.

11.5.7 Distributed Enterprise

We could easily extend any of the figures to a distributed enterprise by connecting multiple switched LANs by a WAN router over Frame Relay. We also add a dial-in component at each site for remote access.

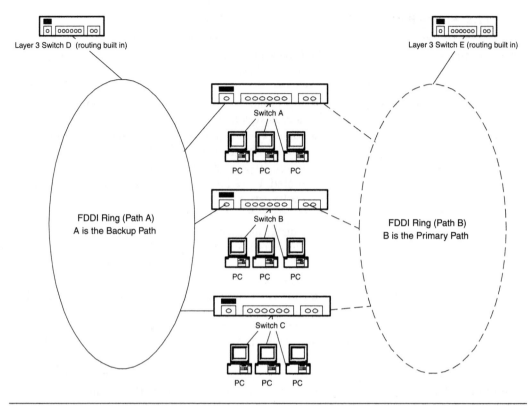

Figure 11.5 Backbone ring with FDDI fault tolerance (dual homing)
Note: FDDI Ring (Path A) and FDDI Ring (Path B) are generally the same physical cable.
They are shown separately only for clarity in the figure.

Table 11.6 Fault-Tolerant FDDI Routed Backbone Design Information

Key Features	■ Leverage fault tolerance of FDDI to minimize the impact of any one switch going down. This design works well in environments where the network must be up 100 percent of the time.
Management Concerns	■ Same as routed backbone. ■ Ensure that if equipment does go down, that immediate notification is made. ■ Monitor FDDI integrity closely.
Scalability	■ Scales well.
Equipment Reuse	■ Same as routed backbone.

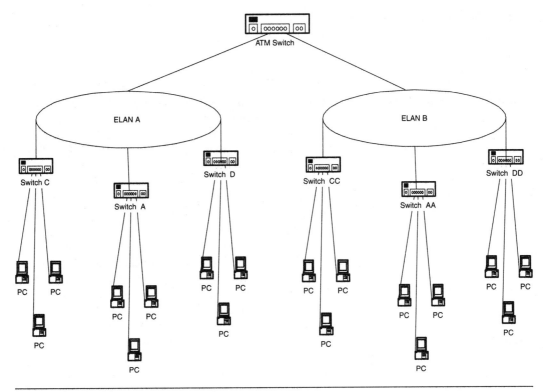

Figure 11.6 ATM backbone of switches

11.6 Management Considerations of Design

There are several management considerations when designing your switched LAN. Your optimal network is one that has high performance and can be easily scaled and managed. The following sections highlight specific areas to consider when designing for manageability.

11.6.1 Cost

You always need to consider the *overall* cost of every purchase; cost is not limited to network device cost. The overall cost includes

- initial purchase cost
- installation costs, including connectors and other small stuff
- training costs for you and your team to learn the new device
- expansion/upgrade costs

Table 11.7 ATM Switch Backbone Information

Key Features	■ State-of-the-art, very fast performance. ■ Containment via ELANs and VLANs.
Management Concerns	■ Key to monitor error rates, collisions, and utilization at each switched port. ■ Attempt to try to segment based on traffic patterns—minimize traffic that crosses ELANs and VLANs. Try to follow 80/20 rule where 80 percent of the traffic is kept local and not routed. Use RMON2 probe/application to determine traffic patterns. ■ Many more technologies (specifically ATM) to understand and monitor. ■ Remember that to be the least common denominator (LCD) switching requires MTU across all technologies. For Ethernet, FDDI, and ATM LANE the LCD is Ethernet: 64-byte minimum frame size, 1518 maximum frame size.
Scalability	■ Scales well. More overhead with additional new users.
Equipment Reuse	■ Easy to reuse a hub or switch. Either can be moved to the edge of another switch to fan out a single port. Be careful of doing too much cascading, though. ■ ATM switches should remain at the core, though; as technology advances, these will be pushed out to the edges as well.

- maintenance costs
- downtime costs (how much the device costs you if it goes down)

11.6.2 Congestion

One of the biggest problems in LANs is traffic congestion so be prepared to spend time eliminating congestion in your LAN. It is difficult to simulate network congestion ahead of deploying your network solution, since traffic is unpredictable by its very nature. It is therefore important that you design your network so that you can monitor congestion. You should also use the 80/20 rule, VLANs, segmentation, traffic prioritization, load balancing, and time-of-day load balancing judiciously to help control congestion. I say "judiciously" because each of these techniques comes with management overhead, and you want to add overhead only when the gain exceeds the burden. In other words, don't overengineer your solution.

11.6.3 Fault Tolerance

How fault tolerant does your network need to be? How critical is it that your network must be operational at all times? Ninety-eight percent of the time? Note that there is a world of difference between 100 percent of the time and 98 percent of the time. Are there portions of your network that should be more fault tolerant?

When you design your switched LAN, you should consider where redundancy and UPSs are necessary and come up with a backup and recovery plan for each network device. WAN connections in particular are slower and less reliable and are good candidates for redundancy. Generally speaking, core network devices should be made more fault tolerant than edge devices; this may mean having a backup network device, backup network paths, and UPSs for all core devices. Again, the level of fault tolerance is dictated by your business needs.

If possible, prototype new solutions outside of your production network. That way you can resolve problems without disrupting your network users. Ensure that before you deploy a new device you have taken the time to make the device fault tolerant.

11.6.4 Security

The level of security is also governed by your business needs. It is important that you take the time to design and secure your network initially and that you monitor your network for security. Security is not something that you do once and forget about; you must constantly monitor for security breaches and augment your security appropriately.

11.6.5 General Management Policy

The last area you should consider is your general management policy.

- How much polling will your management tools do? How frequently? How much will you rely on traps? On trap-directed polling?
- How much bandwidth management will you do? RMON-2?
- Will your management be centralized or distributed? Will you be able to get information anywhere in your network? How much historical data will you save?

- Will your management be in-band (with the rest of traffic) or out-of-band (separate parallel "management" network)? Or a combination? Note that some devices do not support both in-band and out-of-band management.

- How much trend analysis will you do? How much network tuning?

- What will be your policies and procedures for adding new users, moving users, and so on?

- How much of your management effort will be on the backbone as opposed to on the edges?

- What will be the problem notification hierarchy? How will problems be logged, distributed, and recorded for future reference?

- How will you grow your network? How will you introduce new technologies? Prototype network? How will you grow your network and simultaneously minimize user disruption? What are the anticipated future requirements for your network?

11.7 Summary

There are many good "canned" designs that are worth considering. FDDI solutions are popular where nearly 100 percent uptime is required; Ethernet switch solutions are prevalent in small and large businesses because they are easy to build and extend.

It is key that you consider many factors when designing your switched LAN. Overall network cost, potential areas of congestion, fault tolerance requirements, security, and your own business policies should factor into design decisions.

Designing a switched network presents many challenges. It is important that you take the time to design your network and ensure that your network is manageable and will meet your business requirements. You must also ensure that your network can evolve to meet tomorrow's requirements.

Do yourself a favor and take the time to understand your needs, consider different solutions, converge on a solution, and validate the manageability of your solution. Time spent designing up front will be far less costly and will be well rewarded as your network grows.

Developing a Network Management System

12.1 Introduction

Yes, your network is made up of a collection of cabling, switches, routers, concentrators, hubs, servers, and end stations. It employs various protocols and standards and has a configuration that is customized for your environment. Your network is dynamic: end stations come and go, users come and go, and the VLANs managed by your switches are tweaked to reduce broadcast traffic.

Your network is a system. In the same way that a car is a set of components that work together in unison to get you to your desired destination, your network has many interdependencies that keep your network running smoothly so that it can carry data to its required destination.

This chapter wraps up my thoughts on the management of switched LANs. Together we have covered a lot of territory about switched LANs, including the fundamental technologies that comprise switched LANs, the problems associated with switched LANs, troubleshooting tables, and information on how to solve common problems in switched LANs. In the last chapter we discussed switched network design; we are now ready for the final frontier, putting everything together into a network management system.

12.2 What is a System?

The *Random House College Dictionary* defines a system as "an assemblage or combination of things or parts forming a complex or unitary whole" and as "an organized set of computer programs designed to control the operation of computers and associated equipment and to provide various facilities to users of the equipment." *The Microsoft Word 97 Thesaurus* provides "complex," "assemblage," "combination," and "correlation." Two quick analogies extend these definitions and help provide a picture of what a *network system* is.

First, the not-so-pleasant image: Imagine the traffic patterns on a Friday afternoon at 5:30 P.M. in any sizable American city. Too many cars are attempting to get to their destinations as quickly as possible. There are lots of traffic lights, detours, expressways, back alleys, one-way streets, light-sensitive street lamps, toll booths with attendants, buses, oodles of cars, irate taxicab drivers, trucks, pedestrians—all working together as a system. At first glance, all appears unplanned and haphazard—not true. The lights are usually carefully timed, and the number of lanes of many streets are proportioned to traffic flows—at least as far as physically possible. Traffic problems are reported on various radio stations, and traffic is monitored by a local helicopter and video cameras; police are dispatched to resolve key problems and accidents.

Your LAN is not all that different. It, too, has physical constraints. It, too, has unpredictable behavior. Sometimes the need to move large data files simultaneously through multiple points in your LAN will challenge you and your network, just like a Friday afternoon in any sizable American city.

Your LAN also requires various ways to monitor and correct faults in your network in a timely fashion—the overall monitors (helicopters), the network manager (police) responding to and fixing problems, and network outages (accidents blocking the flow of traffic) quickly. Finally, trends such as traffic at Friday at 5:30 P.M. will need to be analyzed in order to predict problems during peak periods and make design decisions accordingly.

Analogy two is far more pleasant: It is the image I try to envision when I think of a finely tuned network. Imagine an orchestra—a carefully chosen group of twenty or more fine musicians. Each musician has a unique part to contribute to the ensemble—complete with a musical part that must be properly played with impeccable timing and tone. Together the members of the orchestra comprise a system that delivers beautiful, controlled music under the leadership of the director.

You, too, can create an orchestrated network system—a system where switch and router configurations are carefully managed and synchronized—a system that plays together beautifully, synchronized perfectly. Unlike an orchestra but like a city's traffic patterns, you must be prepared for the unplanned and prepared to get your system restored and back online as expediently as possible when faults occur. Like an orchestra, you must tune each network device's configuration so that the composite sounds (works) well.

Okay, I think you have the picture. Now let's take a more scientific view of the network management of your switched network.

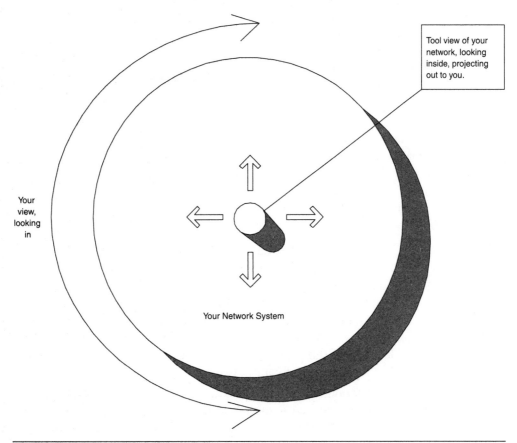

Tool view of your network, looking inside, projecting out to you.

Your view, looking in

Your Network System

Figure 12.1 A conceptual view of a network system

12.3 A Scientific View

Another way to view the network is as a circle with two distinct vantage points: the exact middle and the entire periphery (see Figure 12.1). The circle contains your entire network with all its network devices and users. The larger the network, the larger the circle. For simplicity and focus (for example, if your LAN spans the WAN or many buildings) you may decide to have detail circles that "zoom in" from the large "big picture" circle.

The exact middle of the network is representative of the view of the network that your tools provide. This "view" is used to monitor performance and configuration and provide a means to alert you of problems. This view might collect information from multiple distributed collectors/pollers, or it might collect the data centrally. This view collects lots of data, reduces the data into a useful subset, and provides you with a distinct set of data (the exceptions, the trends, the alarms, the problems) to focus your attention. Great tools provide the entire picture for diagnostics but also management by exception—gaining your attention only when there is a failure or a trend predictive of oncoming failure.

The periphery of the circle is your view of the network. It is the composite view, a 360-degree vision from which you can look at and discern different things about your network, just from the angle and location you choose. Your normal view (or at least the goal) is the direct center, the view that your tools are providing. The more comprehensive your tool set is, the less "walking around" you need to do.

So what happens when you have a problem? This is actually where the circular conceptual model really shines. The scenario goes like this:

1. Your tools alert you to a problem or a distinct set of one or more probable problems. If possible, your tools limit the scope to a pie-shaped portion (a slice of network devices) of the network—two distinct points between which the problem is expected to be confined. Better tools reduce the size of the pie piece (the amount of your network that you must troubleshoot). Sometimes good tools can identify the *exact* location of the problem, an *exact* point in your network, rather than just a pie wedge of your network.

2. At this point you have been alerted, and your tools, hopefully, have narrowed the scope of your problem to just a slice of your network. You then use the problem-solving techniques to reduce the slice further into an exact point or a set of points that make up the problem. Your tools, coupled with your own network expertise, help you narrow the pie piece, identify the problem, and converge on the solution. Figure 12.2 illustrates this process of narrowing down the problem.

There are a few more ideas you can draw from this circular representation of your network system.

- At the core of your system are your management tools; these tools enable you to look into your system, that is, to provide a constant surveillance system for you.

- At the edge of your circle are you and your network management team, managing your network system by viewing what is collected by your tools from the core and the physical makeup of your network.

- If your network is small, so is your network circle; as your network grows, so does your network circle. A small network circle takes less "walking around" to see the entire picture; as the network grows, so do

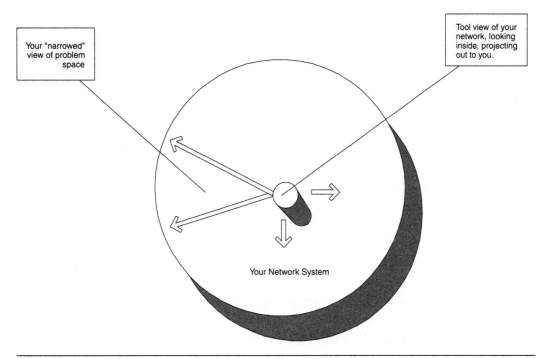

Figure 12.2 A conceptual picture of tools narrowing problem space

the effort and scope of what you must cover to see the entire network. As the circle grows, so does the size of the isolation slices that your tools can provide.

The network circle is a system view of your network. The circle provides the conceptual model to look at your network as a composite, as a single entity rather than as many devices that must all be independently managed. It is this view that will make you successful as a network manager and will open your eyes to the entire problem space, that is, recognizing the importance of the interrelationships of your network devices, enabling you to converge on resolving faults quickly, and scaling your network to meet the needs of your organization.

12.4 Your Switched LAN is a System

At this point you may be saying, This is so abstract—why do I need to think of my switched LAN as a system? There is a simple answer to this is question. Switched LANs have facilitated the next generation and growth of LANs. It is not atypical to see very large switched LANs, LANs that are consistently being extended to service, increasing needs and overall dependencies on networking. Switched LANs grow by adding ports; each port often requires configuration, performance, fault, security, and accounting management. The result? Increased complexity. The need? A solution that scales.

With more traffic come more overhead traffic, more need for management, and more hysteria when the network is down. By always thinking of your network as a system of finely tuned, well-integrated network devices, you will inherently validate network change and growth by looking at the impact on your network as a system. Whether you are adding your next switch or activating idle ports within an existing installation, you need to evaluate the overall impact to your network system (changed traffic flows, increased loads across your backbone, new routes for traffic), not just where to plug things in. This is fundamental to managing your switched LAN, especially as the complexity and size of your switched LAN grows.

12.5 Satisfying ISO Functional Areas as a System

In Chapter 1 we talked about the ISO functional areas as the broad categorizations for network management. We also identified getting the correct amount of granularity and scalability as fundamental to switched LAN management. We discussed the importance of minimizing polling, often by using trap-directed polling and tiered polling, and polling the core of your network more frequently than the edges. And last, we touched on RMON as a way to reduce the "raw" traffic on the network. These techniques enable you to tune your management to focus on the core of your network and not to inundate your network with needless traffic.

It is now time to apply our technical system model to the ISO functional areas and see how we can create a switched LAN management system. This exercise validates our system model against the fundamental functional needs we have.

12.5.1 Configuration Management

In order to satisfy our switched configuration management, we need a system that can set up, baseline, and validate our network . This system periodically validates the integrity of each network device within our switched LAN as well as ensures that the interrelations between the network devices (routing configuration, for example) remains intact. Our system can also be trap triggered; if a configuration trap triggers from a device, the device's configuration is immedi-

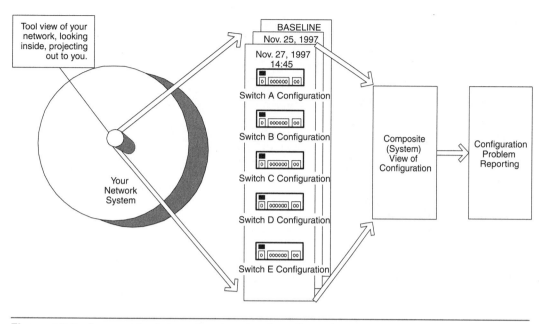

Figure 12.3 A conceptual view of system-level configuration management

ately refreshed. Our configuration system also provides a way to roll back configurations and to zoom in on all configuration changes, given two points in time. And last, our configuration system provides a way to "drag and drop" a configuration onto a new device and prompts us only for the unique configuration characteristics of the device. Drag-and-drop configuration is useful for setting up new devices and quickly replacing failed devices. It might also give you a quick peek at the unique characteristics of any network device's configuration.

Our system model serves us well for configuration (see Figure 12.3). With the aid of our network management tools we periodically take configuration snapshots of our network. Snapshots might be tiered; that is, they might be more frequent and/or comprehensive for the core network devices, or they might not matter so much if your network traffic is minimized. We set up our snapshots to happen periodically in order to verify the integrity of our configuration and to detect unplanned network change automatically. We also can force a snapshot after we make a change; these snapshots can be used to roll back to a known system configuration, to drag and drop a network device's configuration to a new device, and to validate the integrity of our configuration as a network system.

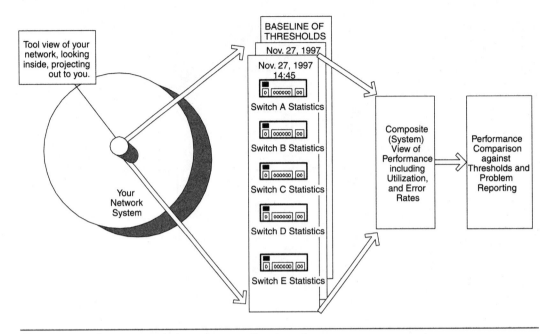

Figure 12.4 A conceptual view of system-level performance management

12.5.2 Performance Management

Performance management follows the same periodic snapshot model (see Figure 12.4). Since poll-based performance management requires more frequent snapshots, it is important to have some sort of data-reduction scheme. A good data-reduction scheme maintains the granularity of data for the most recently collected data and then, as the data age, reduces the granularity. Thus the oldest data (for example, from a week ago) have far fewer "snapshots" than data collected in the last hour. Often the reduced data snapshots become averages of several snapshots. Data reduction enables you to do trend analysis over long periods of time without having to have gigantic storage requirements and super computers to process all the data.

Performance management should as much as possible leverage performance data stored in and computed by network devices. Many network devices calculate utilization internally and often display it interactively using a set of LEDs on the device's front panel. It is important that our performance management system takes advantage of any ways to reduce network management traffic, since adequate performance monitoring requires far more frequent samples than configuration management.

Our performance management system should be triggered by traps as well. Traps that are indicative of network congestion or decreased network response time may trigger performance collection. It may be possible to detect periodic performance degradation trends sooner than periodic polling based on trap-directed polling.

12.5.3 Security Management

Security leverages, trap-directed polling, and periodic polling follow the model of our configuration system—with emphasis on frequency of polling and the collection of passwords, community strings, filters, and data indicative of possible security breaches. Like trap management, security management is more dynamic as security breaches can be devastating to your network. The conceptual picture is very close to our picture (see Figure 12.3) for configuration management.

12.5.4 Accounting Management

Accounting management is all about tracking who uses what. This management is optional, though I expect over the next few years as Class of Service (CoS) and Quality of Service (QoS) gain momentum in the LAN, more emphasis will be placed on accounting management.

The snapshot model here works well with an emphasis on bill creation (reporting) based on usage. RMON and RMON-2 data provide a strong base for usage tracking.

The conceptual picture is very close to our picture (refer to Figure 12.3) for configuration management.

12.5.5 Fault Management

Fault management is the amalgamation of all of our monitoring systems (see Figure 12.5). Our fault management system takes into account configuration, performance, security, and accounting statistics from the other management systems and compares them against a set of "rules" and user-defined policies. Since the data is collected and stored over time, trends that may be indicative of future faults are also evaluated periodically. The rules define the normal state of a network based on a combination of data. For example, a certain configuration might have a defined set of performance parameters associated with it.

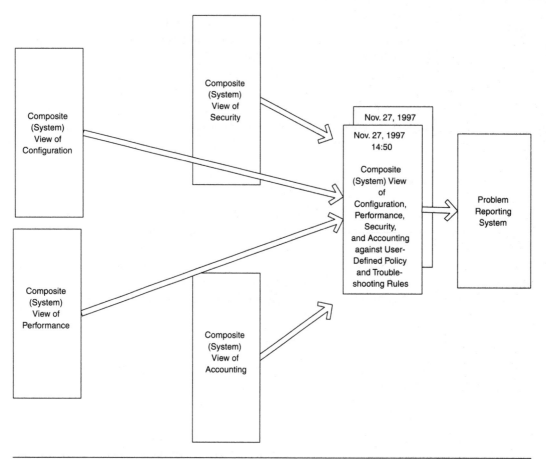

Figure 12.5 A conceptual view of a fault management

As our tools become more sophisticated, they might leverage a set of net-work rules that can be used to detect network faults in advance. These rules are a combination of default rules and rules that you can customize. Network management is only just getting started at this rule-based approach to network management; as tools advance, expect more help here.

12.5.6 Our System Model

Our system model for management satisfies our needs for switched manage-ment by being scaleable, by providing the customizable amount of granularity required, and by making it straightforward to add or modify network devices as our network changes. Optionally, periodic reports might be generated to provide summary information for our network configuration, performance, and fault diagnostics.

12.6 Customizing Your Management System

Every LAN has unique traffic flows, a different set of users, and site-specific requirements. As good as network management tool defaults might be, you should consider customization so that you can fine-tune your management system to an optimal level. Ask yourself a few general questions:

- What are the management goals?
- How comprehensive should management be? What is the cost of failure?
- What reports would be useful?
- Will management be central? Distributed?
- How much of a requirement is there for remote management? For local management?
- How dependent are you on tools? How many human resources do you have? How much automode management do you require?
- Where do you stand on the technology curve? Always on leading edge? Or, do you tend to build on mature, well-proven technologies?

Then consider the following workflows and procedures that define your system processes:

- What are your workflows for adding, deleting, or moving network users?
- What is your workflow for problem reporting and resolution?
- What is your procedure for expanding your network?
- How much network monitoring do you need to do? How frequently should you monitor each device? What is the criticality of any one device failing?

These questions will help you to converge on your network policy. Your network policy customizes your network management system around your goals, network needs, and corporate policy. For example, in some environments security is paramount; in these environments security management should be emphasized. Your network may be growing quickly; hence your policy might emphasize performance monitoring and configuration management. It is important that you "tune" your management system to meet the needs of your LAN; this practice will reduce needless network traffic, improve the quality of your network service, and reduce the overall response time necessary for problem resolution.

12.7 Management Excellence

Management excellence is about continually going beyond the bounds of your own network management goals. Excellence means tuning your management system to optimal levels by providing impressive service levels to your users— virtually no downtime, excellent response time even in times of heavy traffic, and quick resolution of problems. Excellence is about proactive management—identifying and resolving problems even before your network users discover them. Finally, excellence is about creating a LAN that scales—a LAN that is resilient to network changes and the ever-increasing networking needs and users, the thrust and hunger for infinite bandwidth.

Switched LANs can provide the bandwidth your network needs. They do, however, introduce new management needs and more sophisticated management tools that scale. Switched LANs leverage the richness of so many technologies; unfortunately, though, the use of many technologies places more pressure on the management team to understand and provide adequate management of the technology mix.

At this point we have completed the concentrated network management journey for switched LAN management. We have built up our base by covering network management fundamentals, the standards, layer-2 management, layer-3 management, WAN-access management, troubleshooting, and design—all components of our network management system. We recognize that a network is a carefully orchestrated set of hardware and processes that must be managed and thought of as a system rather than as a collection of network devices. Although this journey should leave you with a strong basis and a focus on what is important, achieve excellence by continually improving your own networking prowess.

12.8 Currency

There is no substitute for staying current. Networking technology moves very quickly; subsequently to stay current, you need to read—read a lot. My guess would be that people "in the know" read about 400 pages per week, from about twenty different sources.

There are many fine journals and books that can help tune your understanding of networking. I tend to visit the local general or technical bookstores about every three weeks. It is worth the visit just to see what is new and what is hot. *Business Communications Review* is a particularly good journal on network management. I highly recommend it.

I skim many of the weekly trade presses. These publications tend to be light at times, but they help you stay on the pulse of what's new. Pick a few to concentrate on, and scan the table of contents for articles that meet your focus criteria. Often I rip out the articles I care about (not wise if you are borrowing someone's paper) and read them whenever I have a few extra minutes—much better than reading whatever the dentist selects for his waiting room.

12.8.1 Networking Conferences

Attending network conferences can help you recharge quickly. Good conferences expose you to many different technologies, new and old, and give you an opportunity to explore beyond your normal "fenced-in" yard. I especially like Interop, although I wish it hadn't become so large! Other networking events and shows are also good. I tend to try to spend a day at all local shows; generally it is well worth the expense and effort.

12.8.2 Standards

The IETF meets three times a year to work in committee format on important RFCs. You can learn a lot by reading and tracking RFCs. Pick a few and visit the web site listed in Chapter 2 when your network is operating smoothly.

12.9 Summary

I sincerely hope you found this text useful. I know that I found it very useful capturing these ideas on paper and refining them; I feel a certain freedom from writing this and now will have something to point to when I'm asked my thoughts on switched LAN management.

My last words of advice to you are to keep your switched network management solutions simple. Build a simple system. Somewhere long ago I read, "Simplicity is elegant." This applies to software development, network design, network management, and life in general. Define your processes and workflows as simply and succinctly as possible; keep your network design and network policies simple; replace complex, outgrown solutions with simpler ones. Complexity is usually costly; introduce and use it wisely.

Bibliography

This bibliography includes books and articles that provide additional information on switched LANs. The asterisks indicate my favorite works.

Baker, F. "How Do Routers Work?" *LAN Magazine* (March 1997): 87–91. Describes fundamentals of routers.

Bellman, R. "IP Switching—Which Flavor Works For You?" *Business Communications Review* (April 1997): 41–46.

*Breyer, R., and S. Riley. *Switched and Fast Ethernet*, 2d ed. Emeryville, Ca.: Ziff-Davis Press, 1996. Presents a very well-written, pragmatic approach to building switched networks.

Bruno, L. "Internet Security: How Much Is Enough?" *Data Communications* (April 1996): 60–72. A look at some firewall solutions and their features.

Bryan, J. "LANs Make the Switch." *Byte* (September 1994). Very early article on transition to switching in the LAN.

Cheswick, W., and S. Bellovin. *Firewalls and Internet Security*. Reading, Ma.: Addison-Wesley Publishing Company, 1994. Great book on firewalling.

Deaton, G. "Juggling ATM Traffic." *Data Communications* (April 1996): 130–138. Interesting perspective on traffic management and ATM.

Dickie, M. *Routing in Today's Internetworks*. New York: Van Nostrand Reinhold, 1994. Good coverage of routing.

Dutton, H., and P. Lenhard. *Asynchronous Transfer Mode (ATM)*, 2d ed. Upper Saddle River, N.J.: Prentice Hall PTR, 1995. Concise, easy-to-understand book on ATM.

Enck, J., and M. Beckman. *LAN to WAN*. New York: McGraw-Hill, 1995. Good book on connecting to the WAN.

Feit, S. *SNMP: A Guide to Network Management*. New York: McGraw-Hill, 1995. Comprehensive reference for SNMP.

Ferrero, A. *The Evolving Ethernet*. Reading, Ma.: Addison-Wesley Publishing Company, 1996. Comprehensive coverage of Ethernet.

*Ginsburg, D. *ATM: Solutions for Enterprise Internetworking*, Reading, Ma.: Addison-Wesley Publishing Company, 1996. One of the few solution-oriented books on ATM.

Goehring, H., and F. Kauffels. *Token Ring: Principles, Perspectives and Strategies.* Reading, Ma.: Addison-Wesley Publishing Company, 1992. Good book on token ring.

Held, G. "Virtual LANS Become Reality." *LAN Magazine* (April 1997): 69–74. Discusses basics of VLANs.

———. *LAN Management with SNMP and RMON.* New York: John Wiley & Sons, 1996. Practical book on network management.

Herman, J. "Managing Router Networks: Are We Keeping Pace?" *Business Communications Review* (February 1997): 22–26. Explores the critical need for router management software.

Huitema, C. *Routing in the Internet.* Englewood Cliffs, N.J.: Prentice-Hall, 1995. Strong book on routing.

°Jain, R. *FDDI Handbook: High-Speed Networking Using Fiber and Other Media.* Reading, Ma.: Addison-Wesley Publishing Company, 1994. Best book I've read on FDDI.

Jander, M. "Distributed Network Management: In Search of Solutions." *Data Communications* (February 1996): 101–112. Looks at pros and cons of distributed platform solutions.

———. "Welcome to the Revolution." *Data Communications* (November 21, 1996): 39–53. Explores merits and limitations of Web-based management.

Karvé, A. "Ethernet's Next Frontier." *LAN Magazine* (January 1997): 40–47. Provides high-level coverage of gigabit Ethernet.

Kauffels, F. *Network Management: Problems, Standards and Strategies.* Reading, Ma.: Addison-Wesley Publishing Company, 1992. Provides overview of various network management platforms.

Krapf, E. "Serving Up Gigabit Ethernet." *Business Communications Review* (March 1997): 41–45. Survey of gigabit Ethernet as a backbone technology.

Larson, A. "All Eyes on IP Traffic." *Data Communications* (November 1997): 54–62. Looks at current traffic analysis tools.

———. "Router Management Tools: Up to the Task?" *Data Communications* (November 1996): 101–108. Looks at router management tool offerings and needs.

Leinwand, A., and K. Conroy. *Network Management: A Practical Perspective*, 2d ed. Reading, Ma.: Addison-Wesley Publishing Company, 1996. Good coverage of network management.

Mandeville, R., and J. Johnson. "Forget the Forklift." *Data Communications* (September 1996): 120–134. Evaluation of various LANE solutions.

Martin, J., K. Kavanagh, and J. Leben. *Local Area Networks.*, Englewood Cliffs, N.J.: Prentice Hall PTR, 1994. Well-written book on LANs.

McDysan, D., and D. Spohn. *ATM: Theory and Application.* New York: McGraw-Hill, Inc., 1995. A good ATM reference book.

Microsoft Corp. *Microsoft Word 97.* Redmond, WA: Microsoft Corp., 1983– 1996.

Newman, D., and S. Kumar. "Ethernet Switches: Quantity, Not Commodity." *Data Communications* (November 1997): 85–98. Evaluation of many Ethernet switches.

Nolle, T. "Switching: In Search of the Hassle-Free Network." *Business Communications Review* (March 1997): 35–39. A look at solutions satisfying the apparent "infinite" needs of networking.

*Partridge, C. *Gigabit Networking.* Reading, Ma.: Addison-Wesley Publishing Company, 1993. Provides excellent background information on switching architecture.

*Perlman, R. *Interconnections: Bridges and Routers.* Reading, Ma.: Addison-Wesley Publishing Company, 1992. An excellent source of information on bridging and routing.

Random House, Inc. *Random House College Dictionary.* New York: Random House, Inc., 1973.

Roberts, E. "IP on Speed." *Data Communications* (March 1997): 84–96. Explores some of the emerging layer-3 solutions.

———. "Gambling on Switched Networks." *Data Communications* (May 1996): 66–78. Case study using switching technologies.

———. "Virtual LANs: How Real? How Soon? Here's How." *Data Communications* (October 1996): 66–75. A look at various VLAN solutions.

Rose, M. *The Simple Book: An Introduction to Management of TCP/IP-based Internets*, 2d ed. Englewood Cliffs, N.J.: Prentice-Hall, Inc., 1991. The bible (first edition) on SNMPv1.

———. *The Simple Book: An Introduction to Internet Management*, 2d ed. Englewood Cliffs, N.J.: Prentice Hall PTR, 1994. The bible (second edition) on SNMPv1 and SNMPv2.

Rose, M., and K. McCloghrie. *How to Manage Your Network Using SNMP.* Englewood Cliffs, N.J.: Prentice Hall PTR, 1995. Practical book on management.

Parker, T. *TCP/IP Unleashed.* Indianapolis In.: Sams Publishing, 1996. Good encyclopedia-like reference on TCP/IP.

Schatt, S. *Linking LANs.* New York: McGraw-Hill, 1995. Good reference on WAN connections.

Sheldon, T. *LAN TIMES: Encyclopedia of Networking*, Berkeley, Ca.: McGraw-Hill, 1994. Good quick reference for networking terminology.

Smythe, C. *Internetworking: Designing the Right Architectures.* Reading, Ma.: Addison-Wesley Publishing Company, 1995. A good LAN reference.

Stallings, W. *Local and Metropolitan Area Networks*, 4th ed. New York: Macmillan Publishing Company, 1993. Good survey of LAN technologies.

———. *SNMP, SNMPv2 and RMON: Practical Network Management*, 2d ed. Reading, Ma.: Addison-Wesley Publishing Company, 1996. Good reference for RMON standards.

*Stevens, W. R. *TCP/IP Illustrated,* Vol. 1. Reading, Ma.: Addison-Wesley Publishing Company, 1994. One of three volumes, a strong TCP/IP reference.

————. *TCP/IP Illustrated,* Vol. 3. Reading, Ma.: Addison-Wesley Publishing Company, 1996. One of three volumes, a strong TCP/IP reference.

*Tanenbaum, A. *Computer Networks.* Englewood Cliffs, N.J.: Prentice-Hall, Inc., 1981. My first text book on networking, a classic!

Terplan, K. *Effective Management of Local Area Networks,* 2d ed. New York: McGraw-Hill, 1996. Provides coverage of various tasks, roles, and responsibilities of LAN network management.

*Washburn, K., and J. Evans. *TCP/IP: Running a Successful Network.* Essex, England: Addison Wesley Longman Ltd, 1996. Well-written book on TCP/IP.

Willis, D. "Make Room for Frame Relay." *Network Computing* (February 15, 1997): 73–86. Provides survey of available frame relay services.

Wright G., and W. R. Stevens. *TCP/IP Illustrated,* Vol. 2. Reading, Ma.: Addison-Wesley Publishing Company, 1995. One of three volumes, a strong TCP/IP reference.

RFC References

RFC	RFC Number
Appletalk MIB II	1742
ATM Management MIB	1695
Bridge MIB	1493
Ethernet MIB	1398
FDDI-SMT73 MIB	1512
MIB-2	1213
MIB2 Extensions	1573
OSPF MIB	1850
Repeater MIB	1516
RIP Version 2	1383
RMON MIB	1757
RMON-Token Ring Extensions MIB	1513
SMI	1155, 1212
SNMP	1157, 1901–1908
Source Routing Bridge MIB	1575
Token Ring MIB	1231
UPS Management MIB	1628

Obtaining RFCs (from Chapter 2)

All Internet standards are written in the form of Request For Comments (RFCs), documents used by the Internet community initially to draft and then later optionally to ratify a standard. RFCs are publicly available to anyone; a master index for all RFCs is in a file called `rfc-index.txt` that can be found on the node `ds.internic.net` under the RFC directory. This master location of RFCs is replicated across many sites throughout the world. Using anonymous FTP (log in as user anonymous using a password of your e-mail address), you can retrieve the index and any standard that you are interested in. Or, if you do not have FTP access but do have WWW access, you can get the RFCs at `http://ds.internic.net/rfc`.

Common Networking Acronyms

AAL	ATM Adaptation Layer
AARP	AppleTalk ARP
ABR	Available Bit Rate
ADSP	AppleTalk Data Stream Protocol
AEP	AppleTalk Echo Protocol
AFP	AppleTalk Filing Protocol
ANSI	American National Standards Institute
API	Application Programming Interface
APP	AppleTalk Print Protocol
ARP	Address Resolution Protocol
ASCII	American Standard Code for Information Interchange
ASIC	Application Specific Integrated Circuit
ASN.1	Abstract Syntax Notation One
ASP	AppleTalk Session Protocol
ATM	Asynchronous Transfer Mode
ATP	AppleTalk Transaction Protocol
BER	Bit Error Rate, Basic Encoding Rules (for SNMP)
B-ISDN	Broadband Integrated Services Digital Network
BOOTP	Bootstrap Protocol
BPDU	Bridge Protocol Data Unit
bps	Bits per second
Bps	Bytes per second
BRI	Basic Rate Interface
BUS	Broadcast and Unknown Server
CBR	Constant Bit Rate, Committed Burst Rate
CCITT	Consultative Committee for International Telegraph and Telephone/Telephony
CDDI	Copper Distributed Data Interface
CER	Cell Error Rate
CIDR	Classless Interdomain Routing
CIR	Cell Insertion Ratio, Committed Information Rate
CL	Connectionless Service
CLP	Cell Loss Priority
CLR	Cell Loss Ratio

CO	Connection Oriented Service
CoS	Class of Service
CPU	Central Processing Unit
CRC	Cyclic Redundancy Check
CSMA/CD	Carrier Sense Multiple Access with Collision Detection
CSU/DSU	Channel Service Unit/Data Service Unit
DAC	Dual-Attachment Concentrator
DAS	Dual-Attachment Station
DDP	Datagram Delivery Protocol
DHCP	Dynamic Host Configuration Protocol
DIX	Digital, Intel, Xerox (Ethernet Standard)
DN	Directory Number
DNA	Downstream Neighbor Address
DNS	Domain Name System
DS-0	Digital Signal Level 0 (64 Kbps)
DS-1	Digital Signal Level 1 (1.544 Mbps)
DS-2	Digital Signal Level 2 (6.312 Mbps)
DS-3	Digital Signal Level 3 (44.736 Mbps)
DS-4	Digital Signal Level 4 (274.176 Mbps)
DSP	Digital Signal Processor
DVMRP	Distance-Vector Multicast Routing Protocol
E-1	European Signal Level 1 (2.048 Mbps)
E-2	European Signal Level 2 (8.448 Mbps)
E-3	European Signal Level 3 (34.368 Mbps)
E-4	European Signal Level 4 (139.264 Mbps)
EBS	Excess Burst Size
ECF	Echo Frame
EGP	Exterior Gateway Protocol
ELAN	Emulated Local Area Network
FDDI	Fiber Distributed Data Interface
FPS	Frames Per Second
Frac T1 (FT1)	Fractional T1
FRS	Frame Relay Service
FS	Frame Status
FTP	File Transfer Protocol
Gbps	Gigabits Per Second
GFC	Generic Flow Control
HEC	Header Error Control
HIPPI	High Performance Parallel Interface
HTTP	Hypertext Transport Protocol
IANA	Internet Assigned Numbers Authority
ICMP	Internet Control Message Protocol
IEEE	Institute of Electrical and Electronics Engineers
IETF	Internet Engineering Task Force

IGMP	Internet Group Management Protocol
IGP	Interior Gateway Protocol
IP	Internet Protocol
IPv4	IP Version 4 (current version)
IPv6	IP Version 6
IPX	Internet Packet Exchange
IPX RIP	NetWare Routing Information Protocol
ISDN	Integrated Service Digital Network
IS-IS	Intermediate System to Intermediate System Protocol
ISO	International Organization for Standardization
ISP	Internet Service Provider
Kbps	Kilobits per second
LAN	Local Area Network
LANE	LAN Emulation or LAN Emulation Service
LCT	Link Confidence Test
LEC	LAN Emulation Client
LECS	LAN Emulation Configuration Server
LEM	Link Error Monitor
LER	Link Error Rate
LES	LAN Emulation Server
LLC	Logical Link Control
LRM	LAN Reporting Mechanism
LSA	Link State Advertisement
LSB	Least Significant Byte
MAC	Media Access Control
MAN	Metropolitan Area Network
MARS	Multicast Address Resolution Server
MAU	Medium Access Unit, Multistation Access Unit
MBONE	Multicast Backbone
Mbps	Megabits per Second
MBS	Maximum Burst Size
MIB	Management Information Base
MIB-2	Management Information Base Version 2
MIC	Media Interface Connector
MOSPF	Multicast Open Shortest Path First
MPOA	Multiprotocol over ATM
MSB	Most Significant Byte
MTU	Maximum Transmission Unit
NAC	Null-Attachment Concentrator
NAUN	Next Addressable Upstream Neighbor
NBP	Name Binding Protocol
NCP	NetWare Core Protocol
NDIS	Network Driver Interface Specification
NetBEUI	NetBIOS Extended User Interface

NetBIOS	Network Basic Input Output System
NFS	Network File System
NHRP	Next Hop Resolution Protocol
NIC	Network Interface Card
NIF	Neighbor Information Frame
NLM	NetWare Loadable Module
NMS	Network Management System
NNI	Network Node Interface
NOS	Network Operating System
NSA	Next Station Addressing
NSAP	Network Service Access Point
OC-3	Optical Carrier-3 (155.52 Mbps)
OC-12	Optical Carrier-12 (622.08 Mbps)
OC-24	Optical Carrier-24 (1.244 Gbps)
OC-48	Optical Carrier-48 (2.488 Gbps)
OC-192	Optical Carrier-192 (9.6 Gbps)
OID	Object Identifier
OSF	Open Software Foundation
OSI	Open Systems Interconnection
OSI/RM	Open Systems Interconnection Reference Model
OSPF	Open Shortest Path First
OUI	Organization Unique Identifier
PAP	Printer Access Protocol
PC	Personal Computer
PDU	Protocol Data Unit
PHY	Physical Layer
PIM	Protocol Independent Multicast
PING	Packet Internet Groper
PPP	Point-to-Point Protocol
PPS	Packets Per Second
PRI	Primary Rate Interface
QoS	Quality of Service
RARP	Reverse Address Resolution Protocol
REM	Ring Error Monitor
RFC	Request for Comment
RIP	Routing Information Protocol
RMON	Remote Network Monitor
RMON2	Remote Network Monitor Version 2
RMT	Ring Management
RTCP	Real-Time Control Protocol
RTMP	Routing Table Maintenance Protocol
RTP	Real-Time Protocol
RSVP	Resource Reservation Protocol
SAC	Single-Attachment Concentrator

SAP	Service Access Point, Service Advertisement Protocol
SAS	Single-Attachment Station
SIF	Status Information Frame
SLIP	Serial Line Interface Protocol
SMI	Structure of Management Information
SMP	Standby Monitor Present (Frame)
SMT	Station Management
SNAP	Subnet Access Protocol
SNMP	Simple Network Management Protocol
SNMPv2	Simple Network Management Protocol Version 2
SONET	Synchronous Optical Network
SPF	Shortest Path First
SPID	Service Provider ID
SPX	Sequenced Packet Exchange
SR	Source Routing
SRF	Station Report Frame
STM	Station Manager
STP	Shielded Twisted Pair, Spanning Tree Protocol
T-1	DS-1 (Digital Signal Level 1) (1.544 Mbps)
T-2	DS-2 (Digital Signal Level 2) (6.312 Mbps)
T-3	DS-3 (Digital Signal Level 3) (44.736 Mbps)
TCI	Tag Control Information
TCP	Transmission Control Protocol
TCP/IP	Transmission Control Protocol/Internet Protocol
TELNET	Remote Terminal Protocol
TFTP	Trivial File Transfer Protocol
THT	Token Holding Timer
TPID	Tag Protocol Identifier
TRT	Token Rotation Timer
TTRT	Target Token Rotation Timer
UDP	User Datagram Protocol
UNA	Upstream Neighbor Address
UNI	User Network Interface
UPS	Uninterruptible Power Supply
UTP	Unshielded Twisted Pair
VARBIND	Variable Binding
VBR	Variable Bit Rate
VC	Virtual Channel, Circuit, or Connection
VCC	Virtual Channel Connection
VCI	Virtual Channel Identifier
VCL	Virtual Channel Link
VLAN	Virtual Local Area Network
VMRP	VLAN Membership Resolution Protocol
VP	Virtual Path

VPC	Virtual Path Connection
VPI	Virtual Path Identifier
VPL	Virtual Path Link
WAN	Wide Area Network
WWW	World Wide Web
ZIP	Zone Information Protocol
ZIT	Zone Information Table

Index